Women and Attempted Suicide

Raymond Jack
Faculty of Economic and Social Studies,
University of East Anglia, U.K.

LAWRENCE ERLBAUM ASSOCIATES, PUBLISHERS
Hove (UK)   Hillsdale (USA)

Lawrence Erlbaum Associates Ltd., Publishers
27 Palmeira Mansions
Church Road
Hove
East Sussex, BN3 2FA
U.K.

British Library Cataloguing in Publication Data

Jack, Raymond
  Women and attempted suicide.
  I. Title
  157.7

  ISBN 0-86377-167-X (Hbk)
  ISBN 0-86377-168-8 (Pbk)

Cover by Joyce Chester
Printed and bound in the United Kingdom by BPCC Wheatons, Exeter

WOMEN AND ATTEMPTED SUICIDE

2

Contents

Acknowledgements   iv

Introduction: The Development of Theory and "Attempted Suicide"   ix

Epidemiology and the Neglect of Gender   ix
The Inadequacy of the Pathology Paradigm   x
The Normative Origins of Self-poisoning   xiii

1. Epidemiology and the Neglect of Meaning   1

Epidemiology   1
The Neglect of Gender   10
Suicide and Attempted Suicide   12
The Neglect of Meaning   19
Gender and the Development of Theory   20

2. Current Theories of Self-poisoning   21

Stress   21
Biology   31

Personality Theory 33
Mental Disorder 41
Cognitive Theories 43

3. A Social Psychology of Self-poisoning 55

The Failure of the Pathology Perspective 55
An Interactive Model 59
Locus of Control 61

4. Women and Sex Role Socialisation 69

Sex Roles and Psychopathology 69
Sex Roles and Psychotropic Medication 81
Sex Roles and the Prescription of Psychotropics 102
Sex Roles and Clinical Judgements 109
Sex Roles, Psychotropics, and Self-poisoning 112

5. Learned Helplessness and Causal Attribution 115

The Critique of Learned Helplessness 123
The Reformulation 125
An Attributional "Style" 127
Sex Differences in Attributions and Coping Behaviour 131
Gender Differences in Attributions and Coping 134
Dysfunctional Attributions, Coping Deficits, and
    Self-poisoning 139

6. Causal Attribution and Female Self-poisoning 147

The Functions of Attribution 147
Life Events—Normative and Non-normative Influences 154
Affiliation, Gender, and Sex Role Stereotypes 166
Self-concept, Roles, and Attributions 170
Causes of Causal Attribution 175
Affiliation and the "Specific Vulnerability" Hypothesis 178
Affiliation, Attribution, and Female Self-poisoning 182

7. **An Attributional Model of Female Self-poisoning**   **187**

The Theory Restated   187
An Empirical Investigation   195

8. **Intervention**   **217**

Prevention   217
Secondary Intervention   220
Attribution and Primary Intervention—Prevention   227
Attribution and Secondary Intervention—The "Dilemma
    of Helping"   232
Counselling Self-poisoning Clients   236
Sex Role Socialisation, Social Change, and Female
    Self-poisoning   240

Appendix   **247**

References   **249**

Author Index   **273**

Subject Index   **281**

Acknowledgements

The following figures, tables and extracts which appear in *Women and Attempted Suicide* were reproduced with the permission of the publishers and, where requested, the author(s):

FIGURES

Figures 1.1, 1.5 and 4.8 were reproduced with the permission of the British Medical Association; 1.2 and 4.4 with the permission of the Royal Society of Medicine; 1.4 with the permission of the World Health Organization; 1.6 and 4.7 were reprinted by permission of John Wiley & Sons, Ltd.; 4.1 with the permission of Cambridge University Press; 4.2 and 4.3 with the permission of Lawrence Erlbaum Associates Inc. and the author; 4.5 with the permission of HMSO; 4.9 and 6.1 with the permission of Croom Helm; and 4.10 with the permission of the Royal College of Psychiatrists.

TABLES

Tables 1.1, 1.2, 1.3, 1.4, 1.5 and 4.7 were reproduced with the permission of the Office of Health Economics; 1.1 (top), 4.4 and 4.6 with the permission of HMSO; 4.1 with the permission of Lawrence Erlbaum Associates Inc. and the author; 4.2 and 6.6 with the permission of the American Psychiatric Association; 4.5 with the permission of the Department of Health; 4.12, 4.13 and 4.14 copyright 1978, American Medical Association; 4.15 with the permission of the American Sociological Association; 6.1 and 6.2 with the permission of Tavistock Publications; 6.3 with the permission of the American Psychonomic Society; 6.4 copyright 1975, American Medical Association; and 6.7 with the permission of Cambridge University Press.

EXTRACTS

Extract(s) were reprinted from

Abramson, Seligman, & Teasdale (1978) with the permission of the American Psychological Association

Alloy, Abramson, Metalsky, & Hartlage (1988) with the permission of the British Psychological Society and the author

Anderson (1983) with the permission of the American Psychological Association

Bancroft et al. (1979) with the permission of the British Psychological Society and the author

Baucom & Danker-Brown (1979) with the permission of the American Psychological Association

Beck, Lester, & Kovacs (1973) reproduced with permission of authors and publishers, *Psychological Reports*

Beck, Kovacs, & Weissman (1975), copyright 1975, American Medical Association

Beck (1973), copyright 1973, American Medical Association

Bellantuono, Reggi, Tognoni, & Garattini (1980) with the permission of Adis International and the author

Bille-Brahe & Wang (1985) with the permission of Springer-Verlag

Bond & Demming (1982) with the permission of Plenum Press

Braucht (1979) with the permission of the American Psychological Association

Brewer & Farmer (1985) with the permission of the British Medical Association

Broverman, Broverman, Clarkson, Rosenkrantz, & Vogel (1970) with the permission of the American Psychological Association

Brown & Harris (1978) with the permission of Tavistock Publications

Cafferata, Kasper, & Bernstein (1983) with the permission of the American Sociological Association and the author

Clifton & Lee (1976) with the permission of the Guilford Press

Cooperstock (1978) reprinted with permission of Pergamon Press PLC.

D'Zurrilla & Goldfried (1971) with the permission of the American Psychological Association

Diener & Dweck (1978) with the permission of Lawrence Erlbaum Associates Inc.

Dweck & Goetz (1978) with the permission of Lawrence Erlbaum Associates Inc.

Erkut (1983) with the permission of Plenum Press

Ferguson & Horwood (1987) with the permission of Cambridge University Press

Fleishman (1984) with the permission of the American Sociological Association and the author

Ford & Widiger (1989) with the permission of the American Psychological Association

Forster & Frost (1985) with the permission of Munksgaard International Publishers Ltd.

Fox (1980) with the permission of the American Sociological Association and the author

Goldney & Pilowsky (1980) with the permission of the Royal Australian and New Zealand College of Psychiatrists

Goldney (1981a) by permission of the Royal College of Psychiatrists

Gove (1972) with the permission of the American Sociological Association and the author

Hawton & Goldacre (1982) by permission of the Royal College of Psychiatrists

Hawton & Catalan (1982a) by permission of Oxford University Press

Heshusius (1980) with the permission of Plenum Press

Hirsch, Walsh, & Draper (1983) with the permission of Blackwell Scientific Publications Limited

Hirsch, Walsh, & Draper (1982) with the permission of Elsevier Science Publishers

Holden, Mendonca, & Serin (1989) with the permission of the American Psychological Association

Horwitz (1977) with the permission of the American Sociological Association

Husaini & Neff (1981) copyright by William & Wilkins

Jarvis (1976) with the permission of the American Sociological Association

Kessel (1965) with the permission of the British Medical Association

Kessler, Brown, & Broman (1981) with the permission of the American Sociological Association and the author

Keyes (1984) with the permission of the British Psychological Society

Kreitman et al. (1969) by permission of the Royal College of Psychiatrists

Kreitman & Chowdhury (1973) by permission of the Royal College of Psychiatrists

Kreitman (1977) reprinted by permission of John Wiley and Sons, Ltd.

Landfield (1976) reprinted by permission of John Wiley and Sons, Ltd.

Lipshitz (1978) with the permission of Routledge

Lochel (1979) with the permission of Academic Press

Mant, Broom, & Duncan-Jones (1983) with the permission of Springer-Verlag

Maris (1971) with the permission of the American Sociological Association and the author

Masuda & Holmes (1978) copyright by the American Psychonomic Society

Mellinger (1978), copyright 1978, American Medical Association

Metalsky, Abramson, Seligman, Semmel, & Peterson (1982) with the permission of the American Psychological Association

Mikulincer & Nizan (1988) with the permission of the American Psychological Association

Morgan (1979) reprinted by permission of John Wiley and Sons, Ltd.

Neuringer (1976) with the permission of Grune & Stratton/The Psychological Corporation and the author

Newmann (1984) with the permission of the American Sociological Association and the author

Newson (1976) with the permission of Unwin Hyman/HarperCollins Publishers

Nolen-Hoeksema (1987) with the permission of the American Psychological Association

Oatley & Bolton (1985) with the permission of the American Psychological Association

Parker (1981) by permission of the Royal College of Psychiatrists

Patsiokas, Clum, & Luscomb (1979) with the permission of the American Psychological Association

Paykel, Prusoff, & Myers (1975), copyright 1975, American Medical Association

Philip (1970) by permission of the Royal College of Psychiatrists

Platt (1985) with the permission of Plenum Publishing Corp.

Platt, Hawton, Kreitman, Fagg, & Foster (1988) with the permission of Cambridge University Press

Prescott (1985) with the permission of the British Medical Association

Ramon, Bancroft, & Skirmshire (1975) by permission of the Royal College of Psychiatrists

Robins (1988) with the permission of the American Psychological Association

Showalter (1987) with the permission of Virago Press

Slater & Depue (1981) with the permission of the American Psychological Association

Stengel (1964) reproduced by permission of Penguin Books Ltd.

Stengel (1952) with the permission of the Royal Society of Medicine

Stipek (1982) with the permission of Plenum Press

Strachey (1959) reprinted by permission of Basic Books, a division of HarperCollins Publishers Inc.

Stryker & Gottlieb (1981) with the permission of Lawrence Erlbaum Associates Inc.

Sutherland & Verloff (1985) with the permission of Lawrence Erlbaum Associates Inc.

Taylor (1982) with the permission of Macmillan Accounts and Administration Ltd.

Turner (1980) with the permission of Croom Helm

Weiner (1986) with the permission of the Guilford Press

Weiner (1985) with the permission of the American Psychological Association

Weiss (1957) with the permission of *Psychiatry*, the Washington School of Psychiatry

Weissman, Paykel, French, Mark, Fox, & Prusoff (1973) with the permission of Springer-Verlag

Welch, Gerrard, & Huston (1986) with the permission of Division 35 of the American Psychological Association

Wells (1981) with the permission of the Office of Health Economics

Wexler, Weissman, & Kasl (1978) by permission of the Royal College of Psychiatrists

Williams, Murray, & Clare (1982) with the permission of Cambridge University Press

Wilson (1981) with the permission of the Guilford Press

Wong & Weiner (1981) with the permission of the American Psychological Association

Introduction: The Development of Theory and "Attempted Suicide"

EPIDEMIOLOGY AND THE NEGLECT OF GENDER

In England and Wales between 1961 and 1976 the number of admissions to hospital following deliberate self-poisoning—commonly referred to as "attempted suicide" or "overdosing"—increased from 23,900 to 108,200. Since 1976 there has been an equally dramatic decline in numbers, such that by 1985 admissions had fallen to 77,150 (Wells, 1981; 1988). Beginning its inexorable rise in the late-1950s, this extraordinary phenomenon, previously unknown on such a massive scale, remains largely unexplained.

Observed throughout the western world, wherever it occurred its major characteristic was that women predominated—usually in the order of two-to-one, and frequently by a greater margin (Kessler & McRae, 1983). A second major characteristic was that in over 60% of cases, prescribed psychotropic medication was employed (Wexler, Weissman, & Kasl, 1978).

Despite this, the largely female nature of the phenomenon and its relationship to the 2:1 excess of women among those prescribed psychotropics (Cooperstock, 1982) has been virtually ignored in the literature. Nine major American and European texts published between 1961 and 1986 (see Appendix)—including such seminal works as *The Cry for Help* (Shneidman & Farberow, 1961) and *Parasuicide* (Kreitman,

1977)—fail to devote more than a few paragraphs to sex differences. Similar neglect is evident in the professional journals where, despite a huge increase during the period in articles devoted to research on self-poisoning, few discuss the implications of the sex ratio among their subjects. Many fail even to record the respective numbers of each sex among subjects and, not uncommonly, only male patients are involved.

Perhaps most surprisingly, this predominantly "female malady" has been completely overlooked by feminist scholarship, despite its own re-emergence during the period when self-poisoning was reaching epidemic proportions, and despite its obvious relevance to the debate on gender and mental health to which the contribution of feminist psychology has been substantial.

The popular press has virtually ignored the phenomenon despite its preoccupation throughout this period with drug misuse to which deliberate self-poisoning must be considered a major contributor. Official concern, although leading to the setting up of two government-endorsed working parties (HMSO, 1968; DHSS, 1984) did not extend to the inclusion in official statistics of a discrete category for deliberate self-poisoning and self-injury.

Notwithstanding its neglect in the popular media, self-poisoning soon came to be described as an "epidemic" in the professional journals (Matthew, 1966). The term "epidemic" suggests a phenomenon with a fluctuating temporal course having peaks and troughs in different periods, and indeed self-poisoning has been an enduring social phenomenon with a fluctuating incidence from the mid-19th century to the present. Although demographic aspects of the epidemiology of self-poisoning have received considerable attention—especially during the period of its recent resurgence—little attempt has been made to place this within the much longer time-scale for which records are available, and there has been scant attention paid to the possible influence of social–historical and cultural factors. Such analysis has proven invaluable in understanding other "epidemics", both contemporary and historical, but its comparative neglect in relation to self-poisoning has resulted in this epidemiology making a descriptive rather than an explanatory contribution.

THE INADEQUACY OF THE PATHOLOGY PARADIGM

The development of any convincing and widely shared explanation of self-poisoning has undoubtedly been hindered by the misinterpretation or neglect of several of its definitive features, and the resultant conceptual poverty has both contributed to and been reinforced by conventional theoretical approaches to the phenomenon. Thus, for example, self-poisoning is still often conceived of, both in the professional literature and by the layman, as "failed suicide"—a misconception which has shown remarkable durability despite evidence that the majority of "attempted suicides" are in fact not (Kreitman, Philip, Greer, & Bagley, 1969). Over 90% of "attempted suicides" involve self-poisoning with medicinal agents (Hawton & Catalan, 1982a) and one study found that fewer than 16% of subjects had suicidal intent (Bancroft, Simpkin, Kingston, Cumming, & Whitwell, 1979). For these reasons self-poisoning is a more accurate term and will therefore be employed here. However, it is a term still widely unrecognised outside medicine, which is why "attempted suicide" appears in our own title.

Due at least in part to the confusion of self-poisoning and attempted suicide, theoretical approaches to self-poisoning have been dominated by the assumption of psychopathology. This may be justifiable in relation to completed suicide where there is evidence of significant psychopathology among its perpetrators (Barraclough, Bunch, & Sainsbury, 1974), but among self-poisoners there is little such evidence (Hawton & Catalan, 1982a, p.25).

The evolution of what is now the conventional psychopathology perspective on self-poisoning followed a course shared by perspectives on other forms of deviant behaviour over the last century, progressing through moral, criminal and, most recently, pathological explanatory models. From the early decades of the 20th century the pathology perspective of psychiatry began its ascendancy—"bad" was replaced with "mad" as the underpinning of an explanatory paradigm for many forms of deviance. Drug misuse and a variety of other behaviours previously regarded as moral or criminal transgressions, from murder to shop-lifting, became "pathologised".

Although suicide and attempted suicide remained criminal offences in Britain until 1961, there were comparatively few convictions (Stengel, 1964, p.71) as the intellectual and moral orthodoxies which underpinned this view had begun, by the mid-20th century, to give way to doubts about the nature of attempted suicide and its motivation. The authority of the pathology paradigm grew as psychiatry consolidated its position within the medical profession, the influence of which burgeoned in Britain after the Second World War through the expansion of the newly created National Health Service. It was largely as a result of medical pressure that the Suicide Act of 1961 repealed the ancient law under which suicide and attempted suicide had been criminal acts.

So acceptable had the pathology perspective become that shortly after the Act was passed the Ministry of Health advised doctors and other authorities that attempted suicide was to be regarded as a medical and social problem and that every case should be seen by a psychiatrist. This was an attitude welcomed by one influential contemporary commentator—Erwin Stengel—as "much more in keeping with present day knowledge and sentiment then the purely moralistic and punitive reaction expressed in the old law" (Stengel, 1964, p.72).

All these developments coincided with the almost unremarked beginning in the late-1940s of what was later to be called the "epidemic" of attempted suicide and, long before the official acceptance of the value of the pathology paradigm in the understanding and treatment of self-poisoning, Stengel had suggested that the study of such behaviour was, in turn, valuable to the understanding of psychopathology. Although one of the earliest commentators to identify differences between completed and "attempted" suicide, Stengel none the less promoted the psychopathology perspective in his insistence that: "our knowledge of psychopathology has been greatly enriched by the study of mental mechanisms which enter into suicidal acts". This, despite the fact that, to continue in his words: "one cannot escape the impression that research into the problem of suicide has been almost stagnant for some time" (Stengel, 1952, p.613).

So confident was Stengel of the relevance of a psychopathology perspective, that he stated that notwithstanding its powerful social aspect—what he referred to as its "appeal effect"—there should be no fear of an epidemic of attempted suicide because it is: "... a behaviour pattern which is at the disposal of only a limited group of personalities" (Stengel, 1952, p.620).

Whilst it would be unreasonable to criticise Stengel on the basis of hindsight for his inability to predict the massive increase in self-poisoning which was beginning to gather momentum as he wrote, there is little doubt that it was his belief in the pathological nature of such behaviour which, in his view, clearly precluded its extension to significant numbers of "normal" people. However, the pathology paradigm itself may be criticised not only for its evident lack of predictive power but also on the more serious grounds that as an explanatory paradigm it has proven of equally limited worth.

The full extent of this limitation may be judged by the conclusions of another leading psychiatrist, almost 30 years later, that: "At no point in our discussion so far have we really gained any insight into possible reasons for the epidemic-like increase of deliberate self-harm in most western countries since the early sixties" (Morgan, 1979, p.126). An intimation of the possible reasons for this failure is contained in Morgan's later, rhetorical questions: "... but why has this form of behaviour been chosen instead of others? What new influences are there in society especially concerning young adults and particularly relevant to females?" Finding no answers in his extensive review of the research and practice literature, Morgan (1979, p.126) is forced to conclude that: "At the present time we can only resort to conjecture".

It seems that the replacement of 19th century moral and legal orthodoxies with those of 20th century psychiatry and the pathology paradigm have done little to illuminate the remarkable phenomenon of self-poisoning.

THE NORMATIVE ORIGINS OF
SELF-POISONING

It is, therefore, to a critique of the pathology paradigm and the development of an alternative approach that the present work is dedicated. In view of the fact that since the Second World War self-poisoning with medications has been the most common form of deliberate self-harm, and since women have consistently predominated among self-poisoners, our focus will be on exploring the answers to Morgan's questions—Why women? Why self-poisoning? Why now?

Chapter One begins by describing the epidemiology of self-poisoning, disclosing its predominantly working class female nature. Exploration of its historical context demonstrates how sex differences in motivation and method have been an enduring feature of the phenomenon, and how both can be shown to reflect the social roles occupied respectively by men and women. Thus, for example, female self-poisoning has historically been motivated most frequently by events in the "private" or relational domain, whereas that of men more often is related to events occurring in the "public" realm of work, financial and legal problems. In terms of method, in the days before drugs became readily available women employed household cleaning materials and men industrial toxins with which to self-poison. Since the advent of the National Health Service, women, who have much more contact with this service, employ more prescribed medication than do males.

The early (albeit partial) recognition of these social factors by late-19th century psychiatrists, however, soon gave way to their virtually complete neglect by a later generation of psychiatrists in favour of an asocial pathology paradigm. It is suggested that although several among this second generation of psychiatrists contributed greatly to the understanding of self-poisoning—not least by promoting its conceptual separation from suicide, often alluded to but never fully defined by earlier commentators—the neglect of social context, especially gender, hindered the further development of adequate explanatory models.

Chapter Two supports this contention with a discussion and critique of existing theories and concludes that any satisfactory paradigm must be an "interactive" one capable of embracing both the social and the psychological levels of explanation, and not based on the (largely insupportable) assumption of psychopathology.

In Chapter Three the question of the female predominance is approached. A social psychology of self-poisoning is developed which suggests that if normative social processes can again be recognised as influential in the aetiology of self-poisoning, the study of sex role socialisation should be enlightening. Such socialisation is founded on the belief that members of each sex possess inherently different qualities and therefore are routinely socialised into "sex-appropriate" behaviours and roles. This combination of stereotypic qualities and socially sanctioned roles guides notions of what is "normal" in men and women, but as well as shaping their conforming behaviour it also influences their non-conformity, or deviance. Thus, for example, the perpetrators of aggressive criminal acts are more commonly male, whereas shop-lifting is predominantly a female crime.

Chapter Four examines the literature which describes the differing socialisation of males and females. The influence of the sex role system on forms of female deviance—particularly those relating to health and illness—is explored. It is suggested that the sex role socialisation of women encourages conformity with a dependent, "helpless" stereotype of femininity which both emphasises successful relationships with men and children as central to their social role and self-image and, at the same time, renders them ill-equipped to cope with breakdowns in these relationships. The early experience of parent loss and family breakdown, coupled with a current lack of alternative sources of social and self-esteem may render certain women additionally vulnerable to this helplessness in the face of extreme adversity. Such is indeed the experience of many women who poison themselves which, it is suggested, is the ultimate expression of the helplessness and dependency inherent in the stereotypic female role.

Turning to the second question—Why self-poisoning?—Chapter Four continues with a discussion of the greater use of the health system by women, of the marked excess prescription of psychotropic medication to them, and of the possible reasons for this in terms of stereotypic views (held by both doctors and their female patients) of women as physically and emotionally weaker than men. It is demonstrable that psychotropic medication is more frequently given to women with social and relational problems than to men with similar difficulties and that such medication is subsequently employed in self-poisoning more frequently by women: self-poisoning may then be seen as a form of self-medication reflecting these normative processes, rather than as aberrant behaviour guided by psychopathology.

Emerging from the literature on sex role socialisation comes an understanding of changes in women's roles and in their relationship to an evolving health care system. This provides some illumination of the periodic fluctuations in self-poisoning—and addresses the question, why now?

Having rejected the pathology paradigm an alternative is offered based upon the notion of female helplessness and self-poisoning as both product and reflection of normative sex role socialisation. In Chapter Five, Martin Seligman's theory of learned helplessness (Seligman, 1975) is discussed as potentially forming the basis for an empirical approach to this emerging hypothesis. This theory is concerned with the effects on people of the repeated experience of uncontrollable events—that is of "non-contingency" between outcomes and the individual's attempts to control them. The theory proposes that such experiences of uncontrollability lead to three types of deficit: motivational, where persistence is diminished as a consequence of the expectation that outcomes are uncontrollable; cognitive, where the learning that outcomes are uncontrollable makes it difficult to learn new, potentially effective strategies; and affective, with uncontrollability leading to depression (Abramson, Seligman, & Teasdale, 1978).

Inconsistent results relating to the generalisation of helplessness between situations and to differences in motivational and affective consequences between individuals led Seligman and his colleagues to believe that the original conception gave insufficient importance to cognitive factors in determining how an individual responds to non-contingency and helplessness. The model was, therefore, reformulated in terms of attribution theory, such that the nature and extent of helplessness deficits will depend on the causes to which an individual attributes their inability to affect the environment—i.e. on the process of "causal attribution".

For example, an individual who attributes his failure in a test to internal and stable causes such as "low IQ" will not expect to improve on the next occasion, and is unlikely, therefore, to persist in his studies for resits. One who, on the other hand, makes an external, unstable attribution to "test difficulty", may well expect the next test to be easier and, being more inclined to expect success next time, will persist in his studies. Quite clearly, the former is a dysfunctional attitude to problems which undermines the skills of coping with them. A review of the literature demonstrating sex differences in attribution—with considerable evidence of a dysfunctional female style—concludes Chapter Five.

Chapter Six demonstrates that attribution theory, though not previously applied to this field, is particularly relevant to the understanding of self-poisoning. The occurrence of multiple adverse events has been consistently documented as a feature of self-poisoning and clearly occupies a central role in its causation, with marked sex differences in the nature of precipitant events. Some attempts have been made within cognitive psychology to establish the mechanism linking adverse events to self-poisoning and a consensus is emerging that self-poisoners have deficits in "coping skills"—but concepts have been disparate and an integrative theory has proven elusive. Meanwhile attribution theorists have increasingly recognised adverse events as "provoking agents" in the emergence of dysfunctional attitudes, and most recently that individuals may possess "specific vulnerability" to the emergence of such attitudes when confronted with negative events in particular domains (Alloy, Abramson, Metalsky, & Hartlage, 1988).

In Chapter Seven an emerging vulnerability–stress model therefore suggests that self-poisoners are drawn from among those who are vulnerable to extreme helplessness due to the emergence of dysfunctional attributions provoked by specific types of adverse event. Certain groups of individuals, such as the economically disadvantaged and those with histories of early family disruption, are more vulnerable due to their greater experience of uncontrollability. Women are additionally vulnerable to helplessness, dysfunctional attitudes and self-poisoning due to the effects of the sex role system and the medicalisation of their social and relational problems. The remainder of Chapter Seven is devoted to the results of a study of attributions among 60 self-poisoning patients and the implications of its findings for the continued development of the attributional model.

Turning finally from the evolution of theory to the efficacy of practice, Chapter Eight reviews the literature on primary and secondary intervention with self-poisoners. Here too the influence of the pathology perspective has dominated therapeutic method and, perhaps inevitably, its success has been no greater in practice than theory. While this text is not offered as a practice guide, it is argued that an attributional approach to self-poisoning has implications for intervention which, if integrated into practice, might improve its efficacy.

Although the neglect of gender as an important dimension of self-poisoning amply justifies the focus of the present work, its emphasis on female self-poisoning is not intended to imply that the model offered is inapplicable to that of males. On the contrary the relevance of the suggested model to male self-poisoning is stressed, and the merits of its conceptualisation in terms of gender (a social construction) rather than sex (a biological one) become increasingly apparent as the discussion develops. Much psychological research is criticised by contemporary feminist scholars on two grounds: that it neglects the gender dimension, often not reporting the sex of subjects and frequently employing only male subjects; and a second criticism, to which the present work is more vulnerable, that much research—when it does report sex differences—emphasises these at the expense of the similarities which emerge (Squire, 1989).

In the research described in this book sex differences are disclosed which have a direct bearing on our subject matter. However, these differences are discussed in terms of gender rather than sex—the implication being that the helplessness that is learned during female sex role socialisation may also be experienced by males with particular learning histories involving uncontrollable adversity. None the less, for the present the emphasis remains intentionally female.

Again, the attributional model is not offered as an explanation for all female self-poisoning. Although certain groups are identified as being especially vulnerable to the helplessness consequent on possession of a certain attributional style, "women" are sometimes referred to for purposes of parsimony as if they constituted an homogenous group. They do not and, as individuals differ, so too may the origins of their self-poisoning behaviour. It is not the intention of this work to deny that a small percentage of self-poisoners are mentally disordered and may as a consequence be at great risk of completed suicide. It is the intention to redress the misconception whereby the majority are so regarded.

Similarly, attribution theory is not in reality a single theory and, as yet, is an imperfect and still evolving body of knowledge. Thus the attributional model of self-poisoning described in the forthcoming chapters does not seek to replace the limiting certainties of the pathology paradigm with orthodoxies of a different origin, for in Erich Fromm's cautionary phrase (Fromm, 1947): "The quest for certainty blocks the search for meaning".

CHAPTER 1

Epidemiology and the Neglect of Meaning

Self-poisoning—the deliberate, non-fatal ingestion of medicinal agents in excess of the recommended dose—may with justification be viewed as one of the most dramatic and still largely unexplained phenomena in 20th century social medicine.

EPIDEMIOLOGY

It has been estimated that every year in Great Britain as many as 215,000 people deliberately poison themselves with drugs (Wells, 1981, p.27), although such official records as there are suggest a much lower number because they do not include those self-poisoners who are discharged from casualty departments or who are treated at home by general practitioners. Official statistics do, however, indicate trends in self-poisoning if not its true prevalence, and between 1967 and 1977 the incidence of self-poisoning increased by 90%. The financial cost of treatment for those admitted to hospital in 1977 was conservatively estimated at £20m. (Wells, 1981, p.50). Since then the yearly rate has declined until in 1985 it was officially recorded (for England only) as 77,150 (Table 1.1).

This phenomenon was not limited to Great Britain, however, and similar increases were reported in most western industrialised societies (World Health Organisation, 1982). In America in 1985 it was suggested that as many as 5,000,000 living Americans had at some time

TABLE 1.1
Admissions for Adverse Effects of Medicinal Agents—England and Wales 1957–1985 (Hospital In-patient Enquiry Data)

	England and Wales (HMSO, 1968)	
		All agents
1957		15,900
1958		17,500
1959		20,200
1960		23,300

	England and Wales medicinal and other agents (Wells, 1981)	
	Medicinal	All Agents
1961	23,900	28,400
1962	28,700	34,100
1963	39,000	46,400
1964	42,900	51,000
1965	45,600	54,200
1966	50,300	59,800
1967	57,200	68,000
1968	62,320	74,450
1969	75,550	90,120
1970	79,160	93,180
1971	85,370	99,880
1972	91,440	105,720
1973	92,970	107,170
1974	98,290	113,160
1975	105,290	120,370
1976	108,210	125,240
1977	106,710	121,450

	England (Wells, 1988)
	Medicinal Agents
1978	90,950
1979	87,280
1980	86,810
1981	87,840
1982	85,660
1983	78,160
1984	78,450
1985	77,150

"attempted to commit suicide" (McIntosh, 1985, p.1) while in the European Community a comparable estimate for 1975 was 9,000,000 (Diekstra, 1982, p.10). Not surprisingly in view of these striking statistics, self-poisoning has been described as reaching epidemic proportions in the western world (Matthew, 1966).

Epidemics are often perceived as great "levellers", affecting all without regard for class, creed or other social category. This has not been the case with self-poisoning, for, wherever it has appeared in western societies, it has been a predominantly working class, female phenomenon. Norman Kreitman, a leading commentator on self-poisoning, described a 14-fold excess of class 5 individuals over those from classes 1 and 2 combined among a series of "parasuicides" in Edinburgh (Kreitman, 1977, p.24). International estimates of the prevalence of females among this group have varied from 1.4:1 to 4:1 (Wexler et al., 1978) and among teenagers this has reached 9:1 (Hawton, 1986, p.61), with one study reporting from Edinburgh that 1 in 100 females between 15 and 19 was admitted to hospital each year with self-poisoning (Kreitman & Schreiber, 1979), and another that "self-poisoning has become the most common reason why women are admitted as emergencies to general hospitals" (Hawton & Catalan, 1982a, p.7).

The major aspects of the epidemiology of self-poisoning are illustrated in the tables and graphs on the following pages. Official government records of self-poisoning as such are not kept, and all national data refers to those patients admitted for at least one night to a hospital ward for the treatment of the "adverse effects of medicinal agents". The source of these records is the Hospital In-patient Enquiry (HIPE), which, as noted earlier, must represent a considerable underestimate of the true extent of the phenomenon. It has been estimated from surveys of GP practices and community studies that as many as one-third of such cases do not attend hospital for treatment (Kreitman, 1977) and that at least 10% are discharged from accident departments without admission to wards (Ghodse, 1979).

In view of this, important sources of data are regional centres such as the Edinburgh Regional Poisoning Treatment Centre which has kept records since the late-1920s. The Edinburgh RPTC data have been demonstrated to provide an accurate reflection of national trends (Kreitman, 1977, p.11) and will frequently be drawn upon in this work. The early development of the self-poisoning epidemic (then referred to as "attempted suicide") is shown in Figs. 1.1 and 1.2 which detail the rapid increase in the early post-war years.

National records were first kept by the HIPE in 1953 and Table 1.1 shows trends according to this data from 1957–1985, illustrating the

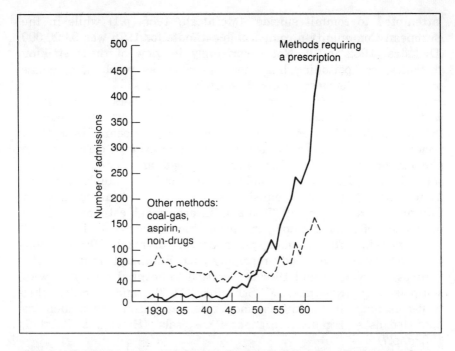

FIG. 1.1. Admissions to Edinburgh Regional Poisoning Treatment Centre 1928–1962 (Kessel, 1965).

massive increase in its prevalence between the early-1960s and 1976 when the rate declined for the first time in 40 years and has continued so to do.

The enduring female predominance among this population is shown in Fig. 1.3 which describes admissions to the Edinburgh RPTC for the period 1973–1985. An interesting aspect of this figure is the marked convergence of the male and female rates towards the end of the period —a point to which we shall return later in the discussion.

National data for 1977 on age distribution (shown in Fig. 1.4) illustrates that the greatest female predominance is among the youngest age groups up to 24 years, after which the differential lessens progressively and rapidly with age, whilst Table 1.2 clearly shows that for both sexes the 25–34 year olds provide the single largest group of self-poisoners.

National trends in female self-poisoning between 1952 and 1982 are shown in Fig. 1.5 which illustrates that the most rapid rate of increase occurred among the younger age groups in the early period and that these groups show the sharpest decline at the end of it.

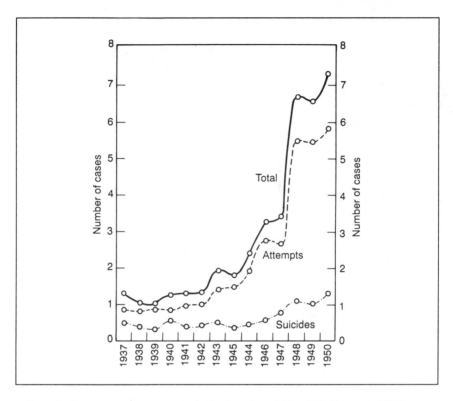

FIG. 1.2. Suicide and attempted suicide, London 1936–1950 (Stengel, 1952).

Detailed characteristics of the self-poisoning population are most readily available from regional data and Tables 1.3 and 1.4 are based on the Edinburgh RPTC admissions for 1978. Table 1.3 demonstrates the striking class differential referred to earlier, with class 5 individuals being massively predominant, and, in Fig. 1.6, having the most rapid rate of increase as the "epidemic" gathered momentum. Although these data refer to males—as the social class of females is less easily established—there is no reason to believe that females would show different patterns. As we shall see, our own data confirm this assertion. Marital status is another important variable in this population and Table 1.4 shows that the divorced of both sexes have the highest rates of self-poisoning, with divorced men having the highest self-poisoning rate of any group. Finally, Table 1.5 describes the incidence of various social problems reported by self-poisoners in Edinburgh in the years 1975 and 1978, showing the relative stability of the nature of such problems over the period but also the marked differences between the sexes.

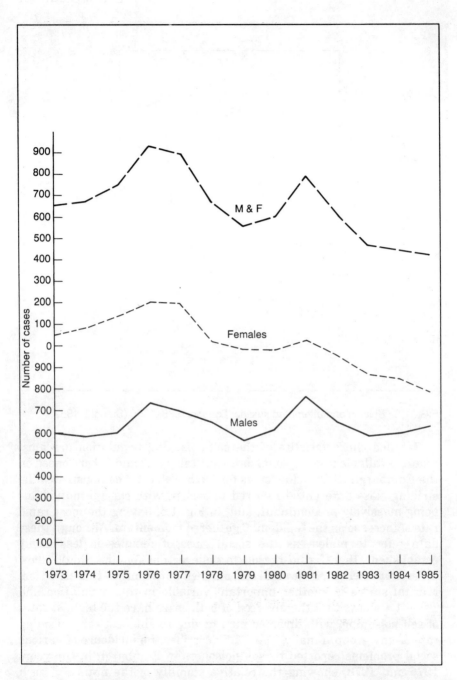

FIG. 1.3. Sex distribution of admissions to Edinburgh RPTC 1973–1985 (Robinson, 1986).

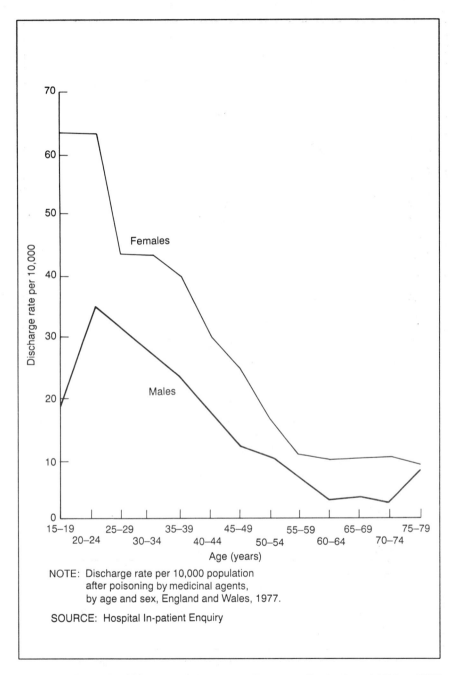

NOTE: Discharge rate per 10,000 population
after poisoning by medicinal agents,
by age and sex, England and Wales, 1977.

SOURCE: Hospital In-patient Enquiry

FIG. 1.4. Self-poisoning, sex- and age-specific rates, England and Wales 1977 (WHO, 1982).

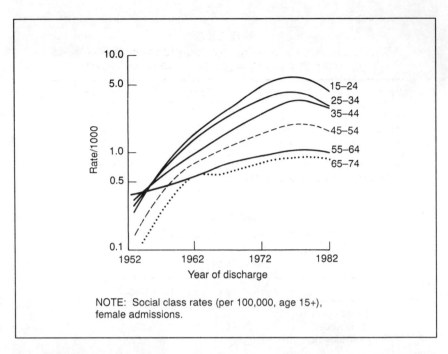

FIG. 1.5. Female self-poisoning age-specific rates, England and Wales 1952–1982 (Brewer & Farmer, 1985).

TABLE 1.2
Discharges and Deaths for Adverse Effects of Medicinal Agents, Age and Sex-specific Rates, England and Wales 1977 (Wells, 1981)

Age Group	Males (%)	Females (%)	All (%)
15-19	11.9	19.2	16.6
20-24	18.9	17.5	18.0
25-34	30.8	25.3	27.3
35-44	17.9	16.5	17.0
45-64	16.1	15.2	15.2
65-74	2.9	4.1	3.7
75 +	2.5	4.0	2.0
Total	100	100	100
Actual discharges and deaths over 15 years	32,220	59,450	91,670

NOTE: Percentage distribution of discharges and deaths for adverse effects of medicinal agents among those aged 15 years and over by age and sex, England and Wales 1977. SOURCE: Hospital In-patient Enquiry.

TABLE 1.3
Male Parasuicide in Edinburgh by Social Class in 1978—Rates per 100,000 Aged 15 Years and Over (Wells, 1981)

Class	Admissions	Patients	First-evers
I & II	122	106	78
III	281	211	131
IV	536	446	275
V	986	721	417

SOURCE: *Annual Report* of the Edinburgh RPTC.

TABLE 1.4
Self-poisoning RPTC Admission Rate by Civil State per 100,000—Edinburgh 1978 (Wells, 1981)

	Males	Females
All ages over 15		
Divorced	1,917	1,129
Widowed	163	155
Aged 15-34		
Single	461	959
Married	370	598
Aged 35+		
Single	351	220
Married	136	227

SOURCE: *Annual Report* of the Edinburgh RPTC.

TABLE 1.5
Social Problems by Sex of Self-poisoners, Edinburgh 1978—1975 in Parentheses (Wells, 1981)

	Per Cent Reporting Problem	
	Males	Females
Overcrowding	14 (12)	12 (18)
Living alone	11 (9)	10 (6)
Criminal record	58 (58)	16 (16)
Debt	21 (17)	16 (17)
Violence used on others	34 (39)	21 (22)
Violence received from relatives	21 (19)	31 (31)
Unemployed	47 (45)	21 (18)

SOURCE: *Annual Report* of the Edinburgh RPTC.

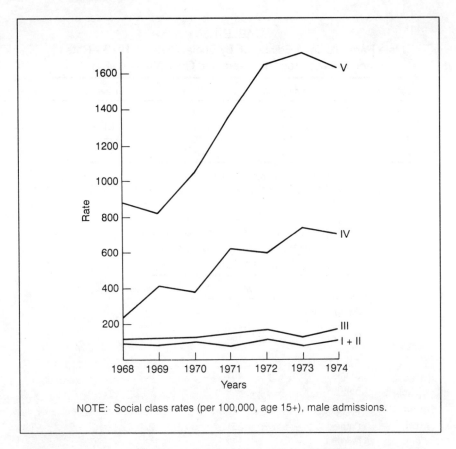

FIG. 1.6. Male self-poisoning by social class, Edinburgh 1968–1974 (Kreitman, 1977).

Much more could be said about the epidemiology of self-poisoning and, indeed, texts concerned with this phenomenon frequently sacrifice theoretical interpretation in favour of its exhaustive description. The predominance of women among self-poisoners is often noted in such work but its implications are rarely considered, and it is to the discussion of this neglect that we now turn.

THE NEGLECT OF GENDER

There is, therefore, clear evidence from British data, and as we shall see, from international sources that females exceed males in "parasuicidal" behaviour: not only this, however, but that they also exceed males in suicidal rumination. Bagley discovered in a survey of

English school children (Bagley, 1975) that 4.5% of boys but 9.7% of girls had entertained "relatively serious suicidal ideation at some time". Paykel discovered a similar disparity when he surveyed a representative sample of the residents of New Haven, Connecticut (Paykel, Myers, Lindethal, & Tanner, 1974). Among his 720 subjects he found that 11.4% of women, as opposed to 5.7% of men had experienced suicidal feelings within the last year. Interesting also was the finding that such feelings were far more prevalent among social class 5 individuals with 11.1% reporting such ideation, as compared to 4.8% among classes 1–3 combined.

Despite these striking statistics, gender is largely ignored in both the theoretical discussion and empirical investigation of self-poisoning. This is amply demonstrated in a recent bibliography by McIntosh (1985). The author describes an explosion of commentary in this field beginning in the early–1960s and points out that an earlier bibliography had listed 2202 references for the 60 years from 1897 to 1957 whilst for the subsequent 13, up to 1970, there were 2300 references. McIntosh's own work, dealing with the period from the mid-1970s to 1983, boasts 2300 entries—mostly from psychiatric sources.

However the impressive growth of commentary (stimulated in part by the massive increase in self-poisoning in these years) did not promote the discussion of gender, and the neglect of these issues is marked, with only 16 entries in McIntosh's bibliography specifically mentioning sex differences in attempted suicide—several of which are reviews describing the results of other papers included in the 16 entries (McIntosh, 1985, pp.64–67). Of 10 major texts devoted to the subject of parasuicide published between 1964 and 1986 (see Appendix), all written or edited by psychiatrists, none give more than passing consideration to gender, and then comment is mostly confined to it as a demographic fact with little apparent theoretical or practical importance.

Despite its unheralded appearance in the post-war years and startling progress to comparative ubiquity in the mid-1970s, self-poisoning, compared for example with drug addiction or child abuse, has received remarkably little public attention. In view of its predominantly female nature this may be seen as even more surprising as its emergence has been contemporary with the resurgence of the women's movement and feminist perspectives on social and medical issues in western society. In the academic sphere sociologists, notwithstanding their enduring interest in completed suicide, with which self-poisoning has been compared, have similarly neglected this phenomenon, and its discussion has been largely confined to the psychiatric literature.

Despite the neglect of gender issues, this body of work has made numerous important contributions to our understanding of self-poisoning: one of these is its gradual conceptual separation of suicide and attempted suicide.

SUICIDE AND ATTEMPTED SUICIDE

Many authors still employ the term "attempted suicide" to describe this phenomenon, and the tendency to regard all non-fatal acts of deliberate self-harm as failed suicides characterises most of the psychiatric literature, at least until the early-1960s. Stengel and Cook's 1958 Maudsley Monograph *Attempted Suicide: Its Social Significance and Effects* (Stengel & Cook, 1958) is frequently cited as the beginning of an appreciation of the differences between the two phenomena, although Stengel himself credited a German epidemiologist—Peller—with first having drawn attention to the distinguishing features of attempted suicide in 1932 (Peller, 1932).

Despite Stengel's generous reference to Peller's work, however, some commentators had shown an awareness of the differing nature of the two behaviours and their motivation long before this—a fact which makes the persistence of the confusion more puzzling. As early as 1838, Esquirol wrote in his *Des Malades Mentales* (Esquirol, 1838) that: "Of 100 persons who attempt suicide only 40 succeed", and Westcott (1885) commented that there were important differences in motivation between those who commit and those who attempt suicide, suggesting that: "It is a common idea that many attempts are made with a view to coerce or influence relations and friends, attempts which in fact are not intended to be successful although they sometimes succeed".

Encouraged by a contemporary dramatic increase in suicidal behaviour similar to that which 50 years later was to prompt Stengel's enquiries, W.C. Sullivan, a deputy medical officer of Pentonville Prison, writing in the Journal of Mental Science in 1900 on the connection of alcoholism to suicide noted (Sullivan, 1900):

> ... in another category of suicidal manifestations, viz. attempts to commit suicide, there has been a similar and even more decided increase. Thus in the period 1867–71 the number of cases of attempted suicide amounted to 35.5 per million inhabitants ... in the period 1892–96 it rose to 57.9 per million, an increase of over 78%.

This dramatic increase is shown in Sullivan's graph (Fig. 1.7) with the attempted suicide rate being the lower curve. At the time attempted suicide was a criminal offence and consequently its reporting in such official data is unreliable—as the apparent excess of suicide in this graph demonstrates. This is, in reality, more due to the comparative ease

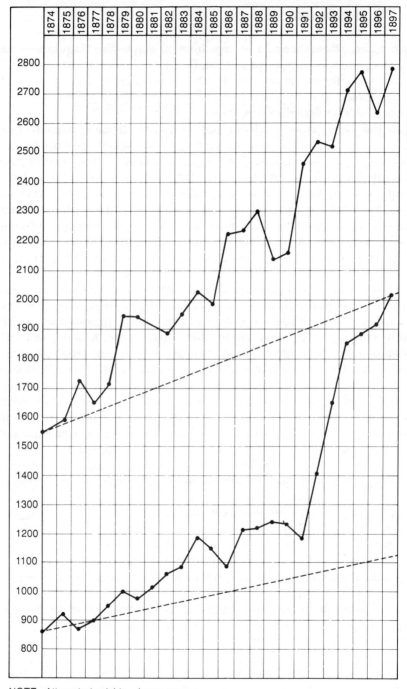

NOTE: Attempted suicide – lower curve.

FIG. 1.7. Attempted suicide in Great Britain 1874–1897 (Sullivan, 1900).

with which attempts could be kept from official notice than to any real preponderance of completed suicide. Despite this inaccuracy the trends shown are informative, especially when it is considered that the extent of attempted suicide shown in these official data must have been considerable underestimates.

In the same paper, Sullivan suggested that these figures, coupled with the evidence of increasing completed suicide, represented a real growth in "suicidal tendency" although cautioned: "... there are decided reasons for thinking that the causation of suicidal attempts is by no means entirely identical with those of the majority of actual suicides". He summarised his comparison of the two behaviours as a difference of motivation, suggesting that differences in their rates of increase, method employed, and in the age incidence of each supported this belief.

The concern to elucidate the difference between attempted and completed suicide was furthered by another prison medical officer, W. Norwood-East, who also noted the considerable increase in "attempted suicide" in the last quarter of the 19th century (Table 1.6). Writing a remarkably comprehensive review of the social correlates of suicidal behaviour in 1913, East noted that there was "a third class (of attempter) the 'workshy' who makes repeated slight attempts to obtain shelter and the comparative comfort of a remand prison", and "of course some cases were trivial, others not genuine". Speaking of the unemployed in the days of the workhouse, Norwood-East (1913, p.460) foreshadowed Stengel's later famous literary allusion on the "Janus face of attempted suicide" by asserting: "Sometimes a twofold idea is present in the man's mind—that if it result in death well and good; if in rescue and employment, also well and good".

He also explored other motivation such as (p.462):

> ... to frighten relatives by making suicidal attempts, the commonest being to stop a wife nagging, to get a wife to return home or to take her husband back, to stop her drinking, to get her to give her lover up. At times to gain sympathy or avoid blame when losing employment through bad conduct or the committal of some crime.

This paper, far in advance of so much that followed it in more recent times, ended with a summary of the differences between suicides and attempted suicides (p.477):

> Attempted suicide and suicide differ ... in the age incidence, and in the methods most frequently adopted; and, whereas attempted suicide is only slightly influenced by civil status, actual suicide is markedly affected. Physical disease is not by itself a common cause of attempted

TABLE 1.6
Suicidal Attempts Known to the Police—Great Britain 1866–1900
(Norwood-East, 1913)

Years	Annual No. of Attempts Known to the Police	Proportion per 100,000 Population	Years	Annual No. of Attempts Known to the Police	Proportion per 100,000 Population
1866–70	704	3.21	1901–5	2304	6.92
1871–75	792	3.38	1906	2497	7.23
1876–80	928	3.71	1907	2514	7.20
1881–85	1099	4.13	1908	2625	7.43
1886–90	1195	4.20	1909	2356	6.59
1891–95	1596	5.35	1910	2462	6.88
1896–1900	1983	6.29	1911	2313	6.40

suicide ... suicide appears to be frequently due to physical suffering. Insanity is more likely to cause suicide than attempts at suicide. In the latter 14.1% were due to this cause.

There are other examples of a recurrent interest in the differences between the two phenomena, with Peller's contribution in 1932, and an English psychiatrist, Hopkins', comprehensive review of all suicides and attempts in Liverpool between 1932 and 1935, which found similar differentiating factors. Of particular interest is Hopkins' (1937, p.90) finding that in at least 30% of cases there was: "no underlying determination to terminate life"; and his assertion that the 2:1 predominance of females noted even then was: "... no doubt due to the hazards of love affairs and of early married life, misfortunes in these circumstances bearing more hardly on the female". This assumption had also been voiced earlier by Norwood-East (1913, p.463) who had remarked in the same context that: "Particularly with regard to lovetroubles it may well be that the age-incidence is different in the two sexes, the love of women differing so materially from that of man".

We shall return to a consideration of sex differences in motivation in later sections of this work, but these remarks and others we shall note when considering the methods employed in attempted suicide demonstrate an early acknowledgement of the influence of sex roles on self-poisoning which was, however, not to be developed by a later generation of psychiatrists.

Thus, evidence exists of an earlier "epidemic" of attempted suicide in the late-19th century and a subsequent continuing, though infrequently voiced, interest in the differences between such patients and completed suicides in epidemiological as well as motivational terms, predating

Stengel by at least 100 years. This seems to have had little impact on the literature, however, and it was not until a paper by Stengel —*Enquiries Into Attempted Suicide* (Stengel, 1952)—and the publication in 1958 of the results of a research survey exploring its assertions (Stengel & Cook, 1958), that these distinctions became widely recognised among suicidologists. These works followed their predecessors in enumerating the demographic differences; however, it was the discussion of motivational differences between the two populations which was to prove to be a watershed in the study of attempted suicide.

Stengel in his 1952 paper asserted that:

> ... research into the problem of suicide has been almost stagnant for some time. This I believe has been due to the preoccupation of the majority of research workers, psychiatrists and sociologists alike, with a retrospective analysis of people who have committed suicide. But we can learn a great deal through the intensive study of those who have survived suicide attempts ... they are, probably, as a group not the same population as those who actually commit suicide, but it would be surprising if a study of that group did not also add to our knowledge of the other. Much has of course been written about attempted suicide, but most writers were concerned with exactly the same problems that had been studied in those who had committed suicide. This is not surprising for most people, including psychiatrists, look on a person who has attempted suicide as somebody who has bungled his suicide.

He went on to suggest that the assumption that a genuine suicidal attempt ought to aim only at death is one that needed challenging, and that:

> It seemed worthwhile to look afresh at attempted suicide, this time as a behaviour pattern, without any preconceived ideas about its aim and biological significance. This we have done with a great variety of patients (and) it becomes obvious that self destruction cannot be the main and only purpose of the suicidal attempt. The self-injury in most attempted suicides, however genuine, is insufficient to bring about death and the attempts are made in a social setting which makes the intervention of others possible, probable or even inevitable. There is a social element in the pattern of most suicidal attempts. In most attempted suicides we can discover an appeal to other human beings.

Stengel goes on to elaborate this alternative motivational hypothesis and we shall explore it at greater length later: however, what is interesting to observe now is his reluctance to completely abandon the notion of a ubiquitous suicidal intent, as is shown by these assertions:

> We regard the appeal character of the suicidal attempt, which is usually unconscious, as one of its essential features, but it certainly is not the only one that determines its purpose. If one had to design a pictorial symbol for attempted suicide one would present this act as Janus-faced, with one aspect directed towards destruction and death, and the other towards human contact and life.

This reluctance to fly completely in the face of what was undoubtedly the conventional wisdom of his day is not surprising and a further insight into his caution may be obtained from one of his concluding remarks:

> I trust that our findings will not give rise to undue optimism, and that inexperienced doctors, in dealing with individual patients, will not adopt the principle "once an attempted suicide, always an attempted suicide".

In 1964 Stengel published his book *Suicide and Attempted Suicide* in which he described much of the material contained in the 1958 Maudsley Monograph, and it is very apparent that his ambivalence about the motivation behind attempted suicide had still to be resolved. He stated (Stengel, 1964, p.80) that his hypothesis offered in the 1952 paper, "that those who attempted and those who committed suicide constituted two different groups or 'populations' was confirmed." But he then went on to qualify this in these words (pp.80–81):

> The formulation concerning the two populations has nevertheless given rise to serious misunderstandings ... Unfamiliarity with this use of the term 'population' and the preference for the simple over the complex proposition, have led to the misconception that these two 'populations' were meant to consist of altogether different and mutually exclusive types of individuals. Some students of suicide readily, though erroneously, accepted this notion, while others, quite rightly, contested it, although it had never been put forward by the present author.

Adding to the confusion, he continued (p.82):

> It is generally believed that most, if not all, people who commit suicidal acts are clearly determined to die. The study of attempted suicides does not bear this out. Many suicidal attempts and quite a few suicides are carried out in the mood 'I don't care whether I live or die', rather than with a clear and unambiguous determination to end life. Most people, in

committing a suicidal act, are just as muddled as they are whenever they do anything of importance under emotional stress.

Stengel concludes this (pp.82–83) with a definition of a suicidal act as: "... any deliberate act of self-damage which the person committing the act could not be sure to survive." This definition would, of course, lead to the exclusion from this category of most of the patients he had described in the 1952 paper where, as we mentioned earlier, Stengel had stated (Stengel, 1952, p.618): "The self-injury in most attempted suicides, however genuine, is insufficient to bring about death, and the attempts are made in a setting which makes the intervention of others possible, probable, or even inevitable". The emphasis of this definition is very different from the one offered in the introduction to the book, which was (Stengel, 1964, pp.14–15): "In this book suicidal attempt (means) the non-fatal act of self-injury undertaken with conscious self-destructive intent, however vague and ambiguous."

Thus Stengel's concern to maintain the centrality of a suicidal intention in attempted suicide in the face of evidence from his own research to the contrary, leads him to offer definitions which are as muddled as he claims the subjects of those definitions to be, a situation clearly shown in his summary of the problem of motivation (Stengel, 1964, p.87): "Most people who commit suicidal acts do not either want to die or to live; they want to do both at the same time, usually the one more, or much more than the other".

In other words the difference is one of degree not kind—a position not too far removed from that which Stengel asserted at the beginning of his research in 1952 that he intended to challenge, namely that: "... most people, including psychiatrists, look on a person who has attempted suicide as somebody who has bungled his suicide".

Although Stengel found it impossible to abandon entirely the suicide analogy and its terminology, psychiatrists such as Kessel and Kreitman, working in the Regional Poisoning Treatment Centre in Edinburgh, confronted with the second wave of the epidemic increase in the behaviour which had begun in the early-1960s, and finding a similar lack of suicidal motivation, rejected Stengel's suicide analogy and sought a more adequate terminology. Kessel (1965) declared: "If the term attempted suicide were just meaningless, it could be tolerated, but it is positively wrong and should be discarded". He therefore suggested that the phrase "deliberate self-poisoning" should be adopted to describe the behaviour, and, four years later, Kreitman added: "The term attempted suicide is highly unsatisfactory for the excellent reason that the great majority of patients so designated are not in fact attempting suicide." The term "parasuicide" was offered (Kreitman et al., 1969).

Although contentious at the time, empirical evidence mounted demonstrating that the definitive characteristic of this behaviour was certainly not its suicidal intent. Thus Bancroft found that only one-third of his patients claimed that they had wanted to die—even fewer (16%) were assessed by psychiatrists as having intended to die (Bancroft et al., 1979), results replicated in Hawton's study of adolescent "attempters" (Hawton, Cole, O'Grady & Osborn, 1982b).

The eventual abandonment of the suicidal analogy by many leading commentators not only resulted in a more appropriate terminology but also facilitated the development of a variety of alternative motivational hypotheses. None the less, the inadequate earlier conceptual framework of suicidologists, which emphasised suicidal intention and mental disorder, had the seriously limiting effect of discouraging the exploration of the personal and social meaning of parasuicide. The assumption had been entrenched in the psychiatric paradigm that the behaviour was irrational, the manifestation of mental disorder, and therefore quite literally "meaningless". This pathology perspective led to the neglect of normative influences and their role in the promotion of self-poisoning. Thus, whilst the terminological debate was won, and the suicidal analogy largely abandoned, the pathology paradigm persisted.

THE NEGLECT OF MEANING

Whilst the contribution of psychiatric enquiry to the description of self-poisoning has been great, its relative neglect by social science has led to the predominance of the psychiatric perspective and an emphasis on psychopathology and psychiatric epidemiology. This is clearly illustrated by Stengel's remarks in his exploration of the social and interpersonal aspects of attempted suicide (Stengel, 1952, p.620), that despite its social effects and interpersonal meaning it remained: "... a behaviour pattern which is at the disposal of only a limited group of personalities".

This statement, made on the eve of the most phenomenal increase in self-poisoning ever known, must have been the cause of some subsequent regret although its central contention is one that continued to be propounded in the psychiatric literature, much of which is devoted to a search for mental or personality disorder among self-poisoners and to the description of their socio-demographic characteristics. Again, this contribution should not be underestimated for there has evolved an exhaustive body of descriptive material relating to the incidence of psychopathology among this population and a definitive account of its demographic and ecological distribution. However, as might be expected of a discipline whose strength in part has been founded on the sophistication of its system of description and classification, there has been a neglect of subjective and social "meaning".

This is to say that mainstream academic psychiatry—as opposed to psychodynamic psychology—with its entirely legitimate concern to improve the description, classification and treatment of pathological states, has tended to regard self-poisoning as a symptom of such disorder and therefore to regard the behaviour itself as essentially "meaningless". Much as the anorexia, sleep disturbance and retardation associated with "endogenous depression" are seen as symptoms of an organically based illness to be cured rather than as in any sense purposive action with subjective and social meaning to be discovered and understood. Where this denial of meaning is not associated with the declared organicism of much mainstream psychiatry, it may be seen at least in part as stemming from the historical conception of self-poisoning as attempted suicide. It is established that many completed suicides occur among those clearly suffering from severe depressive or other psychotic mental disorders (Barraclough et al., 1974), and suicidal ideation and behaviour in this context frequently spring from hallucinations or delusions which are by definition irrational and "meaningless".

GENDER AND THE DEVELOPMENT OF THEORY

The neglect of social meaning in self-poisoning has both contributed to and been promoted by the parallel neglect of gender as a definitive characteristic of this predominantly female phenomenon. Where purposiveness and meaning is afforded to self-poisoning—that is, where evidence is lacking of enduring mental illness as is the case in the majority of episodes (Hawton & Catalan, 1982a, p.25)—the pathology orientation inherent in the psychiatric paradigm is inclined to impute the "manipulative" or "aggressive" motivation of the "hysterical", "inadequate", or "psychopathic" personality. This, as we shall see, is particularly true for female patients who are frequently, and apparently with little justification, diagnosed as "hysterical personality".

As we turn now to a consideration of current theories of self-poisoning it will become clear that an explanatory model based on the assumption of psychopathology has permeated most commentary on self-poisoning. It will be argued that this model has little empirical justification and has hindered, rather than enhanced, the development of theory capable of illuminating the many facets of this phenomenon; not only those related to psychopathology, but, perhaps more importantly, those related to gender.

CHAPTER 2

Current Theories of Self-poisoning

STRESS

Neil Kessel, in an early paper on the human ecology of self-poisoning (Kessel, 1965), proposed that: "The ecology of self-poisoning can be simply summed up: high rates are associated with living in overcrowded, poor surroundings, with living in bad conditions". Despite its concern with social factors, much of this type of analysis has been described as "psychiatric sociology" in that it is frequently put to service within a conceptual framework inextricably bound up with individual pathology (Goldie, 1979).

Finding that self-poisoning occurs predominantly among working class, often impoverished and unemployed people with multiple family and social problems, the reductionist perspective interprets the phenomenon as an aberrant response to stress. This perspective suggests that stress is external to individuals and emanates from those social conditions which govern their everyday lives. When the individual is subject to stress, so much can be tolerated, but no more, and when this point is reached pathological, internal processes (such as depression) are said to take over.

Now, it is proposed, the individual responds with abnormal behaviour governed, not by the social organisation and process which previously regulated their actions, but by the irrational impulses of the disordered psyche, or inadequate personality. Thus the social constraints and processes which regulate "normal" behaviour and which afford social action purpose and meaning are held not to determine the nature of the "abnormal" response to social stress. Despite the social nature of the ecological and epidemiological data accumulated on self-poisoning, the explanation and its theoretical underpinning remains indisputably psychological: ironically, in trying to place this particular form of deviant behaviour in its social context, such theorists have denied its pervasive influence.

This point is eloquently made by Cloward and Piven (1979, p.654), two American writers on the meaning of various forms of female deviance:

> If the study of social life has taught us anything, however, it is that social behaviour is socially regulated. How people think about their circumstances and act upon them is influenced by powerful and pervasive forces by which world views are transmitted to them; by which social, economic and political structures enmesh them; and by which elements of age, sex, social class and religious socialisation are imposed upon them. Taken together these regulatory influences define the parameters of possibility.
>
> Given the large influence of these regulatory processes, why should people cease being subject to them as they gravitate toward deviant behaviour? After all, deviant behaviour is still social behaviour. Is it imaginable that people would cease being subject to their particular world view? Or to the modes of social organisation that variously link and divide them? Or to the myriad socialising influences that regularly impinge upon them? The classical paradigm is based on the assumption that, in the evolution of deviant adaptations, people are suddenly freed from the historically specific social context that has already determined what they are or can be ... Social context can not be ignored ... The possibility that the content of deviant behaviour, the particular ways in which people deviate, may be a function of other features of social context has not been generally understood.

The relationship between the deviant behaviour of the individual and the social processes which give rise to it has been illuminated by another writer on theoretical approaches to suicidal behaviour—Steve Taylor—who also commented on what he considers the fallacious and heuristically harmful division between external (social) and internal (psychological) explanations. Taylor (1982, p.133) asserts:

> We can argue that the states of different social environments do differently regulate individual actions (as seen for example by differing suicide rates), or we can argue that this is not the case and that suicide

is in fact caused genetically or whatever. What we can not do is argue that society's influence can be turned off like a tap.

Taylor is critical of both internal and external orientations and (p.130) proposes that: "The majority of works in both approaches tend to favour a narrow empiricism which is suspicious of both abstract theoretical analysis and studying human behaviour as essentially meaningful social action".

Once it is allowed that what Taylor terms "suicidal behaviours" are indeed meaningful, then it must also follow that actors (p.136): " ... do not just construct any meanings for their actions; meanings are related to social situations and are developed in terms of (or are constrained by?) generally shared values and meanings".

Returning to the work of Cloward and Piven, we find a similar position being taken. In their critique of the external explanations offered by stress theories, and the difficulty such theories have in accounting for the different ways in which people react to the externally similar stressful circumstances, they argue (Cloward & Piven, 1979, p.654) that:

> Stress is being made to explain too much. Stress itself does not typically aggregate or disperse people, and thus tells us nothing about the likelihood that people will seek private escape from torment or join together in revolt against it; stress does not create social ideologies, and thus tells us nothing about the likelihood of social, religious or political deviance; stress does not impose normative rules through the socialisation process, and thus tells us nothing about the limits and possibilities for deviation by age, sex, and social class. In other words, the classical paradigm renders social context irrelevant to the structuring of rule violations.

Once it is accepted that deviant behaviour is purposive and has meaning, then explanation of the different ways in which people, and particular groups sharing social characteristics, react to apparently similar events becomes possible. The meaning people attribute to events is a product of their experience. Cloward & Piven continue (p.655):

> Stressful conditions are thus never experienced in raw form; they are interpreted by thinking people guided by a particular cognitive and moral framework. Such a framework is not invented de novo by people under stress; it is a feature of the social structure within which they live out their ordinary or rule-abiding lives, and it also guides them when they are prompted to break the rules.

The Subculture of Parasuicide

An example of one attempt to apply an ecological analysis to the interpretation of self-poisoning comes from Norman Kreitman who proposed the existence of a "parasuicide subculture" (Kreitman, 1977, pp.64-75). Although this theory does not explore the social-structural, normative influences on the way people interpret stress, it does propose that socio-cultural factors may influence their behavioural response to it—may "guide them when they are prompted to break the rules".

Kreitman studied the relatives and close friends of a series of 135 parasuicides—mostly self-poisoners—admitted to the Edinburgh RPTC in a ten week period in 1967. Of these contacts he found that 17 had themselves been admitted to the RPTC following parasuicide within the previous 4 years—a rate 4 times higher and significantly greater ($p > 0.001$) than would be expected according to the usual incidence of parasuicide among a population such as that which made up the contact group. This led Kreitman to suggest that a subculture of parasuicide may exist within which self-poisoning in particular represented a "language" through which distress was communicated and which was the equivalent of a generally understood signal. He proposed (p.66) that such a subculture:

> Is likely to be one in which there is a relative lack of emphasis on verbal communication with greater value attached to the immediate discharge of emotion and the use of physical methods to convey meanings. There is also likely to be an emphasis on short-term relief of feelings as against long-term planning and hence possibly a greater use of violence. There are analogies here with the "delinquency subculture".

Thus the mode of response to stress according to Kreitman's communication theory is perhaps a product of the subculture within which an individual exists, and that, in this case, self-poisoning is a "preformed message ... a ritual" generally understood by members of the subculture as signalling intolerable stress. Although bearing superficial similarity to the theory of Cloward and Piven, Kreitman does not consider that wider, social-structural features determine either the values of this subculture or the particular form of deviance which it promotes as the legitimate language of stress. Instead he proposes that its members must not only possess: "similar attitudes and beliefs; it also necessitates their being socially interrelated".

Kreitman's reluctance to cast the net wider in search of the social-structural influences on parasuicide may be due to the fact that the results he obtained would not in any case support such an effort. No significant effects on the distribution of "positive contacts" among the self-poisoners were found stemming from class, marital status, or gender. It therefore becomes difficult to imagine what this subculture does share apart from parasuicide. The theory encounters further problems when it is recalled that only 17 out of 135 parasuicides had a positive contact—i.e. someone within their close kin or friends who had previously been admitted for parasuicide. Thus only 12.5% of parasuicides could be thought of as members of the subculture of parasuicide. Finally, in view of the fact that there was no significant difference between male and female parasuicides in the extent of their positive contacts, the theory also has difficulty explaining the preponderance of women among self-poisoners.

A later study by Platt (1985), designed to explore the possible existence of such a subculture, included control groups of people who were not parasuicides and compared geographical areas with respectively high and low incidence of self-poisoning. Platt found some support for the notion of a subculture as far as people in the high risk area differed from those in the low risk area in that they had more "feelings of fatalism when confronted with life's problems"—feelings which, as we shall see later, have been associated with self-poisoning. However no evidence was discovered within the high risk area for "a greater degree or preference for ... a present time orientation or for an emphasis on action and activity" (Platt, 1985, p.285). Kreitman had earlier suggested both as characteristic features of the parasuicide subculture.

In addition, Platt discovered that controls in the high risk area "found the parasuicidal act less understandable, more deserving of punishment, more morally wrong and more suicidal" than controls in the low risk area. This is not in keeping with Kreitman's subcultural hypothesis that such behaviour is more normative in high risk areas. However, as Platt points out, it is in keeping with the notion that among certain groups this form of behaviour may have particular potency as a shock tactic employed in the absence of any equally powerful, normatively acceptable alternative.

Finally, Platt found no difference between parasuicides and controls in either high or low risk areas in the extent of their contacts with other parasuicides. In other words, people who were not parasuicides had as many contacts with parasuicides as did parasuicides themselves. Not surprisingly, Platt concludes that the notion of a subculture of parasuicide, at least in the form presented by Kreitman, is unsupported by his findings.

Kreitman (1977, p.73) is reluctant to surrender the pathology paradigm entirely, as this assertion demonstrates: "... these findings are in accord with what is known of other forms of 'communicated' psychopathology, such as epidemic hysteria and *folie à deux*". However, his theory is a departure from the classical stress paradigm criticised by Cloward and Piven in that it at least appears to accept that "parasuicide" is meaningful and may have normative origins—in their terms it understands that deviant behaviour is socially regulated.

None the less, although the theory is prepared to accept that certain features of parasuicide may be the product of normative, subcultural influences—for example towards impulsivity and action—it fails to consider why women should be more subject to its influence than men, or the possible normative influences on its particular method (self-poisoning with medicinal agents). This means that Kreitman's view of self-poisoning as the language of stress is essentially uninformative in terms of the three central questions of our work—Why women? Why self-poisoning? Why now?

Role Stress

Simple ecological models of stress emphasise its origins in factors such as poor housing, population density, and poverty. Kreitman went beyond this to a human ecology perspective interested in the interaction between such external factors and sub-cultural influences guiding individuals' responses to them. Another apparently socio-cultural theory takes a somewhat wider perspective and is concerned not so much with identifying sub-cultures of deviant behaviour, but rather explores the normative social roles and associated behaviours, the boundaries and nature of which are widely endorsed throughout society. Such theories suggest that stress can arise when individuals occupy, or aspire to, roles which have conflicting demands—for example the wife working outside the home who is torn between the demands of her paid employment and those of her family. Again, individuals as they progress through the life span and enter and leave roles, the demands of new roles may conflict with the values and behaviours developed in occupying the old ones. Thus the adolescent may find the transition from the dependency of childhood to the relative autonomy of adulthood stressful—the values and behaviours acquired to facilitate the dependent role are not those required for autonomy.

Walter Gove is a major exponent of this perspective and specifically applied his theory of role stress to an analysis of the sex difference in "attempted suicide" (Gove, 1972). He suggested that role conflict may be a source of stress leading to mental disorder and attempted suicide. Gove claimed that since World War Two the rate of mental disorder in women had exceeded that in men, whereas before the war the men had exceeded women. On closer examination he found that the disparity since World War Two was almost entirely accounted for by the marked excess of married women. Thus single women had lower rates than married women, whereas single men had higher rates than married men. This led Gove to the conclusion that marriage protected men from mental disorder but made women more vulnerable to it.

Gove (1972, p.205) explained these disparities by asserting that since World War Two the status of the domestic role traditionally occupied by women had been eroded and that, as a result: "... married women, as opposed to married men, find their role to be restricting in scope and their instrumental activities to be relatively unrewarding". In turn single women were more favourably placed in their roles than men in that:

"... single women are more likely to have close personal ties, and such ties appear to be very important in maintaining a sense of wellbeing".

Gove did not carry out his own study to test these hypotheses in relation to attempted suicide: rather he employed data gathered from a previous study of admissions to a state mental hospital and from police records. He also used data drawn from a survey of telephone callers to a suicide prevention centre carried out some 20 years earlier. He found that, as predicted by the theory, married women had higher rates of attempts and threats than did single women and the reverse was true among men.

Gove's assertions have met with severe criticism—especially those in relation to the changing ratio of mental disorder since World War Two, which are the foundation of his argument. A protracted debate with the Dohrenwends centred on Gove's definition of mental disorder which, it was claimed, did not include those disorders most frequently diagnosed in men (such as psychopathy) and therefore underestimated the rate of male disorder (Dohrenwend & Dohrenwend, 1976). More recently, Fox has taken issue with the fact that Gove's theory is based almost exclusively on rates of hospitalisation, rather than on 'true' rates as shown from community studies. In this sense, therefore, they ignore possible sex differences in patterns of helpseeking, referral and treatment (Fox, 1980). Fox (p.260), using data on untreated mental disorder from three national surveys found that "women are more likely to be mentally ill than men regardless of marital status".

In relation to Gove's assertions on what he describes as "attempted suicide" there are similar problems with the data in that his sample is atypical of self-poisoners, most of whom are not admitted to mental hospitals, and who have been shown to differ in important respects from callers to suicide prevention centres (Kreitman & Chowdhury, 1973). It is apparent that his hypothesis is not borne out by the data from the

Edinburgh RPTC on the marital status of parasuicides (Table 1.4). The rates of single women under 34 greatly exceed those of married women in the same age group (959 and 598 per 100,000 respectively) and are almost twice those of single men (959 vs. 461 per 100,000 respectively). This latter comparison was not reported by Gove and, in conjunction with the former, seriously undermines his contentions.

It is unfortunate that one of the very few studies devoted to the sex difference in parasuicide should be so methodologically flawed, especially as it, unusually, adopts a sociological approach. The importance of social roles and sex differences in them is almost entirely neglected, as we have seen, within the pathology paradigm. This is not to suggest that Gove does not adhere to such a paradigm—he does, in that he believes women who "attempt suicide" are mentally ill as a result of the stress caused by their occupation of inherently frustrating roles. Thus Gove has no need to consider the particular form their disorder takes as meaningful in its own right—rather it is seen as symptomatic of the depression and associated "suicidal" tendencies caused by stress. Thus, although Gove's sex role theory of parasuicide attempts to address the normative origins of this type of female deviance its methodology is flawed, its results are unsupported by other studies and, despite its apparently sociological approach, it ultimately relies on the pathology paradigm to explain its particular form.

No single stress theory has shown itself capable, therefore, of addressing all three of the central questions posed earlier. Simple ecological models cannot explain why women should respond to the stress of unfavourable conditions more than men and in this particular, self-poisoning way. Kreitman's more sophisticated model completely ignores sex differences as an issue to be explained, and Gove's theory in its recourse to psychopathology fails to escape criticism as "psychiatric sociology" (Goldie, 1979). However other social role theorists have been more successful in avoiding this fate.

Sex Roles and Social Acceptability

Marsha Linehan (1973) similarly emphasises the importance of cultural norms and social acceptability as influences on suicidal behaviour and her theory explicitly seeks to explain sex differences in both completed and attempted suicide. Noting that the male rate of completed suicide is approximately twice that of women, whereas among attempted suicides females predominate over males by a similar factor, Linehan proposes that these differences reflect the influence of sex role stereotyping. Females are stereotyped as more passive, dependent and emotionally expressive than males, who are stereotyped as decisive, strong, successful and inexpressive (Broverman, 1972). Thus these stereotypes may permit females to make less serious attempts, expect more help when they do make an attempt, and seek help more rapidly having poisoned themselves. In Schneidman and Farberow's oft quoted terminology the "cry for help" is more socially acceptable coming from females (Schneidman & Farberow, 1961). The male stereotype however does not promote indecisiveness in any attempt, neither does it permit help seeking before or during suicidal actions. In short it does not permit failure. These assumptions would predict the observed male predominance in completed suicide and the female excess among non-fatal self-poisoners.

Linehan supported her theory that completed suicide is perceived as a more masculine activity than attempted suicide by employing Osgood's semantic differential with male and female college students. She found that both males and females who completed suicide were indeed seen as more masculine and potent than males and females who engaged in non-fatal acts.

In a later series of studies exploring the influence of sex role stereotyping on suicidal behaviour Stillion, McDowell & Shamblin (1984) demonstrated that females consistently sympathise more with suicidal target figures than do males and, in a further study employing the Personal Attributes Questionnaire (Spence & Helmreich, 1978), that females and feminine males sympathised more with suicidal target figures than did males and masculine females (Stillion, McDowell, Smith, & McCoy, 1986).

Although the social acceptability hypothesis has some support from these attitude tests the results based upon them are vulnerable, as are so many studies in this field, to the criticism that subjects' attitudes evoked through vignettes—as these were—may be only indirectly related to behaviour. Furthermore the studies did not involve self-poisoners whose attitudes may be entirely different from student research subjects. Finally, the results of another study by White and Stillion herself further weaken the argument (White & Stillion, 1988). Pointing out that earlier studies had not employed vignettes of non-suicidal but equally troubled target figures, the authors suggested that the gender differences in sympathy ratings might reflect a general tendency for females to be more sympathetic than are males to troubled figures whether such figures are male or female, suicidal or not.

The use of a non-suicidal comparison condition disclosed, as White and Stillion predicted, that female sympathy ratings were not influenced by the suicidal or non-suicidal status of the vignette figures, or their sex. Equal sympathy was expressed to all troubled figures and there appeared to be a generalised tendency for women to be more sympathetic regardless of the situation. There is therefore no support here for the proposal that females may make more attempts because they expect to receive sympathy afterwards. The results in relation to male responses suggest that even less sympathy might be forthcoming from males in that they reported less sympathy with troubled female target figures than troubled male ones, whether or not the females made attempts. This undermines the social acceptability and the "cry for help" hypotheses: it also questions the "manipulative woman" theory of female self-poisoning which suggests that such women are attempting to regain the affections of lost male partners.

There was some support, however, for the hypothesis that attempted suicide is an unacceptable option among males as it affronts stereotypic masculine attributes. White's male subjects showed more sympathy with troubled males who did not attempt suicide than with troubled males who did. This might be regarded as support for Linehan's theory in relation to the lower incidence of male self-poisoning compared with that of females, although at the same time it undermines her argument on the sex differences in completed suicide as it seems unlikely that males would sympathise more with completers than non-attempters.

The work of Linehan, Stillion and White, although ultimately coming to something less than definitive conclusions, at least furthers the often neglected consideration of sex differences in self-poisoning and suicide. In so doing it goes beyond Kreitman's emphasis on subcultural factors to suggest that wider normative influences based on sex role socialisation may be influential, and unlike the analysis of both Kreitman and Gove it is not ultimately reliant on the assumption of psychopathology.

These are perspectives which will become increasingly central to our discussion as we continue to explore current theories of self-poisoning, and recent feminist writers have contributed stress models which integrate the valuable features of all those we have described but without ultimately returning to the pathology paradigm. One such author is Michelle Wilson (Wilson, 1981) who suggests that "attempted suicide" is a means of coping with stress and also signalling distress employed by those whose social roles deny them any other source of influence. As women and men differ in the roles they occupy so too do they differ in the stress to which they are exposed and the resources available for coping with it. We shall return to explore such models in more detail later, but as we have seen their impact on the study of this phenomenon has been inhibited by the dominance of psychiatry and the reluctance of its commentators to abandon the pathology paradigm. This itself is rooted in the biological differences between the sexes and their often incorrectly assumed psychological sequaele—most of which it seems are unfavourable to women and potentially suicidogenic.

BIOLOGY

Women—the Stronger or Weaker Sex?

In any explanation of sex differences in behaviour the most obvious causal candidate is biology. It has thus been suggested that women, because they are said to be biologically the stronger sex—an assumption founded on the lower neo-natal mortality rate of female infants, and the greater longevity of women—survive "attempted suicide" whereas men do not. As we have suggested, the conflation of suicide and "attempted suicide" has been found to lack any empirical justification. While one study found that more than 3% of self-poisoners had killed themselves within 3 years of their first episode (Buglass & McCulloch, 1970) in the majority of cases there is little or no evidence of suicidal intent.

Another reason to dismiss this form of biological theory is that there is convincing evidence that in some ways women are not the "stronger sex". Thus it is well documented that women have more physician consultations, are more frequently hospitalised, and suffer from more acute disorders, all of which is the case even after health problems related to child bearing are excluded (Nathanson, 1977; Verbrugge, 1989).

A final rebuttal is provided by the fact that the other major biological argument makes precisely the opposite claim—that because women are weaker they cannot inflict fatal injuries with the facility of the physically stronger male. Such notions are undermined by the fact that when method is controlled, the sex difference in rate of completed suicide disappears—i.e. among those who use guns, men and women have the same suicide rate (Wilson, 1981, p.133). This theory is associated with another claim which is that women use less violent means than do men and therefore, it is claimed, have a greater chance of survival. While it is true that sex differences exist in methods chosen, as Linehan points out, this theory too is fallacious because if it were true the overall incidence of suicidal behaviour would be the same for men and women, whereas when actual suicide and all forms of parasuicide are added up, women still massively exceed men (Linehan, 1971).

Hormones and the Menstrual Cycle

Another aspect of the biological theory is based on the proposition that the hormonal fluctuations of the menstrual cycle render women vulnerable to depression and associated suicidal ideation. This has been a persistent claim, as it has been in accounting for many other forms of female deviance such as violent behaviour, criminal acts such as shop-lifting, and various forms of psychiatric disorder (Dalton, 1980).

The work of Katrina Dalton and others on the "pre-menstrual syndrome" has gradually established the medical credibility of this disorder in terms of its physical and, to a lesser extent, its psychological effects (Taylor, 1983), and indeed several court cases in the recent past have accepted pleas of diminished responsibility on the grounds of pre-menstrual syndrome in murder cases. However, no undisputed link with self-poisoning has been established.

None the less there are several studies of self-poisoning women which have claimed to establish an association between the pre-menstrual and menstrual phase of the cycle and this behaviour—the most recent being a 1986 French survey (Fourestie et al., 1986). This study claimed to have identified a significant excess of suicide attempters in the first week (menses) and after the fourth week of the cycle, when oestrogen—a female hormone previously associated with depression when deficient—is at its lowest ebb.

However Fourestie's conclusions were later dismissed in the same journal by a paper which pointed out that the division of the menstrual cycle into four weekly phases is arbitrary, as many women do not conform to such a pattern and the length of cycles normally may vary by a week or more. Thus the apparent excess of women in the "first" and after the "fourth" week would disappear if another way of dividing the cycle was employed (Magos & Studd, 1987). Additional criticism stems from the fact that a causal relationship may not be assumed from the finding of low oestrogen among self-poisoners in any case because self-poisoning and hormonal fluctuations may both be a response to a third factor such as emotional or physical trauma.

A recent paper examining the relationship between women's expectations of the emotional and behavioural effects of the menstrual cycle highlights further difficulties with self-report surveys. Firstly it was found that the concurrent daily records women kept of physical and affective states throughout the cycle differed from the states they later recalled as associated with each phase and any changes were exaggerated in recall. Secondly, these recollections were biased in keeping with the individual's menstrual beliefs. Thus, the more a woman believed in the menstrual distress syndrome the more she exaggerated in recall the negativity of her symptoms during her last period. Finally it was found from the concurrent records that whereas physical symptoms did vary with cycle phase, affective ones did not (McFarland, Ross, & De Courville, 1989).

The methodological problems involved in such surveys are legion and an exhaustive review of the literature dealing with this claimed association was carried out by Birtchnell and Floyd (1974). They found not only that those studies which claimed an association had similar methodological problems as that of Fourestie, and that the statistical analysis of the data was either absent (as in Dalton's research) or flawed, but also they were unable to replicate the results of earlier studies. In addition Birtchnell and Floyd point out that almost every phase of the cycle has been implicated in some form of female deviance or other.

Accounts of the historical development of the assumed relationship between female hormones and behaviour, and convincing rebuttals, are to be found in much feminist literature, where the promotion of such beliefs is interpreted as evidence of male chauvinism in the interests of excluding women from positions of responsibility and power (Weideger, 1978; Laws, Hey & Eagan, 1985).

Biological theories adduced to account for sex differences in self-poisoning, therefore, have been unable to establish conclusive evidence in their favour and are, in addition, completely unable to account for the socio-demographic distribution of the phenomenon. If biological factors are causally implicated, why should working class women be more vulnerable than those from the middle class and, indeed, why should men appear at all among this population?

PERSONALITY THEORY

A second group of "internal" theories of self-poisoning may be termed personality theories, which, although apparently psychological, on closer examination, are ultimately biologically based.

Female Masochism

Freud believed that female children, having discovered the genital difference between the sexes, compare the clitoris as an instrument of sexual pleasure unfavourably with the penis. They therefore abandon their active, clitoral sexuality and this becomes transferred to the "passive", receptive mode of vaginal sexual expression. This, Freud believed, leads to a general relinquishment of the active and aggressive behaviour which is characteristically masculine, and hence to the adoption of passive, receptive "feminine" behaviour. Unfortunately this pattern of normal female development has a high price because in Freud's view (Freud, 1933, in Strachey, 1965):

> The suppression of women's aggressiveness which is prescribed for them constitutionally and imposed on them socially favours the development of powerful masochistic impulses, which succeed, as we know, in binding erotically the destructive trends which have been diverted inwards. Thus masochism, as people say, is truly feminine.

These ideas were developed later by Helene Deutsch, an early psychoanalytic patient of Freud, in her *Psychology of Women* (Deutsch, 1945). She claimed that women were inherently masochistic, narcissistic and passive. Deutsch felt that the transfer of sexual orientation from the active, penetrative penis to the passive, receptive vagina naturally led to female masochism as, in order to experience sexual pleasure the woman has to be penetrated—overpowered—by a man.

The Freudian notion of penis envy furthered the view of female development as inately self-defeating or self-destructive. According to Freud in Strachey (1959) pp.186–197:

> After a woman has become aware of the wound to her narcissism, she develops, like a scar, a sense of inferiority. When she has passed beyond her first attempt at explaining her lack of a penis as a punishment personal to herself ... she begins to share the contempt felt by men for a sex which is the lesser in so important a respect.

Female behaviour—such as self-poisoning—which is thought of as self-destructive is therefore seen as symptomatic of this self-hatred and represents its masochistic outcome.

Freud proposed that penis envy leads women, in addition to feelings of inferiority and shame, to be inately narcissistic, in an attempt at concealment of their "scar", and "less ready to submit to the great necessities of life". As well, they are "more influenced in their judgements by feelings of affection or hostility" (Freud in Strachey, 1959, p.197).

Narcissism is thus believed to explain the importance of relational breakdown as a common precipitant of female "suicidal" behaviour. Women, convinced of their inferiority, seek evidence of their worth through their attractiveness to and relationships with males, who possess what the female imagines she lacks. This tendency is exacerbated in certain women who have experienced real or fantasied rejection by their fathers, and who, it is said, suffer from unresolved Oedipal problems. Such women are excessively dependent, dissatisfied and demanding in relationships with men in an effort to satisfy their need for validation as a worthwhile human being and resolve their Oedipal crisis. This in turn promotes the likelihood of these relationships breaking down. Thus those women whose self-esteem and self-image is most dependent on heterosexual relationships are the least able to maintain them and are particularly prone to self-destructive behaviour following their breakdown.

Freud (in Strachey, 1959, pp.191–2) also thought that: "The hope of some day obtaining a penis in spite of everything and so of becoming like a man may persist to an incredibly late age and may become a motive for the strangest and otherwise unaccountable actions".

Self-poisoning, it might be assumed, would be included among these "strange and unaccountable actions", and the commonplace attribution to female self-poisoners of aggressive, manipulative and hysterical character represents a fairly accurate account of Freudian notions of female personality development.

A startling example of this perspective is to be found in McCulloch and Philip's book on *Suicidal Behaviour* (McCulloch & Philip, 1972, p.62): Women who are socially deviant are more dominant and aggressive than non-deviant women, so that, if men in this category are 'loners', the women appear to be 'harridans'.

An example of a rather more sophisticated model, though one still based upon the notion of female narcissism, is that of Ronald Maris (Maris, 1971) who termed female "self-destructive" behaviour "deviance as therapy". In keeping with the theory described above, Maris suggests that women who have experienced disruption in early family life, especially parental abandonment, suffer chronically low self-esteem. In order to cope with this, he asserts (p.120):

... most of the female subjects make a narcissistic recovery. This primitive narcissism is a fragile veneer covering up feelings of basic personal inadequacy. In many cases feelings of personal inadequacy develop into sociopathic behaviour, in which the patient complains of being unable to meet even minimal interpersonal demands ... Most women studied made an effort to fend off their depressions and to get the affection and respect denied them by becoming sexually deviant.

Maris asserts that sexual deviance and also drug abuse constitute "coping behaviour" which, in that they fend off feelings of total worthlessness, avoid severe depression and thus may actually prevent completed suicide. He proposes that attempted suicide is often associated with such behaviour patterns and may be termed "secondary deviance" (i.e. it is a reaction to the stigmatisation and isolation resulting from the primary deviance of sexual deviation and drug abuse). In that it represents "a dramatic plea and communiqué to a public that has stigmatised and ostracised them", female attempted suicide may be thought of "... as partial self-destruction to the end of making life possible—not ending it".

Maris concludes that in this way the apparently self-destructive deviance of women actually constitutes a form of therapy and that to remove the "defence" of attempted suicide may leave such women with no choice but to finally kill themselves in order to escape the shame and worthlessness of their unresolved Oedipal crisis.

Apart from the doubts described earlier, which surround the concept of female narcissism, it is apparent that Maris's description of his sample of attempted suicides bears little resemblance to those commonly encountered in the literature. Although self-poisoning does occur among drug abusers and prostitutes, they are hardly representative of this population. Consideration of his various definitions of the characteristics of subjects however makes this puzzling discrepancy more explicable. Thus "sexual deviation" includes "indiscriminate sexual intercourse with 20 or more different partners prior to marriage" or in the absence of marriage "was determined more by the indiscriminate nature of the intercourse than by the number of partners". "Drug abuse" is similarly catch-all in that it includes "utilising prescribed tranquilisers or amphetamines in excess of the dosage recommended"; and finally, "stigmatisation", we are led to believe, may be defined to include abortions, venereal diseases and foster homes as a child.

Another problem with Maris's theory is that his study did not include male attempters—he therefore has no means of knowing that what he has observed differs in any way from the circumstances or behaviour of male patients. Thus it cannot be described as a theory of female deviance—because it is all about women it is not about women at all. The absence of a control group of any sort imposes similar limitations on the interpretation of his results.

Despite these shortcomings Maris's hypothesis begins to go beyond the restrictions of the pathology paradigm. By interpreting attempted suicide as a form of deviance similar to others such as crime and prostitution and involving similar social processes, he suggests that attempted suicide is not only functional (therapeutic) for the patient but also for "straight" society in that such deviance defines normative boundaries. The relationship between normative roles and relationships and female deviance will become central to our later discussion and Maris's theory alludes to the importance of this.

However, while he can envisage that the deviant behaviour of attempted suicide may contribute to the maintenance of normative structures, Maris cannot concede that it may also originate within and be an expression of them. He neglects the possibility that the dependence of many women on relationships with males and the form of their response when these break down may be a product of social roles and relations, and not symptomatic of narcissistic psychopathology. Thus, despite his assertion that his theory of deviance as therapy "should not strain the sociological imagination" (Maris, 1971, p.114), neither does it strain the pathology paradigm in its ultimate reliance on the theory of female narcissism.

The Critique of the Theory of Female Masochism. It is beyond the scope of this work to enter into a detailed critique of Freudian personality theory: this has been done to good effect elsewhere, perhaps most notably in the work of Hans Eysenck (1986). He criticises the reliance of psychodynamic theory on case study material derived from the records of analysts, its lack of empirical validation, and the apparent inefficacy of the treatment based upon its contentions. However, the theory of female masochism—which one feminist critic has referred to as "viewing personality traits as secondary sexual characteristics" (Heshusius, 1980, p.847)—is central to our own concerns and merits more detailed commentary.

Paula Caplan's work *Women's Masochism—The Myth Destroyed* (Caplan, 1986), as the title suggests, is an extensive description and rejection of Freud's theory. Dismissing the perception of female vaginal sexuality as inherently passive, inevitably painful or masochistically subordinate, Caplan asserts (p.32) that: "The focus on penetration as the cornerstone of women's personality leading her to become generally masochistic seems completely misguided. It is also incorrect to assume that women's role in heterosexual intercourse is necessarily passive". Caplan refers to the American nationwide survey of female sexuality (Hite, 1976) as contradicting the view that penile penetration is the essence of female sexual experience. Women have a variety of means of achieving sexual pleasure. Additionally, the missionary position during intercourse—regarded by Deutsch as evidence of subordination and passivity—is neither necessarily painful nor biologically necessary as conception is no more likely. Finally, the vagina is not a passive organ but is grasping, secreting and pleasure-giving through its own functions—rather than through any alleged eroticisation of pain.

Caplan points out that the fact that certain female experiences have pain as an accompaniment—such as childbirth and, sometimes, menstruation—has been used to support the contention that female suffering is somehow natural. Eryk Erikson (1964, p.275), for example, suggests that women have an ability to "stand (and to understand) pain as a meaningful aspect of human experience in general and of the feminine role in particular". However, as Caplan (1986, p.31) asserts, "menstruation is not an option for women ... and what women seek through pregnancy is children, not the pain of childbirth". The fact that women sometimes experience pain does not mean they seek it out or enjoy it. The confusion of what is with what "ought" to be in Freud's thought—the naturalistic phallacy—has been pointed out by Cavell

(1974) who wrote: "The important distinction between what is the case and what could be the case, between human nature as we find it in a given situation or culture and human nature as it might be, is so often lacking in Freud's work".

For this reason Freud's theories have been described as ethnocentric and phallocentric—i.e. they assume that females experience their genitalia as the absence of a penis, make unfavourable comparisons with the male, and consequently envy their possession of the (more valued) penis (Sayers, 1982).

In their thorough, and by no means hostile review of empirical evidence in relation to Freudian theory, Fisher and Greenberg (1985), when discussing penis envy categorically assert (p.199):

> It can be immediately declared that Freud was wrong in his assumption that the average woman perceives her body in more negative and depreciative terms than the average man ... if anything women are more comfortable with their body experiences than are men ... consistent evidence exists that the female exceeds the male in general body awareness, sense of body security, adaptability to changes in body sensations and appearance, and ability to integrate body experiences in a fashion meaningfully consistent with life role. The male is clearly less accepting of, and less comfortable with, his body than is the female.

There is also empirical evidence that the personality traits Freud claimed as essentially female are in fact socially, not biologically acquired. Studies of hermaphrodites who are born with undeveloped or sexually ambiguous genitalia, for example, grow up to show the interests, behaviours and personality characteristics of the sex in which they are raised (Money & Erhardt, 1972). As well, it has been demonstrated that normally sexed individuals acquire much of their "sex-appropriate" behaviour and characteristics through the influence of social expectations inherent in the sex role system—through "nurture" rather than "nature" (Delamont, 1980, pp.14–29; Chetwynd & Hartnett, 1978).

Although measures of hostility and aggression have frequently been applied to self-poisoning patients, results have been equivocal. Philip (1970) discovered that "attempted suicides were much more hostile than normals or neurotics". Vinoda (1969) found that high risk patients showed high inner-directed hostility, though among low risk patients hostility was other-directed. Possibly in keeping with this, Kreitman found that differences between normals and self-poisoners were only marked among character disordered patients (Kreitman, 1977, p.88), while Cantor's (1976) study of female self-poisoners found they "had a tendency toward externalised aggression". She reminds the reader that Stengel (1964) and Farberow and McEvoy (1966) proposed that externalised aggression is more typical of attempters, and that Freud originally applied his concepts to completed suicides.

These mixed results lend conviction to Heshusius' (1980) conclusion that:

> Theories on suicide have considered suicidal behaviour a form of internalised aggression, although it must be noted that no causal relationship between aggression and suicidal behaviour has been established and that the internalised aggression theory exists at a level of clinical intuition.

Freud's theory of female masochism is open to severe criticism and its application to female self-poisoning is, at best, lacking in support. Freud himself was aware of the limitations of his personality theory in relation to women, which he described as "incomplete and fragmentary" (Freud, 1933, in Strachey, 1959). However, it has remained influential and the notion of the hysterical woman—a further derivative of female narcissism and envy—continues to underpin certain approaches to self-poisoning.

The Hysterical Woman

If the evidence for certain aspects of Freudian personality theory is limited, so too has it proven difficult to establish the widespread existence of these or any other personality traits among self-poisoners in general, or female self-poisoners in particular.

Philip's (1970) study of the "traits, attitudes and symptoms" of a group of 100 "attempted suicides"—50 men and 50 women—began by reviewing the literature and deduced:

> All the major tests in the psychological armamentarium have been used, with varying degrees of sophistication, in the quest for the "suicidal personality". Such a quest has been unsuccessful, the results from projective techniques and questionnaire methods alike being equivocal in many instances and contradictory in others.

Philip, in his own research, which employed the Symptom Sign Inventory of Personal Disturbance and Character Disorder (Foulds & Hope, 1968) found that "no significant sex difference occurs" and concluded: "There is no unique 'suicidal personality' ".

Norman Kreitman (1977), reviewing two psychometric studies carried out with parasuicides by the Edinburgh Regional Poisoning Treatment Centre, summarised the results thus (pp.90–91):

Although parasuicides as a group differ quite strikingly in some respects from normals, such characteristics are not ubiquitous nor are they confined to the population under study: there is no "suicidal personality" ... Demographic, social and personality factors are so interwoven that to search for a "suicidal personality" is to don a conceptual strait-jacket which restricts the researcher to a very simplistic notion of personality.

Robert Goldney, in a 1981 study specifically to test the assumption of hysterical personality in young female self-poisoners, administered a personality questionnaire to 110 women aged 18–30 who had taken an overdose. These results were compared with those of a control group consisting of women attending a community health centre who had no history of self-poisoning. Goldney (1981a, p.141) stated:

Young women who had attempted suicide did not score in a more hysterical manner than women in a comparison group ... These results ... do not support the clinical view that young women who attempt suicide exhibit marked hysterical traits.

It is perhaps fitting to conclude this consideration of personality theory as it has been applied through the pathology paradigm to self-poisoning with a further quote from Goldney (1980a, p.145), who is himself a professor of psychiatry:

... the question arises as to why clinicians have previously considered such subjects to be hysterical ... contributing factors appear to be that attempted suicide has, by its very nature, a dramatic impact on others; that it is an act which is seen in an unfavourable light by a large proportion of health professionals, and the term hysterical has no doubt been used in a pejorative manner; and that it has predominantly been carried out by young women, a group who, *ipso facto*, have frequently been labelled as hysterical. Whilst it would be inappropriate to suggest that the term hysterical should never be applied to these subjects, at the very least the present study is in accord with previous objective work which indicates that caution should be exercised before applying the hysterical diagnosis to those who have attempted suicide.

MENTAL DISORDER

Depression, Suicide and Self-poisoning

Another strand of the "internal" pathology explanation is that relating to the frequent finding from both hospital and community based studies, that depression is twice as prevalent among women as men (Weissman & Klerman, 1977). In relation to self-poisoning, it is assumed that as twice as many women suffer with depression it is to be expected that twice as many will poison themselves. This assumption is based on the notion that suicidal ideation is associated with depression, and that self-poisoning reflects such ideation.

Perhaps the first objection which may be raised against this perspective is that any suicidal ideation is markedly absent among many self-poisoners— thus Hawton and Catalan (1982a, p.30) claim: "Of course in some cases the individuals will have had unequivocal suicidal intent. Such individuals are relatively rare among those who are admitted to hospital having survived attempts".

Indeed Bancroft and his colleagues in a study of the motivation underlying self-poisoning, found that 56% of the patients sought respite from an "unbearable situation" and that there was, in fact, a negative association between a "wish to die" and the "need to escape from an impossible situation" which was identified as the motivation of the majority of patients (Bancroft, Skirmshire, & Simkin, 1976).

Although enduring suicidal ideation is therefore uncommon among self-poisoners, as might be expected, depression is commonly diagnosed. However, a study of psychiatric symptoms among self-poisoners by Newson-Smith and Hirsch (1979) found that just as common are feelings of nervous tension and irritability. In addition it was discovered that, while such symptoms were common, most did not reach clinical significance and less than one-third of patients were deemed to have a definite psychiatric illness. When interviewed a week later the number with definite disorder had diminished to 24%. It seems, therefore, that the symptoms of frank mental disorder are absent in the vast majority of self-poisoners, and when they are present they are usually transient and secondary to the severe social and relational problems self-poisoners have in most instances. Hawton and Catalan (1982a, p.25) conclude that: "perhaps between 5 and 8% are suffering from severe psychiatric illness".

Further doubt is cast on the relevance of this pathology paradigm by the results of a recent study (Newmann, 1984) addressing the common finding of excess depression among women. This concluded that much of the so-called depressive illness found in community studies is in fact not clinical depression but rather "normal distress", and its author asserts (p.137) that:

A central and defining feature of depression as a clinical disorder is the presence of dysphoric mood, consisting of feeling sad, blue, discouraged or depressed. However such feelings are ubiquitous in a normal population and do not necessarily indicate clinical impairment.

In her study of almost 1000 randomly chosen residents of Wisconsin, Newmann employed a measure widely used in community studies of psychiatric disorder—The Psychiatric Evaluation Research Interview (Dohrenwend, Shrout, Egri, & Mendelsohn, 1980). She found that mean scores for a variety of symptoms rarely demonstrated significant sex differences and (Newmann, 1984, p.146):

> In fact the results reveal small differences for the most severe symptoms
> ... and substantial differences only for those symptoms judged by
> clinicians to be the least indicative of poor mental health, i.e. feelings of
> sadness.

This pattern of results is different from those usually found on the basis of the PERI scale, Newmann claims, because the scores on each part of the scale are usually aggregated to give an overall score and this disguises the fact that the pattern of mean differences for men and women is not constant across the items comprising the scale. It is in those areas least regarded as evidence of clinical depression that women score most differently and which lead to their elevated aggregate scores—hence giving the false impression of higher levels of female depression.

Support for Newmann's views, specifically in relation to the diagnosis of depression among self-poisoning women is derived from a paper by Goldney and Pilowsky (1980). These workers reviewed the literature relating to the incidence of depression in this population and found that estimates varied from 10% to 79%. However they note (p.201) that of the 23 studies reviewed: "There appears to be a lesser proportion of subjects designated as depressed when clinical diagnosis alone is employed than when objective measures are used."

Newmann's scepticism about the meaningfulness of claims derived from community surveys using aggregated questionnaire scores was reflected in the classic study of female psychiatric disorder by Brown and Harris (1978) in London. Finding that depression at "a case level" was widespread among working class women in Camberwell, the authors write (p.283):

> Does this suggest that what we have been discussing is so common that
> it cannot be considered a medical phenomenon; being part of daily life it
> is just a particularly unpleasant form of unhappiness?

There seems good reason therefore to doubt that the claimed excess of depressive illness in women is an adequate explanation of female self-poisoning because:

1. Two-thirds of self-poisoners do not show enduring psychiatric disorder of any sort;
2. What is commonly described as "depression" among women is not comparable to that level of clinical depression associated with suicidal ideation; and
3. As we have seen, most self-poisoners do not express suicidal ideation.

There is some evidence that this has become increasingly recognised among psychiatrists involved with self-poisoning in that, at least among those patients referred to the Edinburgh Regional Poisoning Treatment Centre, the incidence of diagnosed psychiatric disorder has declined over the years at the same time as the prevalence of the behaviour increased (Dyer, Duffy, & Kreitman, 1978). Recognition of this may also be seen in the change in Health Department policy in relation to the assessment of self-poisoning, such that from December 1984 it has no longer been the recommended policy that all such patients should be assessed by a psychiatrist (DHSS, 1984).

COGNITIVE THEORIES

The inability of "internal" theories based upon concepts of personality or psychiatric disorder to illuminate "suicidal behaviour" gave rise to another school of internal explanation based on cognitive psychology. Charles Neuringer, a leading exponent in this field, asserts (Neuringer, 1976, p.235):

This movement reflects the direction found in most mental health endeavours and seems to be the product of the disappointments, equivocalities, and cul-de-sacs that have resulted from the failures associated with personality and motivation-dominated research in suicide. These disappointments may be traced to the disregard of cognitive variables as they affect and determine the course of the individual's employment of his sensory inputs and affective systems.

Neuringer, noting the association of stressful events and suicidal behaviour, but also recognising the ubiquity of such adversity in society, suggests (p.234) that:

What is particular is the manner in which people perceive, interpret, and react to their external stresses and affective pressures. What is different is the manner in which the stress is interpreted. Each man has a cognitive coding system which serves to shape, mould and interpret the inputs arising from the environment. It is that coding system, or cognitive-interpretive system, which supplies the dimensions to stress. How life's experiences are perceived, coded, organised, and understood is the basic clue to the explanation of why a person acts to end his existence.

Dichotomous Thinking

As is apparent from this quotation, Neuringer does not subscribe to the absolute differentiation between suicide and "attempted suicide" —rather he views both as points on a continuum. He employed Osgood's Semantic Differential (Osgood, Suci, & Tannenbaum, 1957) to assess the meaning individuals attach to concepts along various dimensions of evaluation—is the concept good or bad, active or passive, strong or weak. The subject rates each concept on a scale from one extreme to the other. Neuringer (1976, p.238) found that "suicidal" individuals show "dichotomous thinking" in that:

> They organise their characterisations in polar dichotomies in a much more rigid and extreme manner than do non-suicidal persons regardless of neuropsychiatric status. All people think dichotomously but most individuals have the capacity to moderate or even ignore the dichotomies ... suicidal individuals lack this flexibility and cling to extreme polarised views. (This) precludes the possibilities for moderation, compromise and shifting of perspectives ... (which) leads to diminished problem solving and adaptation ... Dichotomous thinking can be lethal because if an individual is dissatisfied with something in his life he finds it difficult or impossible to modulate his extreme polarised expectancies—he cannot conceptualise compromise.

This was conceived as a cognitive style which could lead the suicidal person to experience the world as a continuously narrowing set of possibilities for relief and change, such that death becomes the only escape from an impossible situation. Thus (p.240): "It is generally felt that the suicidal individual, because of his rigid mode of thinking, finds it difficult to develop new or alternative solutions to debilitating emotional difficulties".

Neuringer, noting the almost complete absence of research into suicidal women, specifically sought to establish whether such cognitive patterns were evident in women. Studying a group of female "threateners" who presented to a suicide prevention centre, he established that, in those considered to have a high level of suicidal potential, such cognitive processes were indeed evident (Neuringer & Lettieri, 1982).

Whilst Neuringer's attempts to escape the inadequacies of personality theory are informative and his interest in sex differences in suicidal behaviour unusual, because the study was devoted entirely to women it cannot be regarded as particularly illuminating in relation to sex differences in this behaviour. In addition his study on women threateners is of questionable relevance to actual self-poisoners as early-1970s research by Kreitman and Chowdhury (1973) in Britain indicated that those people who present to suicide prevention centres, in this case Samaritans' clients, are not necessarily representative of self-poisoners. Although Neuringer and Lettieri (1982, p.93) assert that their findings add to the evidence against the proposition of biologically based personality theory in the rather colourful sentence: "This should not be surprising, since there is no evidence that having or lacking a penis implies a difference in brain structure and function". In keeping with those other examples of internal explanations we have explored, Neuringer, despite this professed disenchantment with the results of theories based on psychopathological models, elsewhere remains adamant (Neuringer, 1976, p.246) that: "There is a difference in the cognitive structures and activities of suicidal individuals as compared to those of individuals who are considered normal". He suggests that the origins of these differences may lie in various areas and he speculates (p.249):

> Some of the characteristics of suicidal thinking bear a resemblance to those found among brain damaged persons. Might there be subtle inherited or traumatic neurological anomalies in suicidal individuals? The evaluation of the incidence and extent of neurological and psycho- neurological deficit in suicidal individuals may prove to be of great interest.

These speculations seem to fly in the face of the fact that he has no means of knowing whether his group of threateners subsequently indulge in suicidal behaviour or not, and if, as one might be entitled to assume, the majority did not, then his assertions on the relationship of his findings to actual self-poisoning or suicide is at best tenuous, and his imputation of brain damage to those who merely call on suicide prevention centres—numbered in many hundreds of thousands in both Britain and America—surely lacks credibility.

Neuringer, is therefore, extremely reluctant to consider that the cognitive differences he claims to separate "suicidal individuals" from "normal" ones could have social origins: this is especially so in his 1976 paper where social variables are not considered at all. The recurrent themes of perceived constraint and lack of alternatives are never considered as evidence of the real limitations imposed on women by the sex role system, which effectively denies them access to a diversity of social roles and resources and hence inhibits their problem-solving capacity. However, in his later book *Suicidal Women*, which extends to over 100 pages, Neuringer does devote the last half paragraph to a consideration of the possible effects of women's roles, and states (Neuringer & Lettieri, 1982, p.94):

> The successful filling of these female roles in our society is difficult for the most capable of women, and it is surprising that the suicide level among women is as low as it is. The low level of female self-destruction may be attributed to the suicide-attempt escape valves allowed to women. Will this escape valve be closed off as women's roles change? The answer will probably be yes if women have to assume male emotional stoicism in addition to their existing female tasks. The suicide level of women may surpass that of men if women have to be executives/ managers in addition to being mothers, lovers and companions. These new demands on women seem to be the media model of female liberation, but such an ideal is a dangerous one for women. Women, in order to be liberated will have to cast off many of the traditional female role attributes if they are to survive.

This is strongly reminiscent of the dire warnings of those 19th century psychiatrists described by Showalter in her history of women and psychiatry who, on noting the increasing rates of female admission to asylums, explained it by reference to women's increasing education which was thought to overtax their naturally inadequate mental equipment (Showalter, 1985). As did his predecessors, Neuringer fails to consider the possibility that as female roles change so too could those of males, and hence the male may be able to share some of the "female tasks", thereby reducing the burden on women. In this sense, despite the apparent willingness to view present female attributes and roles as socially determined, Neuringer's contentions imply inherent danger in changing the existing, and by implication, natural order of things even though, under this order, suicide attempts may be the only safety valve left open to the distressed female. Despite these criticisms of Neuringer's work, and specifically the conclusions he reaches on the basis of it, his attempts to escape the conceptual strait-jacket of the pathology model are instructive. This is especially so in his proposition of the possibility of a dysfunctional cognitive style which might inhibit adequate coping by reducing expectations of improvement in those adverse conditions known to precipitate self-poisoning.

Coping Skills

Support for the significance of cognitive factors in parasuicide continues to emerge in the more recent literature which, in addition to providing confirmation of some earlier findings, has begun to focus on the implications of these various cognitive characteristics for the skills required to cope with adverse events. Thus, Patsiokas and colleagues using the Alternate Uses Test (AUT; Wilson, Christenson, Merrifield, & Guilford, 1975), found that "suicide attempters" were significantly less able to generate alternate uses for well known objects than a group of non-suicidal psychiatric controls, leading to the conclusion (Patsiokas, Clum, & Luscomb, 1979) that this might result in:

> ... an inability to display diversity in coping with their stressors. The cognitively rigid person has difficulty conceiving and following through suggestions of new behaviour options and may be deterred from contemplating anything other than his stressful situation.

However the mechanism linking poor performance on the AUT and inadequate coping remained unexplored and a more recent study by Schotte and Clum (1982) found that in a group of student suicide ideators, cognitive rigidity as assessed on the AUT was not related to problem-solving skills measured by the Means–Ends Problem-Solving Procedure (MEPS; Platt, Spivack, & Bloom, 1975).

Asarnow, Carlson, and Guthrie (1987) more directly investigated cognitive strategies for dealing with stressful events among parasuicides and ideators by employing a Coping Strategies Test (CST). This was developed by the authors and involved children (aged 8–13) providing solutions to hypothetical stressful situations. They found that "suicide ideators", when compared with "non-suicidal" children, were significantly less likely to generate active cognitive coping strategies— defined as solutions involving self-comforting statements or instrumental problem solving as opposed to those involving physical or verbal aggression, suicide or running away. Asarnow and her colleagues concluded that parasuicidal children may resort to this behaviour as a consequence of their inability to spontaneously generate cognitive mediational strategies to regulate their affective and behavioural responses to stressful life events.

The reliability of these results is questionable, however, in view of the small sample sizes involved—only eight actual parasuicides were included—and their generalisability to adult parasuicides is also doubted by the authors.

Schotte and Clum (1987), building on their earlier work, further tested what they describe as the "diathesis–stress–hopelessness model" by comparing 50 hospitalised patients classified as suicidal with 50 non-suicidal psychiatric patients. They were concerned to explore the exact nature of the problem-solving deficits leading to hopelessness in the face of adverse events known to characterise parasuicides. They employed the Means–Ends Problem-Solving Procedure measure (MEPS, Platt et al., 1975) which demonstrated that suicide ideators were able to generate fewer than half as many potential solutions to interpersonal problems selected from their own lives as similarly depressed control subjects. In addition, ideators tended to focus to a greater extent on the potential negative effects of implementation than did the controls and were less likely to implement these solutions once generated. All these conclusions were found to be predictive of levels of suicidal intent on the Beck Suicide Ideation Scale (Beck et al., 1975a).

However, as in their earlier paper (Schotte & Clum, 1982), the authors found that a simple correlation between degree of hopelessness and interpersonal problem-solving skills was not established and suggested that hopelessness arises not from deficits in interpersonal problem-solving skills but rather a maladaptive general orientation toward problems.

Once again these results must be treated with caution as the suicidal subjects had not—at least recently—engaged in parasuicide and 85% were diagnosed as schizophrenic. The generalisability of the findings is open to question as such psychopathology is rare among self-poisoners. However this is a common failing in studies concerned with parasuicide which do not employ self-poisoners as subjects—studying instead students (Cole, 1989), suicide ideators (Schotte & Clum, 1987) threateners (Neuringer & Lettieri, 1982), or attenders at various types of crisis centre (Holden, Mendonca, & Serin, 1989).

None the less, the recent Holden et al., (1989) paper lends support to Schotte and Clum's conclusions, finding that among a large group of adult suicide ideators the relationship between hopelessness and suicidal intent was mediated by a general sense of capability, or "self-efficacy", which, as measured on a social desirability scale (Jackson, 1984), reduced the positive association between hopelessness and suicidality. Holden et al., (p.503) conclude:

... both negative cognitions about the future (i.e. hopelessness) and the interaction of these pessimistic expectations with a lack of self-efficacy ... are associated with suicide. Conversely, cognitions of self-capability reduce the link between suicide and hopelessness.

Cole (1989) supports these conclusions with his finding that among adolescent non-patients—contrary to the well documented findings with adults—depression was more strongly related to suicidal behaviours than was hopelessness. He also found a strong negative association between suicidal ideation and survival coping beliefs as measured on the Reasons for Living Inventory (RFL; Linehan, Goodstein, Nielsen, & Chiles, 1983) which taps self-efficacy and the belief a person has in their ability to solve personal problems. Relating this to Schotte and Clum's findings, Cole suggests that positive beliefs about one's survival coping abilities may act as a buffer between hopelessness and suicidal behaviour.

Cole claims support for his findings in the commonly reported "personal fable" found among adolescents—the belief that they are "special, unusually capable and fortunate individuals, and that accidents or catastrophes that could befall others will not happen to them" (Elkind, 1967, 1985; Lapsley, 1985). Cole (1989) suggests that multiple failure experiences, common among parasuicides, may "dissolve the myth of omnipotence and well-being that buffers against suicidal thoughts".

Cognitive approaches indicating deficits in problem-solving skills as the mechanism linking adverse events and self-poisoning have considerable empirical support, although concepts are disparate and results sometimes conflicting. There remains an acknowledged need for an integrating theory. However, the most recent literature has moved away from the rather global concept of "cognitive rigidity" as measured on such tests as the Alternate Uses Test and the Semantic Differential, to cognitive constructs more easily operationalised in considering coping behaviour, such as the Means–Ends Problem-Solving Procedure. These have greater heuristic value in model building and, as a result, more sophisticated interactive models are evolving with the most recent empirical findings suggesting that what has previously been referred to as cognitive rigidity involves a negative cognitive set towards problems in general which may be related to both specific deficits in problem-solving skills and the hopelessness known to be characterstic of self-poisoners. The most influential account of the role of hopelessness in self-poisoning is that of A.T. Beck.

Hopelessness

Using the term "suicide" to include "suicidal behaviour", Beck, Kovacs, and Weissman (1975) begin with these words (p.1146):

The phenomenon of suicide presents a puzzle to students of psychopathology as well as to the lay public; what mysterious force drives a person to violate one of the most hallowed notions of human nature—the "survival instinct"? Of the multitude of explanations by various writers, few seem to ring true or have even minimal empirical support.

Beck and his colleagues are critical of previous pathology models which employ the explanation of internalised aggression, pointing to their own empirical work which found no support for such a contention (Beck, 1967). They propose (Beck et al., 1975b, p.1147) that this work led to a belief that concentration on depressive illness in the study of attempted suicide had led to a neglect of cognitive factors—specifically that of hopelessness:

> Beck's thesis of suicidal behaviour incorporates two themes that occur in the historical survey of suicide; namely, the concepts that hopelessness is the catalytic agent and that "impaired reason" plays an important role in most cases of hopelessness and, consequently, in suicidal behaviour. The main thrust of Beck's argument is that suicidal behaviour is derived from specific cognitive distortions: the patient systematically misconstrues his experiences in a negative way and, without objective basis, anticipates a negative outcome to any attempts to attain his major objectives or goals.

"Hopelessness" is defined as a: "system of cognitive schemata that share the common element of negative expectations". There is reference to earlier work by Minkoff (Minkoff, Bergman, Beck, & Beck, 1973) which found that hopelessness was a more sensitive indicator of suicidal intent than depression *per se*. This study had also demonstrated that: "Suicide attempters who were not depressed showed a substantial correlation between hopelessness and suicidal intent" (Beck et al., 1975b, p.1147).

The study set out to replicate Minkoff's findings with a much larger sample of 384 suicide attempters who had been admitted to two metropolitan hospitals—160 men and 224 women, over two-thirds of whom had employed drugs in their attempts. The authors concluded that depression had a bearing on suicidal intent only by virtue of its association with hopelessness, as measured on a scale devised by Beck and others (Beck, Weissman, Lester, & Trexler, 1974), such that: "For the present data, hopelessness accounts for 96% of the association between depression and suicidal intent" (Beck et al., 1975b, p.1148).

Having employed both psychometric and clinical assessment of depression and hopelessness, it is asserted (p.1148) that: "Whether measured psychometrically or clinically, hopelessness, defined operationally in terms of negative expectations, is a stronger indication of suicidal intent than is depression".

The authors feel that this finding goes some way to unravelling the "puzzle" of suicidal behaviour among the non-depressed, in that it: "pinpoints hopelessness as the missing link between depression and suicidal behaviour", and that it might help the clinician to: "get a hold of the situation by targeting in on the hopelessness rather than by dealing with (the patient's) overt self-destructive acts". Despite this, as had Neuringer, they remain attached to a pathology view describing (p.1147) the negative schemata of hopelessness as "cognitive distortions", within which the patient: "... systematically misconstrues his experience in a negative way and, without objective basis, anticipates a negative outcome to any attempts to attain his major objectives or goals".

None the less Beck and his colleagues display an ambiguous attitude—again in much the same way as Neuringer—towards the possible role of normative socialisation in creating these cognitive distortions. They devote their last brief paragraph (p.1149) to the following speculation, where enthusiasm for personological explanation and person-oriented interventions is tempered by recognition of a sociological dimension:

> In addition the "hopelessness" formulation of suicidal behaviour has provided the rationale for active cognitive and behavioural approaches directed at correcting the pervasive misconceptions inherent in such an attitude.The techniques for cognitive-behavioural treatment of suicide have been described elsewhere. When the negative expectations are related to various reality factors in life, the current findings might help to identify a starting point for professionals whose ultimate goal is constructive social change.

Intimations of Social Context

The paper described above does not specifically discuss the implications of gender and sex role socialisation to self-poisoning, but in an earlier contribution to a volume dealing with the cognitive therapy of depression in women (Beck & Greenberg, 1974b) Beck's ambiguous position about the relationship of normative socialisation, sex roles, and psychopathology is further demonstrated. Here (p.129) Beck seems to accept that:

It is indubitably true that women have been offered, throughout history, only the narrowest range of alternatives in choosing their life-styles. Rarely has a woman had the opportunity to direct her own life, to realise her personal conception of happiness and fulfillment.

Earlier in the piece he had accepted that these restricted roles—"their subservient posture as secretaries, nurses and assistants and especially those duties that attend housewifery and motherhood"—might in themselves be inherently depressing. Beck accepts (p.116) that it is indeed tempting:

... to postulate ... a kinship between the subjective feelings of helplessness in depression and the objective helplessness and powerlessness of women in American society, when compared to the prestige of men in male oriented professional and business worlds.

He even refers to Phyllis Chesler's assertion in her feminist account of women and mental health (Chesler, 1972) that the symptomatology of depression is merely an intensification of traits which normal socialisation processes induce in women: "passivity, dependence, self-deprecation, self-sacrifice, naivete, fearfulness and failure", and that therefore:

If, as Chesler and other feminists assert, depression is a normal response to rigid, exploitative sex role definitions in a male-dominated, authoritarian society, then the role of psychotherapy may be limited to encouraging revolutionary sympathies in individual patients (from Beck & Greenberg, 1974b, p.118).

However, daunted perhaps by this prospect, Beck then proceeds again to temper this sociological account by suggesting that alternative schools of thought on depression give rise to "more optimistic views" on psychotherapy, and his approving account (p.127) of the behavioural treatment of a depressed housewife leaves little doubt as to his preference for the "personological" approach:

When a depressed housewife is unable to function in the home, the therapist may give her tasks of increasing difficulty to perform, at which she has a good chance of succeeding. At first she may be required only to make the beds, then to cook a meal, and so on. When she has clearly succeeded at a task her lethargy decreases and she is motivated to try more.

This seems perilously close to an exhortation to accept that there are no alternatives available, and that, rather than direct effort at attempts to broaden opportunity, the "patient" must learn to function more efficiently within the roles she is allowed.

Beck concludes his paper with several startling examples of the belief that society's influence can be "turned off like a tap"—as described by Cloward and Piven, and Taylor earlier in this chapter in their critiques of the pathology perspective. Thus it is asserted:

> But women, both as a group and as individuals, will go nowhere unless a critical decision is reached—that is, despite socialisation and precedent, to accept responsibility for their lives, goals, families, careers, and psychological symptoms without falling back on the easy excuses of masculine preference, social appearances, difficult times and circumstances ... The fundamental challenge remains what it has been all along—to master and command trying circumstances and thereby transcend them into an acceptable and even rewarding way of life.

And later (p.130):

> Young women will do well to concentrate on preventing future depressions by cultivating habits of self-respect and self-reliance and by leading a balanced life, participating in a variety of activities rather than depending on family ties alone for emotional and intellectual sustenance ... In their subordinate posture, women are vulnerable and continuously on the defensive, overvalue looks, health, youth and other undependable assets, and panic when they think them threatened. Finally, by restricting their attention to the "feminine" sphere in the age of supertechnology and the "global village", women sacrifice a sense of the objective reality that exists beyond domestic confines.

If these decisions and choices were available one can only wonder why women do not choose them, and Beck's assertions must surely be viewed as exemplary of the tendency, prevalent in such functionalist accounts, of "blaming the victim". Having outlined in some detail the sociological reasons women are unable to choose—because of their socialisation and the objective absence of alternatives—he then, "turns off" these influences, returns to the personological perspective of individual dysfunction, and blames them for not so choosing. What, then, is the "more optimistic" solution than that of "encouraging revolutionary sympathies"? Beck concludes his paper (p.130):

When depression progresses to the clinical stage, professional help can make it possible for the depressed woman to weather the crisis and lay the groundwork for more effective responding in the future.

A conclusion which recalls another of Chesler's statements to the effect that "women have to lose in order to win" (Chesler, 1972, p.47).

CHAPTER 3

A Social Psychology of Self-poisoning

THE FAILURE OF THE PATHOLOGY PERSPECTIVE

The review in Chapter Two of current theories of self-poisoning has suggested that the pathology paradigm which underpins them has proven unilluminating in relation to female self-poisoning. The reluctance, or rather inability, of the exponents of this perspective to go beyond the individual, has led to the neglect of social context, and of the interaction between individual and context. An insistence on pathology, or at least, "difference" between self-poisoners and "normal" people has blinded students to the similarities. An example of this is to be found in McCulloch and Philip's account of *Suicidal Behaviour*, where the striking class differentials in self-poisoning—Kreitman described a 14-fold excess of class 5 individuals over those of classes 1 and 2 (Kreitman, 1977, p.24)—are swept aside with the statement (McCulloch & Philip, 1972, p.13):

There is no doubt that in trying to understand the behaviour of these people, social class is largely irrelevant. We suggest that persons who have suicidal behaviour as a common experience are more like each other than they are like persons of their own social class who do not manifest this behaviour.

The "puzzle" of self-poisoning, and particularly the predominance of women, has not been solved by the psychopathologists: a fact acknowledged by one of their number (Morgan, 1979) in this plaintive remark occuring after 126 pages of a volume recounting all the "facts" of epidemiology and psychopathology in self-poisoning:

> At no point in our discussion so far have we really gained any insight into the possible reasons for the epidemic-like increase of Deliberate Self Harm in most Western countries since the early-1960s. The imitative contagion-like effect in younger persons undoubtedly is relevant here, but why has this form of behaviour been chosen instead of others? What new influences are there in society especially concerning young adults and particularly relevant to females?

Later the author, as did Neuringer and Beck before him, conjectured about women's roles, devoting one sentence to the following possibility:

> Young women often find themselves in a dilemma when their emancipation is hindered by continued restraints such as unequal job opportunities or domestic commitments which are not shared by their male partners.

and again:

> Most of the increased incidence has been due to overdoses with one or more psychotropic drugs, usually obtained through medical prescription. Have these agents become more available in recent years? They most certainly have ... It does seem that availability through medical prescription is mirrored closely by the frequency with which a drug is used for the purpose of deliberate self-harm ... Are such drugs used inappropriately as a panacea for individuals whose problems are not resolved by them?

The next obvious question is not, however, posed—do those women whose "emancipation is hindered" receive excessive prescriptions over males, and do they then poison themselves with them when their problems remain unresolved? Later in this work it will be proposed that the answer to both is yes, and that the same social/psychological process underpins both phenomena as well as several other aspects of self-poisoning unaccounted for in the pathology paradigm—such as why the breakdown of interpersonal relationships more frequently precipitates self-poisoning in women than men. However, before this can be undertaken it is necessary to explore why existing models have failed to provide satisfactory explanation.

Steve Taylor in his account of suicidal behaviour (Taylor, 1982) suggests (p.135) that there has been a dearth of theory building as a result of the emphasis in psychiatry and epidemiology on fact gathering:

> Explanation neither emerges, nor is derived from data, it has to be invented. By confining ourselves to the data ... we become trapped in a world of descriptive particulars.

and again:

> However, such research, rather than "building up" into an increasingly "general" explanation has rather tended to go the opposite way and, as might be imagined, "broken down" into more and more particular explanations ... With no clear theoretical framework, explanation does not order data, rather data orders explanation, with each "new" discovery demanding its "own" explanation.

Taylor therefore concludes (p.130):

> The majority of works ... tend to favour a narrow empiricism which is suspicious of both abstract theoretical analysis and studying human behaviour as essentially meaningful social action.

Cognitive psychology, as exemplified in the work of Neuringer and Beck, began to acknowledge the importance of the individual's interpretation of events in relation to their self-poisoning. There is even some acknowledgement that sex role socialisation is an important determinant of the meanings individuals attach to events. However, as we have seen, these authors too insist that the cognitions of self-poisoners are "distorted" and "without objective basis" (Beck et al., 1975b, p.1147), and therefore deny the behaviour based upon such cognitions' legitimacy as meaningful social action. Both turn off the socialisation tap at the point of self-poisoning, and therefore are unable to account for those social divisions, especially that of gender, which are definitive of this phenomenon, yet remain unexplained.

This failure of pathology theory to provide explanation is clearly inherent in its insistence on the division between social and psychological, internal and external, normal and abnormal. Taylor (1982, p.18) suggests that this is a relatively late development in the study of suicidology, comparing it with the Durkheimian approach in this way:

Of course Durkheim was interested in the boundaries between sociology and psychology, but it was a later generation of students who created the disjunction between supposedly "internal" and "external" factors in the explanation of suicide. Durkheim was concerned with the way society superimposes itself on individuals, but his sociology was not an attempt to show that social facts impinge on individuals from without and, as it were, propel them like billiard balls in given directions; but rather that society, the collective experience of humanity, "lives in" the subjective experiences of individuals. When Durkheim wrote about society being external, he was not advocating some crude social determinism where forces physically outside individuals push them in given directions, but rather that society is external to each individual considered singly.

The exhortations of Neuringer and Beck to women to cast off the oppressive limitations imposed by society have within them such an implicit "crude social determinism". As oppression is viewed as external, their perspective assumes that it can be resisted, and that "despite socialisation and precedent", those individuals whose cognitive processes are "normal" can "accept responsibility for their lives ... and psychological symptoms" and "master and command trying circumstances and thereby transform them into an acceptable and even rewarding way of life" (Beck et al., 1974b, p.129). In other words, women can cast aside the external regulation of sex role socialisation and instead employ self-regulation to combat its pejorative effects. But, as Taylor asserts (p.133):

Where, we may ask, does this self regulation come from? ... from the individual ... but this is inconsistent: either society does influence individuals or it does not. We can argue that the states of different social environments do differently regulate individual actions ... or we can argue that this is not the case and that suicide is in fact caused genetically or whatever. What we can not argue is that society's influence can be turned off like a tap and that in some way an individually based regulation takes over.

None the less Beck, casting aside the pervasive influence of socialisation, turning off the tap, asserts that: "The possibilities for change inherent in current attitudes go far beyond what has already become incarnate in social habit and legal actuality" (Beck et al., 1974b, p.129), and that those who are unable to resist these external forces are seen as having "distorted" cognitive processes which lead them to:

... fall back upon the easy excuses of masculine preference, social appearances, difficult times and circumstances (and) sacrifice a sense of objective reality that exists beyond domestic affairs.

AN INTERACTIVE MODEL

Although the shortcomings of the pathology model are inherent in its basic assumptions, the same cannot be said of those derived from cognitive psychology. It remains possible to base an account of gender variables in self-poisoning upon normative cognitive processes and theories of sex role socialisation without resort to the pathologising conclusions of Beck and Neuringer. Such an account, in that it seeks to integrate the "social" and the "psychological" is an interactive one, the general tenets of which have been described by Nicholas Braucht (1979, p.665) in relation to suicidal behaviour in these terms:

(a) that such real-life behaviours cannot adequately be understood by recourse to either individual difference variables alone or environmental variables alone; (b) that neither individuals nor environments can be understood to be pathological in themselves; and that (c) behaviour is not viewed as sick or well, but is defined as transactional—an outcome of reciprocal interactions between specific social situations and the individual.

An interactive analysis, based on such tenets, is particularly apposite to self-poisoning because of the well documented characteristics which were described in detail in Chapter One. To briefly recap: these are that wherever it has occurred in western society it has been a behaviour predominantly adopted by young, working class women; it became ubiquitous between 1960 and 1980 in these societies, in some places with a rate of one per cent of teenage women being recorded and outnumbering men by a ratio of two to one or more; it is usually unaccompanied by psychopathology, although it has often, it seems erroneously, been attributed to hysterical personality in women; it frequently involves the ingestion of prescribed sedative medication, among the recipients of which women outnumber men by two to one; and it is precipitated by adverse life events which show clear gender differences in their nature, most commonly in women the breakdown of interpersonal relationships, and in men financial or legal problems.

It has been demonstrated that these social, and particularly gender, divisions in the phenomenon cannot be explained adequately either by the "internal" accounts of the pathologists, or the allegedly "external" accounts of the ecological or stress model. In the absence of psychopathology it must be accepted that this behaviour is meaningful and purposive, carried out within social interactions and informed by those normative processes which shape other forms of social behaviour. The cognitive theories of Neuringer and Beck have much to offer in their initial emphasis on the meaning individuals attach to those events which occur in their environment, as the importance of an accumulation of adverse events in the precipitation of self-poisoning is well attested. Thus Neuringer and Lettieri (1982, p.27) describe the cognitive approach as seeking: "... to delineate the meaning of the suicidal act for the individual and how that meaning developed from particular intellectual styles". And Beck (1963) noted on the basis of long-term psychotherapy of suicidal patients that: "The suicidal preoccupations ... seemed related to the patient's conceptualisation of his situation as untenable or hopeless".

That these "intellectual styles" and "conceptualisations" and the self-poisoning behaviour associated with them represent, not distortions of normative cognitive processes, but rather are the product of them is denied by these writers in their insistence on dichotomising normal from abnormal, social from psychological. That these cognitive processes reflect and reinforce the social structural divisions so clearly evident in the phenomenon is not considered, nor can they therefore accept that, in the words quoted earlier of Cloward and Piven (1979, p.655):

> Such a (cognitive) framework ... is not devised *de novo* by people under stress; it is a feature of the social structure within which they live out their ordinary rule-abiding lives, and it also guides them when they are prompted to break the rules.

They are therefore unable to explain these social and gender divisions—why should women have more distorted cognitions than men? Why should this particularly occur during certain historical periods more than others? Why should females have distorted cognitions specifically in relation to interpersonal relationships in the private or "affiliative domain", and men in relation to financial, work or legal matters, i.e. the public or "achievement domain"? Why should self-poisoning with prescribed medication be the particular manifestation of these cognitions? Any theory which hopes to illuminate these questions must be interactive in that it should be able to conceive of the individual's cognitions associated with self-poisoning as, not random, illogical distortions, but, instead patterned by the social/structural context within which the individual exists—as part of the social process, not as an aberrant, pathological response to it.

Beck, in his hopelessness theory of suicidal behaviour, asserts that hopelessness is "a primary feature in suicidal intent" and that it is "defined operationally in terms of negative expectations". As both Beck and Neuringer acknowledged, the sex role system is a dominant feature of the socialisation process and is one which has particularly disadvantageous effects for women—in particular, young, working class women whose aspirations and opportunities are most constrained by it. However, neither is prepared to acknowledge that the cognitive framework of negative expectations characteristic of self-poisoning women are the result of this socialisation process and are the basis of its legitimation. Expectations, negative or otherwise, do not arise in isolation from a social context, they are social constructions based on social comparisons and cannot therefore be dismissed as "distorted" or "without objective basis" simply because they are associated with apparently deviant behaviour.

An important contribution to the understanding of the relationship between cognition and social context in self-poisoning comes from the application of Rotter's *Theory of Generalised Expectancies*, often referred to as "locus of control".

LOCUS OF CONTROL

In the concept of locus of control, Rotter suggested that individuals differ in their experiences through time of their ability to control reinforcements, both positive and negative. People with early experience of success in controlling their environment would tend to expect success in the future, i.e. develop "generalised expectancies for internal versus external control of reinforcements"; conversely those with experiences of an inability to control outcomes would expect failure in the future, and develop an opposite generalised expectancy (Rotter, 1966).

Rotter and others developed a forced choice scale to measure individual's beliefs about the locus of control, which, referred to as the "I–E" scale, involved paired statements such as "what happens to me is my own doing" as opposed to "sometimes I feel that I do not have enough control over the direction my life is taking". Obviously one of each pair implies that reinforcements come unpredictably from the environment, the other that they are contingent on the individual's actions. Individuals who believe that they can actively control their fate may be described as having a sense of internal control whereas those who attribute the course of their lives to fate, chance or other causes beyond their control possess a sense of external control.

This concept has been widely employed as a suggested mediator of the effects of stressful life events. Subjects with greater externality, when confronted with adverse events and life changes, demonstrate more anxiety and depression than those with internal locus (Lefcourt, 1981). It has been demonstrated that there are class differences in locus of control orientations, with working class individuals possessing external, fatalistic orientations. Early work by Battle and Rotter (1963) demonstrated that locus of control beliefs are related to class, with middle class people showing a more internal style than working class, and to educational attainment, where those high in attainment possess the more internal style (McGhee & Crandall, 1968). A more recent study of the well established inverse relationship between depression and socio-economic status sought to explore the importance of life event frequency and locus of control to this finding.

Husaini and Neff (1981) in a study of 713 rural American adults found, as has been consistently reported elsewhere, a higher incidence of depression among their lower class respondents. They failed to confirm the findings of other research of a higher rate of adverse events among the lower class respondents, and concluded that stressful events alone could not be responsible for the class differential in depression. Instead they proposed that the individual's perception of where control lies mediates between events and affective response. They found support for this in that locus of control, as measured on a shortened version of Rotter's scale, was related both to social class, rated in terms of education and income, and levels of depressive symptomatology, as measured on the Centre for Epidemiologic Studies – Depression Scale (CES–D). They concluded (p.645) that: "Lower class individuals tended to perceive themselves as being victims of their environment (i.e. externally oriented), and this tendency has a marked influence on their level of symptomatology".

In relation to gender, a study of women who had recently given birth surveyed their utilisation of health service and other formal and informal helping networks (Westbrook & Mitchell, 1979). Comparing the use of such services by middle and working class women respectively, it was found that working class women, although they expressed more positive attitudes to childbirth and childcare, also demonstrated fatalistic attitudes to the effect that they felt that "what would be would be" irrespective of their actions. This, the authors felt, accounted for the relative underutilisation of ante-natal services by working class women, and in terms of a "coping style" left such women ill prepared for adversities which their middle class peers anticipated, and felt more able to control. Thus, their fatalistic orientation led to coping which was less instrumental because their external orientation led them to expect that they were powerless to affect the course of events.

There is therefore consistent empirical support in the literature for the contention that working class individuals possess more external orientations than those from other socio-economic groups and that this renders them more vulnerable to distress in the face of adverse events and less able to mobilise effective coping behaviours. This begins to suggest that normative socialisation—in this case social class—affects cognitive styles in patterned ways thus supporting Cloward and Piven's (1979, p.655) assertion referred to earlier that:

> Stressful conditions are thus never experienced in raw form (but) are interpreted by thinking people guided by a particular cognitive and moral framework (which) is not devised *de novo* by people under stress (but) is a feature of the social structure within which they live out their ordinary rule abiding lives, and it also guides them when they are prompted to break the rules.

Empirical support for these contentions comes from one of the few large scale epidemiological studies of self-poisoning which attempted to build a theoretical model in relation to its socio-structural findings. This Canadian study (Jarvis, Ferrence, Johnson, & Whitehead, 1976) set out to explore the significance of age and sex patterns in self-injury, including in this both parasuicidal behaviour and actual suicide.

In an unusually thorough case finding effort which included cases treated not only in hospitals but other institutions such as jails, psychiatric institutions and by GPs, the authors collected a variety of demographic and ecological data much of which reflected the findings of other surveys, in that among parasuicides young women from lower socio-economic groups, living in depressed city centre areas predominated. A rate of over 1 in 100 women aged 20–24 was found which led the authors to coin the phrase, subsequently oft quoted, that self-injury on this scale could be regarded as "a technique in human relations". In attempting to account for these patterns in self-injury, Jarvis et al. (1976) developed a theoretical model which views self-injury as one of a possible range of responses to stress. They proposed (p.151) that:

> Individuals react to this strain in terms of the resources at their command, the means and skills they have learned are necessary to impinge their will on the environment.
> Classes of individuals differ in the extent to which they determine the conditions under which they function. Relatively high determination of one's environment could be termed "high control". To the extent that individuals have high control, or are permitted this by the roles they

occupy, they will be able to restructure the environment when it threatens. Techniques of implementing control are learned and later reinforced through socialisation in association with particular roles and statuses.

People with high control are found in all categories of the population, but come disproportionately from among males rather than females, from those in the economically productive years of mature adulthood, from the upper and middle classes ... A person with little control or who is relatively ineffective at conventional controlling techniques, would be more likely, when facing a serious problem to adopt a method of control such as self-injury ... The more youthful, the traditional female and the lower class person would tend to fall into this category.

These conclusions lend support to the locus of control theorists who have shown that the construct is able to differentiate in some ways those groups who predominate among self-poisoners, i.e. working class women, and there are a very small number of studies which apply the concept directly to groups of parasuicides, to which we now turn.

The notion that suicidal behaviour is a variety of "risk taking" is an early example of the proposition that such behaviour is characteristic of those with an external orientation. Thus, Weiss (1957, p.389) described the connection in these terms:

Many suicidal attempts have at least in part the character of a gamble with death, a sort of Russian roulette, the outcome of which depends to some extent on chance. The attempts are consciously or unconsciously arranged in such a manner that the lethal probability may vary from almost certain survival to almost certain death; and fate—or at least some force external to the conscious choice of the person—is compelled in some perhaps magical way to make the final decision.

In a later paper Raymond Firth applied this idea to an analysis of suicidal behaviour in Tikopia—a Pacific island where suicidal individuals either swam out into shark infested waters in the case of women, or paddled out in canoes if men. Survival was therefore dependent on the elements or upon the urgency of the ensuing search by those left behind. Perhaps a more dramatic example of gender differences in suicidal behaviour than we have so far described, though undoubtedly one which, in terms of the apparent balance of risk, seems to show a similar disadvantage inherent in the female sex role (Firth, 1971).

There are six subsequent examples of papers which apply Rotter's construct of internal-external locus of control—however two of these did not apply it to parasuicide patients, but rather to the ubiquitous "introductory psychology students". For this reason these studies will not be described in any detail as their findings must be merely conjectural. The study of Williams and Nickels (1969), which is often quoted in this context, employed Rotter's I–E scale with a group of 235 students who were also asked to complete two different scales to measure "suicide potentiality". Externally oriented subjects generally scored higher on the suicidal potentiality scales.

The second such study (Lambley & Silbowitz, 1973), again employing student samples, asked subjects to complete a "short questionnaire detailing the number and frequency of their suicidal thoughts and attempts". The results of this when correlated with results on Rotter's scale found no significant differences between contemplators and non-contemplators. As the study distinguishes neither between those who may have made attempts and those who had not, nor between males and females, and in view of the ubiquity of both self-poisoning and of suicidal rumination in the general population (Paykel et al., 1974) these findings may legitimately be regarded as lacking in credibility.

The first study to apply the scale to parasuicide patients was that of Friedrich Wenz who, in 1977, reported the results of a comparative study of male and female attempters (admitted to hospital following their attempt) and threateners (people who telephoned a suicide prevention centre). A control group of staff from that agency and others in the locality was used who "made no threats of suicide or attempts during their lives". The attempters were found to be significantly more external than the controls, although no difference was found between attempters and threateners (Wenz, 1977). Problems with this study include the fact that the controls differed significantly on numerous socio-demographic variables, including level of education which, as we have seen, itself is related to locus of control, with the better educated showing more internality. For this reason alone therefore one would expect those differences which were found between their scores on the I–E scale and those of less well educated attempters.

An unpublished doctoral study by Martin Levenson which examined *Cognitive and Perceptual Factors in Suicidal Individuals* found no significant differences between attempters and either non-suicidal psychiatric patients or a control group of hospital workers. This study employed small numbers—16 in each group—and was confined to males (Levenson, 1972).

A more recent study carried out by Luscomb, Clum, & Patsiokas, (1980) similarly confined itself to male subjects, and its controls were limited to hospitalised psychiatric patients. However, in an attempt to broaden the construct internal-external, they delineated two dimensions at the external end—described as the "congruent external" and the "defensive external".

The congruent external is he who believes that reinforcers are not contingent upon his behaviour—as in Rotter's original conception. The defensive external, on the other hand, uses externality as a means of blame projection—they verbally put forth an external point of view as a defence against failure, "whereas, in reality (manifested in their behaviour) they are striving, ambitious internals". The researchers identified the latter types by employing an Interpersonal Trust Scale, low scores on which had been shown elsewhere to be related to congruent externality (Hamsher, Geller, & Rotter, 1968). The results indicated that for congruent externals there is a relationship between the amount of life change experienced and parasuicide, although no such relationship was observed in relation to externals as a whole.

The final, and most sophisticated, of the studies using parasuicide patients, is that of Robert Goldney (1982), an Australian study which examined the locus of control orientations of a group of 110 women aged between 18 and 30 who had taken overdoses. The Adult Nowicki-Strickland Internal-External locus of control scale was used as the author claims it requires less verbal fluency than the Rotter Scale (Nowicki & Duke, 1974). Scales measuring depression, hopelessness and perceived childhood distress were also employed. The control group consisted of women attending a community health centre.

Goldney divided the patients into high, medium and low lethality groups according to how life threatening their attempt was and found significant differences between them. Overall the self-poisoners scored higher on externality than did the controls. However it was found that within the parasuicide groups, those of highest lethality in fact scored more internally than did the less lethal groups, a finding reminiscent of those of Krause and Stryker (1984) which suggested the possibility of a curvilinear relationship between locus of control scores and stress. These authors, finding that moderate externals experienced more distress in the face of comparable levels of stress than did extreme externals, suggested that maybe extreme externality acted as a defence against feelings of overwhelming guilt, relatively diminishing anxiety and depression. Goldney's high lethality group, being in comparison less extreme externals than the lower lethality groups, would therefore lack this defence. Support for Beck's assertion of the importance of hopelessness in parasuicide and its relationship to external locus also comes from the Goldney study. He found that locus of control scores did not remain significantly correlated with depression when controlling for hopelessness, although there was a significant correlation with hopelessness when controlling for depression. Finally support was forthcoming too for the work of Bryant and Trockel (1976) in Goldney's finding that there was a significant positive correlation in his self-poisoning group between externality and perceived childhood stress. Bryant had earlier discovered that among college women subjects, uncontrollable childhood events promoted an external locus of control orientation.

The Goldney study is clearly superior to those which employed students in preference to parasuicides, and, in that it employs greater numbers of subjects, controls for levels of depression and suicidal intent, and uses non-patient controls, is superior to those few others which do apply the construct of locus of control to parasuicide patients. Its findings are in line with those predicted by the theory, and the only anomaly—that of the comparatively lesser externality of the high lethality group compared with the moderates—can be accounted for in terms of the Krause and Stryker model of non-linearity.

Although the findings from locus of control studies and parasuicide have not always been consistent, and the methodology of most of those is questionable, external locus orientations have been shown to be linked conceptually to fatalistic orientations and to hopelessness in parasuicides. Although there seems to be little in the literature employing Rotter's locus of control scale to the study of gender differences in such orientations, Goldney's study, while not being comparative in gender terms, at least demonstrates that self-poisoning women are indeed characterised by external locus orientations. The conceptual links with Beck's Hopelessness Theory of self-poisoning are strong in that the notion of non-contingency in external locus orientations could be seen as giving rise to those negative expectations he identified as central to hopelessness.

The early findings of Battle and Rotter which indicated greater externality in working class people, their subsequent confirmation by Husaini and Neff, and Westbrook and Mitchell's description of fatalistic coping styles in working class women begin to point convincingly to the importance of social structural factors in the evolution of cognitive styles associated with self-poisoning which, as we have seen, was not denied by Neuringer and Beck in their cognitive approach to suicidal behaviour but was not explored in any detail, and was subsumed in their search for pathology. This, it is contended here, has led to a neglect of social context and the implications of normative socialisation—in particular the sex role system—in female self-poisoning.

Having found support for the proposed role of normative socialisation processes in the aetiology of self-poisoning, it is to a consideration of sex role socialisation and its relationship to female self-poisoning that we now turn our attention.

CHAPTER 4

Women and Sex Role Socialisation

SEX ROLES AND PSYCHOPATHOLOGY

In the Introduction it was proposed that there are three questions which, although central to an understanding of female self-poisoning, the literature leaves largely unexplored. These were: Why women? Why self-poisoning? Why now? Having argued the case for the abandonment of the pathology paradigm on the grounds of its descriptive inaccuracy and explanatary inadequacy, and having established the need to place the phenomenon firmly within its social context we can now approach that body of knowledge which can offer some enlightenment on these questions.

Kay Clifton and Dorothy Lee suggest that female "suicide proneness" represents the "self-destructive consequences of sex role socialisation". They conclude that due to sex role socialisation, women tend to:

extrovert (turn outward on others) their positive feelings in pleasant situations and to introvert (turn blame on themselves) their negative reactions to unpleasant situations. Men do the reverse ... women are self-destructive in passive ways, reflecting their lack of self-favourability and confidence and manifested by failure to react to everyday situations in ego building ways.

It will be recalled from our examination of stress theories in Chapter Two that Michelle Wilson (1981) offered a model which integrated many of the positive features of Kreitman's parasuicide-as-communication theory, Maris's view of "attempted suicide" as a form of coping behaviour, and Gove's sex role theory of female "suicidal behaviour"—without resorting ultimately to the assumption of pathology. Her summary (p.139) of this model is worth repeating in full as it provides an eloquent and concise account of the bedrock of our own developing approach:

> Attempted suicide is the means of telling others that one is unable to deal effectively with stress. Modes of suicidal behaviour can be thought of as coping mechanisms because they involve the use of available resources for dealing with stressful situations. Women and men have very different resources not only in obvious ways, such as physical strength and economic power, but also in terms of autonomy, power over others and self-concept. Given the difference in the social location of women and men, it is also logical that they would experience different sources of stress as well as have available different forms and rates of reaction. Given that some change is occurring in the society, it is likely that gender specific rates of suicidal behaviour will change as a consequence.

Another author who has added to this line of reasoning is Lous Heshusius who, employing Jarvis's often quoted phrase, proposed that female self-injury represents "culturally reinforced techniques in human relations". Like Jarvis, in his epidemiological study referred to earlier, Heshusius suggests that such behaviour is resorted to by women more than men because a "woman's place" does not offer her the resources to deal effectively and adequately with the environment. Unlike men, women lack access to the sources of financial, political, job related and even physical power and, typically lacking such resources women are taught to be helpless—and to resort to self-injury as a culturally reinforced technique in human relations.

Cloward and Piven, whose work we have considered before, propose that female deviance is typically individualistic and self-destructive: examples given are prostitution, drug and alcohol addictions, and physical and mental illness. This characteristic form of deviance, they suggest, is not the result of aberrant behaviour but reflects the passivity and powerlessness inherent in the female role. They propose that deviant behaviour represents a protest against constraints imposed by socio-structural forces, and is moulded by the socialisation which forms "non-deviant" behaviour (Cloward & Piven, 1979).

They then go beyond this analysis which is shared with Clifton and Lee, Wilson, and Heshusius to consider that aspect which these authors neglect—why self-poisoning with medicinal agents? As Stengel had done 30 years earlier in pointing to the growth of "attempted suicide" after the establishment of the British National Health Service in 1947, Cloward and Piven point to the role of the medical establishment in the growth of female self-poisoning. They propose that the increasing influence and authority of the health system leads to the greater medicalisation specifically of female problems, which stem, in reality, from their disadvantaged social roles not their inherent mental or personality disorder. This influence is seen as encouraging women to act out (p.669): "more than ever before the individualised and self-destructive patterns of resistance to which they have been limited in the past".

These assertions seem to offer the promise of enlightenment on all three of our questions. Sadly, however, the authors offer little in the way of empirical evidence for their intuitively convincing arguments. We shall explore the evidence for the proposed influence of the sex role system on the medicalisation of female problems in the next chapter, but first we turn to the relationship between sex roles and psychopathology.

The notion that the gender specific forms taken by deviant behaviour are reflections of normative socialisation is a familiar one—whether the behaviour is described as criminal or psychopathological. The predominance of males, and virtual absence of females, among those committing violent crimes causes little surprise and may be seen as a consequence of that aspect of male sex role socialisation which emphasises assertiveness, dominance, aggression and power as appropriate male attributes. Similarly the female predominance among those convicted of prostitution reflects certain aspects of the female role emphasising sexual submissiveness and also the everyday employment of female nudity as an instrument of commodity marketing (Schur, 1983).

The influence of the sex role system on forms of female psychopathology, and its diagnosis and treatment has been the subject of a considerable literature in recent years—an early and now classic contribution to this literature being Chesler's (1972) *Women and Madness*. However, despite its wide application to numerous forms of criminal and psychopathological phenomena within the sociology of deviance, this perspective has rarely been applied to self-poisoning as a form of female deviance. The brief contributions of Kay and Clifton, Cloward and Piven, and Heshusius reported above and a few paragraphs in Chesler's book seemingly exhaust such application, but the recent work of Elaine Showalter, an American feminist historian of psychiatry, while it too neglects female self-poisoning, adds to our understanding of this approach through its analysis of an earlier "female malady"—the late-19th century epidemic of hysteria (Showalter, 1987).

The Hysteria Analogy

Showalter's analysis of the way in which cultural ideas about what constituted "proper" feminine behaviour shaped the forms, definition and treatment of female psychopathology over 150 years, seeks to demonstrate that such psychopathology represents a consequence of, rather than a deviation from, the traditional female role. Although the work is concerned with a range of predominantly female disorders—"female maladies"—its discussion of the 19th century epidemic of hysteria is of particular relevance to our present interest. As we have seen, female self-poisoning has frequently been explained in terms of the hysterical personality supposedly common among its perpetrators, and its form—unconsciousness and physical dependence—has even, in a brief aside, been compared with that of the swooning of the hysterical woman (McCulloch & Philip, 1972). This was commonly described in 19th century romantic novels, and usually occurred, as with self-poisoning, within the context of traumatic interpersonal relationships.

Although this disorder was mainly documented among middle class women, it was not exclusively so, as the case records of the "father" of hysteria, Charcot, and also English asylum superintendents of the time show. The *Oxford English Dictionary* defines "epidemic" as: "… disease, literally or figuratively, prevalent in community at special time", and Showalter suggests that what was "special" about this time was the educational and professional aspirations of middle class women, and the ensuing stress they encountered due to the conflict between such expectations and an absence of socially sanctioned roles to enable their expression. Hysterics were described as predominantly young women often quarrelsome, determined, manipulative—all qualities typically attributed to a later generation of women who had poisoned themselves—and, as one F.C. Skey, a lecturer at St. Bartholomew's Hospital noted in 1866, with unusually interfering and controlling parents. Recording these observations Showalter (1987, p.133) proposes: "… it is precisely in a reaction against this kind of supervision that hysterical women were led to violate the expectations of the female domestic role".

Thus hysteria has been described as a "hidden protest", a "vocabulary of dissent", and its symptoms of paralysis as "an inarticulate body language". The inertia, anergia, and general debility, sometimes leading to total invalidism, were, it is argued, reflections, not of aberrant behaviour caused by a pathological state, but, instead an extreme version of the frailty, sensitivity, dependence and confinement to the domestic sphere which were definitive characteristics of femininity in that era. To escape the confines of these domestic roles inevitably involved the loss of female identity, the only way to retain this whilst rejecting these roles was to enter the only other acceptable female role—that which has been described as the "hyperfemininity" of the invalid.

Hysteria was not the only example of the increasing predominance of women of all classes among the ranks of the "insane". Showalter (1987) has demonstrated, using both asylum records and national statistics, that until the 1850s males outnumbered females in asylums by about 30%, but after this time the predominance of women mounted inexorably so that (p.52):

> ... by 1872 of 58,640 certified lunatics in England and Wales, 31,822 were women ... by the 1890s the predominance of women had spread to all classes of patients and all types of institutions.

Industrialisation, urbanisation, and changes in the family due to declining fertility and a gradually decreasing infant mortality rate affected the roles of women in all classes. However the relationship between poverty and insanity was well documented by 19th century psychiatrists as one of the moral causes of insanity—women were the majority of recipients of poor law relief and poor people were more likely to be committed to institutions than those from the middle or upper class (Scull, 1982). As Showalter suggests (p.27):

> For the poor the public asylum was a welcome alternative to the workhouse ... Given the barely liveable conditions that many working class families had to endure, patients were materially better off in the asylum than they would have been at home.

A major role for female patients in asylums became that of housekeeping with the most enlightened asylums providing occupational therapy consisting of their re-education in those domestic duties their "insanity" had led them to neglect. The 1845 Lunatics Act obliged all local authorities to build asylums, resulting in a massive increase in their number and therefore contributing to the quadruple increase of pauper asylum patients by the end of the century—when they constituted 91% of all institutionalised mental patients (Showalter, 1987, p.27)—three quarters of whom were women, as we have seen. Thus at the same time as changing conditions challenged traditional social and family roles of women and threatened their ability to maintain them, a socially sanctioned means was provided for the expression, explanation and control of this "failure"—female mental debility.

While the epidemic of female maladies was being documented in late-19th century Britain, in Western Europe and America (Smith-Rosenberg, 1972) evidence was accumulating of an alarming growth in the incidence of another psychiatric phenomenon—that of suicidal behaviour. As with the epidemic of insanity which had earlier occurred in Britain and elsewhere, this new phenomenon would also become a predominantly female malady.

As was briefly noted earlier, Sullivan a deputy medical officer of Pentonville Prison writing in 1900 asserted that suicidal behaviour had, since 1874, "grown in a degree entirely out of proportion to the increase in population". Using the *Criminal Statistics* which were the main source of such data at that time, he demonstrated a growth of more than 100% in "attempted suicide" between 1874 and 1897 (Sullivan, 1900).

Norwood-East offered further evidence of this in his 1913 paper, in which he gave evidence of the number of attempts known to the police between 1866 and 1900, which similarly showed a 100% increase—from 3.21 per thousand population to 6.29 (Norwood-East, 1913).

Although for a variety of reasons—including the reluctance to report such incidents due to their, then, illegality—these data will clearly represent an underestimate, they demonstrate unequivocally a dramatic increase in incidence over a period of three decades, and one which was to be repeated in the more recent epidemic of self-poisoning which we have observed in our time.

Showalter (1987), pointing to the association between social change, sex roles, social class and the increase in all types of mental disorder among women, writes (p.18):

During the decades from 1870 to 1910, middle class women were beginning to organise on behalf of higher education, entrance to the professions and political rights. Simultaneously, the female disorders of anorexia nervosa, hysteria and neurasthenia became epidemic.

The omission of self-poisoning from Showalter's argument does not detract from its relevance in pointing to the importance of changing social roles—and in particular sex roles—in the social construction of female psychopathology. The importance of social roles and changes in them in this context is perhaps most impressively illustrated by the manner in which the epidemic of female hysteria drew to its conclusion.

The incidence of female hysteria began to wane with the beginning of the First World War, during which women of all classes gained a certain measure of emancipation through their admission to professional and industrial roles previously filled by men. However as cases of female hysteria disappeared from the asylums and consulting rooms of Europe and America, they were replaced by soldiers returning from the slaughterhouse of Mons and Ypres, men who showed all the classic symptoms of hysteria—paralysis, amnesia, blindness and mutism, none with any organic aetiology. This too adopted epidemic proportions such that in 1916 it was estimated that 40% of casualties were such cases and that by 1918, 80,000 cases had been observed. Indeed many of the asylums built to accommodate the victims of the explosion in female insanity now were among the 20 military hospitals devoted to the treatment of shell shock.

Founded as it was on a biological determinism and belief in the fundamental difference of the sexes, not only physiologically but also psychologically in terms of the aetiology of mental disorder, the psychiatric establishment initially responded by inventing another term (war neurosis) to describe this disquieting evidence of the possibility of male hysteria. The reluctance to ascribe this archetypal female diagnosis to these shattered "heroes" was inevitable in a chauvinist era which was characterised by rigid, mutually exclusive sex roles, and masculine ideals of stoicism and emotional restraint. Gradually however medical personnel and psychologists came to recognise that this phenomenon was intimately related to the conflict between these rigid social expectations of the masculine role and the intolerable reality of trench warfare. War neurosis came to be seen therefore, in the words of Salmon (1917), as: "... an escape from an intolerable situation" from which physical flight was "rendered impossible by ideals of duty, patriotism and honour".

There were class differences too among the victims of this male epidemic, as there had been within the female disorders of hysteria and neurasthenia. Showalter (1987, p.175) describes them in this way:

... the hysterical soldier was seen as simple, emotional, unthinking, passive, suggestible, dependent and weak—very much the same constellation of traits associated with the hysterical woman—while the complex, overworked neurasthenic officer was much closer to an acceptable, even heroic male ideal. Interestingly, mutism, which was the most common shell shock symptom among soldiers and non-commissioned officers, was very rare among officers. To be reduced to a feminine state of powerlessness, frustration and dependency led to a deprivation of speech as well ... Ernst Simmel argued that mutism was a symptom of the soldier's repressed aggression towards his superior officers, a censorship of anger and hostility by turning it in upon the self. Thus shell shock may actually have served the same kind of functional purpose in military life—defusing mutiny—that female hysteria served in civilian society.

The parallels with the 20th century epidemic of female self-poisoning, itself often described by its subjects as "an escape from an intolerable situation" (Bancroft et al., 1979), and by psychiatrists as symptomatic of the "hysterical personality", are striking. Characterised by an elective mutism and passivity induced through unconsciousness, and predominant among working class women whose self-esteem is threatened by failing familial and social relationships of a distressing and uncontrollable nature, self-poisoning may indeed be seen as both a response to and reflection of female powerlessness.

The Historical Perspective

The analogy drawn between the 19th century epidemic of female hysteria and that of self-poisoning has historical, theoretical and clinical justification. Since classical antiquity hysteria has been regarded as the archetypal female disorder, a fact emphasised by its name (derived from the Greek word *hysteron*) womb. The association of female mental disorder with the reproductive system has persisted into our own time and has exercised a powerful, and it has been argued, constraining influence over the understanding of self-poisoning in women.

Equally constraining has been the ahistorical perspective inherent in the pathology paradigm which renders it unable either to learn from or contribute to the understanding of historical changes in the prevalence of deviant behaviours. Although it would represent too great a diversion here, and so a brief excursion must suffice, it is possible to construct an account of the historical fluctuations in female self-poisoning reflecting periods of intense change in women's domestic and social roles and the expectations associated with them.

The late-19th century increases in suicidal behaviour coincided with changes in women's roles fostered by demographic and industrial developments. These increases were concurrent with similar increases in other "female maladies"—anorexia and hysteria. Although the literature nowhere recognises it as such, the rapid increase in self-poisoning after World War Two may be seen, therefore, as the second such epidemic, and this too coincided with considerable changes in women's roles and expectations following the emancipation from domestic confinement brought about during the war by war work and after it by the boom in female employment fostered by the inevitable labour shortages.

Throughout the 1960s and early-1970s changing sexual mores and practices related to the availability of the contraceptive pill, increased access to educational and occupational opportunity, earlier marriage and childbirth and the readier availability and greater acceptability of divorce and cohabitation all had important implications for women's roles in both the private and public sphere. During this period self-poisoning inexorably increased from 15,900 in 1957 (HMSO, 1968) to 108,210 in 1976, with two-thirds of all cases being women (World Health Organisation, 1982, p.28)

These trends have been illustrated earlier and are largely based on data from the Edinburgh Regional Poisoning Treatment Centre which, unusually, has records of self-poisoning dating back to the late-1930s.

Self-poisoning reached its height in 1976, since when it has declined each year and now stands at about 75% of its peak prevalence—falling from 99,404 to 77,150 (Wells, 1988). During this period there have been further changes in socio-economic structure: for example, decreases in male participation in the labour force can be contrasted with similar levels of increase in female participation (HMSO, 1987, p.70) and the reversal of previous marriage trends with teenage marriages showing a 50% decline and cohabitation a marked increase (HMSO, 1988, pp.40–41). Unemployment among males (Platt, 1985) and teenage marriage among females (Kreitman & Schreiter, 1979) have both been implicated in the aetiology of self-poisoning, and a recent study comparing regional trends in Edinburgh and Oxford (see Fig. 4.1) confirms both the general decline and that the rate of this decline is greater among women than men (Platt, Hawton, Kreitman, Fagg, & Foster, 1988). Similar trends were found in an earlier study from Edinburgh (Robinson, Platt, Foster, & Kreitman, 1986; see Fig. 1.3) which reported that the sex ratio was therefore reduced to its lowest level since 1967 (i.e. 1:1.1).

Kessler and McRae (1983) reviewing 45 American studies of "attempted suicide" involving 29,124 cases carried out between 1940 and 1980 note a similar convergence in the ratio of male-female suicidal behaviour and suggest that the convergence is due to the increasing occupation by women of non-traditional sex roles. They note that in America women towards the end of this period were marrying later, deferred childbearing, had smaller families and were employed outside the home more. They enumerate evidence from other sources showing that women with these characteristics—especially those in employment—demonstrate lower rates of psychological distress than do women in more traditional roles, and propose that women in conventional roles have less effective coping styles than non-traditional women. When confronted with problems in family and relational spheres, women in traditional roles rely on other people for emotional support and do not know how to garner help when this is not available. Referring to Martin Seligman's work, they suggest that this style is one of "learned helplessness".

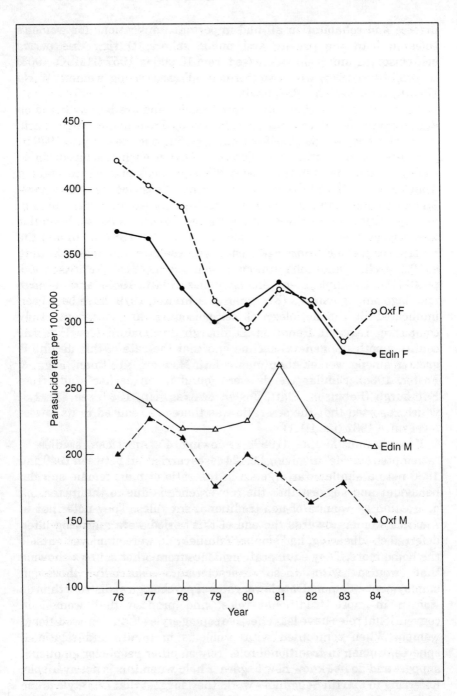

FIG. 4.1 Self-poisoning in Edinburgh and Oxford, 1976–1984 (Platt et al., 1988).

Changing social roles, Kessler and McRae suggest, have afforded women more coping resources: they point to the fact that although the divorce rate has increased the emotional and practical impact on women of divorce may be lessened by the greater financial and social independence consequent on their greater participation in employment. Males, on the other hand, may well experience these developments as challenging their traditional domination in certain public and private roles, and suffer a loss of self-esteem and effective coping as a result: especially might this be the case where high levels of male unemployment prevail. Thus, Kessler and McRae assert there is a "convergence of coping styles" with males more frequently demonstrating that style traditionally characteristic of female coping, and that as styles have converged so too has the rate of male and female self-poisoning.

The credibility of this hypothesis is enhanced by the results of a study by Sutherland and Veroff (1985) who measured the "need for achievement" of two cohorts of young Americans: those who were aged 13–16 in 1972 were assessed then and at the age of 19–22 in 1979, and those who were aged 9–12 in 1972 were assessed first then and later when aged 15–18 in 1979. Briefly, the results showed that adolescent females demonstrated higher achievement scores in 1979 than did adolescent girls in 1972, although the reverse is true for males (Table 4.1 and Figs 4.2 and 4.3).

This leads the authors to suggest (p.175) in an assertion reminiscent of Kessler and McRae:

... something very critical happened during the 1970s that changed the achievement orientations in adolescent boys and girls ... the later cohort groups of each sex deviated from the patterns created by the earlier, more traditional, cohort groups. The later birth cohorts showed result patterns similar to those of the opposite sex in the earlier cohort group. Whether this means that the younger generation is becoming androgynous with respect to achievement motivation is not clear ... we may very well be at a transition period. Once we pass this transition point, when the expectations for both men and women in their roles will be truly parallel, perhaps the results for both men and women will be similar.

This conclusion to our brief historical review of trends in self-poisoning returns us to Elaine Showalter's work which reconstructed the conceptualisation of female hysteria and other mental disorders by adopting an historical perspective and, eschewing narrow biologism, emphasised the social construction of these disorders through social roles and relationships. When considering developments after the

TABLE 4.1
Changes in Male and Female Achievement Orientation—USA 1972–1979
(Sutherland & Veroff, 1985)

Year	Males		Females	
	Earlier Cohort	Later Cohort	Earlier Cohort	Later Cohort
1972	2.61	2.73	2.50	2.52
	(N = 18)	(N = 26)	(N = 22)	(N = 27)
1979	2.35	1.47	1.50	3.21
	(N = 28)	(N = 30)	(N = 26)	(N = 24)

NOTE: Mean n achievement scores in 1972 and 1979 for earlier and later birth cohorts (by sex).

First World War, with the decline of female hysteria and the new epidemic of male "war neurosis", Showalter (1987, p.90) suggests that the changing pattern of male and female distress had common origins with sources far more profound than the semantic evasions of the psychopathologists were prepared or able to recognise:

What had happened to make these men so unstable, so emotional, in a word, so feminine? Women understood the lesson of shell shock better than their male contemporaries: that powerlessness could lead to pathology, that a lasting wound could result when a person lost the sense of being in control, of being an autonomous actor in a manipulable world.

This analysis has offered not only an account of how the sex role system influences forms of female deviance, but in its emphasis on the role of powerlessness or helplessness, it is also able to illuminate the participation of certain groups of males (notably the unemployed and recently divorced) in that particular form which is our concern—self-poisoning. Unlike the pathology paradigm it can also offer explanation for its changing prevalence and sex ratio over time. The question this analysis of the influence of the normative socialisation process has so far not addressed is why self-poisoning with medicines became the favoured method of expressing this helplessness.

We began this chapter with an assertion from Cloward and Piven that through its growth, and extension into almost every aspect of women's lives, the health care system promoted and legitimated the stereotype of female helplessness. Through the "medicalisation of female problems", it is suggested that not only does this system encourage women to view themselves as inadequate but, having done so, it then prescribes remedies for their inadequacy which serve only to foster that self-image—psychotropic medication. Self-poisoning—now viewed as

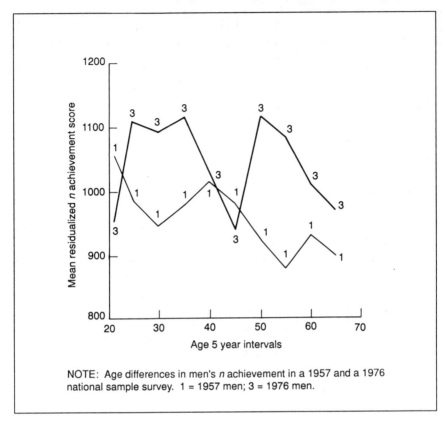

NOTE: Age differences in men's *n* achievement in a 1957 and a 1976 national sample survey. 1 = 1957 men; 3 = 1976 men.

FIG.   4.2.   Changing age patterns in achievement orientation–American males 1957–1976 (Sutherland & Veroff, 1985).

self-medication—may then be understood as the product of this normative socialisation process, rather than as the aberrant response to stress of the mentally disordered or the hysterical personality.

It is to an exploration of the relationship between women and medicine, and the implications of this for the understanding of female self-poisoning, that we now turn.

SEX ROLES AND PSYCHOTROPIC MEDICATION

The view that the epidemic of self-poisoning was a reflection, not of aberrant mental states, but rather of the normative influence inherent in the increasing medicalisation of social problems, was not limited to the sociologists of deviance. Neil Kessel, a psychiatrist and influential

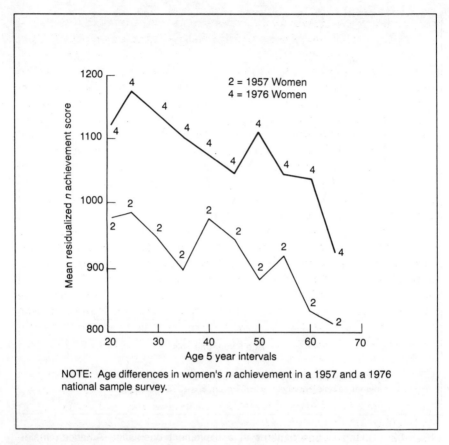

FIG. 4.3. Changing age patterns in achievement orientation–American females 1957–1976 (Sutherland & Veroff, 1985).

student of self-poisoning, described this process succinctly by suggesting (Kessel, 1966) that: "Doctors are the designers of the fashion of self-poisoning". Kessel was referring here to the dramatic increase in self-poisoning which occurred from the mid-1950s, to the equally impressive growth in the prescription of psychotropic medication which had accompanied it and, in that a majority of such patients had taken psychotropics, seemed to fuel it. Trends since the late-1950s in self-poisoning (Figs. 4.4 and 4.5), psychotropic prescription (Tables 4.4 and 4.5) and the drugs employed (Figs. 4.6 and 4.7, Tables 4.6 and 4.7) are illustrated on the following pages. However, as we have shown earlier, the phenomenon of self-poisoning does have an historical continuity the understanding of which can usefully inform our appreciation of the modern epidemic to which Kessel referred.

Early Methods of Self-poisoning—the Domestic
Focus of Female Forms

Kessel briefly alluded to the historical context in one of his early papers
(Kessel, 1965), reminding the reader that in Shakespearian times the
notion of taking poison with the intention of inducing sleep rather than
death was exemplified in the story of Romeo and Juliet. There the
heroine feigns death by taking a herbal sleeping draught in order to
escape the controlling influence of her family. Kessel, using the data
derived from the records of the Edinburgh Poisoning Treatment Centre,
showed that prior to the establishment of the National Health Service
in 1947, and before the advent of widely available medicinal drugs, the
most common forms of poisoning were by coal gas and household
cleaning and disinfecting agents such as *lysol*, and iodine.

The popularity of such agents extended back into the late-19th
century, when poisoning was even then favoured over the more violent
methods characteristic of completed suicide, such as hanging, drowning
or "immersion" as it was called when not fatal, and wounding. Reviewing
data for the 1890s in Britain, W.C. Sullivan (1900) noted that among
attempters there was: "... a marked predominance of drowning and
poison (57.3%) over hanging (7.6%) (a) reversal over the conditions found
in actual suicide, where hanging is the chief method". Norwood-East
(1913) records that in 1910 the commonest method of "attempted
suicide" was poisoning—employing a variety of substances including:
"... carbolic acid, coal gas, salts of lemon and various liniments".

By the 1920s, an American study of 1000 attempted suicides
(Lendrum, 1933) found that poisoning was the most common method
for attempts constituting three-quarters of their total and that iodine
headed the list being especially favoured by women who employed it
twice as often as men (see Table 4.2). This latter fact led the author to
welcome its comparative harmlessness "since it is the favourite recourse
of disappointed lovers". The sex difference in choice of poisons was
emphasised by the author who pointed out (p.497) that poisoning in men
commonly resulted in fatality because:

Men have access ordinarily to the strong mineral acids of industry, such
as nitric or hydrochloric acid, whereas women more commonly employ
comparatively innocuous disinfectants from the home medicine cabinet,
such as iodine, mercurochrome or potassium permanganate.

The domestic focus of the female choice of poisons is given added
poignancy by the author's laconic remark (p.498) that: "... potassium

TABLE 4.2
Methods of "Attempted Suicide" by Sex—Detroit 1927–1930 (Lendrum, 1933)

Agent or Method	Male		Female	
	Patients	Died	Patients	Died
Asphyxia	51	2	63	0
Hanging	10	1	1	0
Drowning	9	0	11	0
Firearms	17	8	2	0
Cutting or piercing	58	7	15	1
Wrists	(20)	.	(7)	.
Throat	(33)	.	(5)	.
Other parts	(5)	.	(3)	.
Jumping from height	1	0	3	0
Crushing (beneath vehicle)	1	0	2	0
Miscellaneous	3	0	1	1
(*Male:* Swallowing razor blades; Pounding head on bars of cell; Setting fire to clothes. *Female:* Injection of mercuric chloride)				
Poison	213	23	539	29
Iodine	89	0	179	0
Solution of cresol (lysol)	35	6	113	10
Mercuric chloride	20	4	60	7
Phenol	13	2	31	7
Barbital (veronal)	7	0	25	2
Potassium permanganate	0	0	30	0
Mercurochrome	1	0	18	0

NOTE: Sixteen women and four men, however, used two agents; three women used three agents, and one man used four.

TABLE 4.3
Methods of "Attempted Suicide" by Sex—Liverpool 1932–1935 (Hopkins, 1937)

Method	Attempted suicide		Suicide	
	Males	Females	Males	Females
Coal-gas poisoning	123 (34.3)	110 (36.9)	135 (46.7)	76 (69.1)
Cut throat	75 (20.9)	20 (6.7)	30 (10.4)	2 (1.8)
Liquid and corrosive poisons	68 (18.9)	106 (35.6)	34 (11.7)	20 (18.2)
Sedative poisons	6 (1.7)	13 (4.4)	4 (1.4)	1 (0.9)
Immersion	26 (7.3)	25 (8.4)	14 (4.8)	2 (1.8)
Cut wrists, stabbing, etc.	10 (2.8)	4 (1.3)	1 (0.3)	none
Strangulation, hanging	19 (5.3)	13 (4.4)	45 (15.8)	5 (4.5)
Jumping from heights or in front of vehicles	19 (5.3)	7 (2.3)	22 (7.6)	4 (3.6)
Gunshot	2 (0.6)	0	4 (1.4)	0
Miscellaneous	10 (2.8)	0	0	0

NOTE: First number given is actual number of individuals, number in brackets gives the percentage of the total.

permanganate has been popular only since women began to receive it as a douche".

In Britain, Hopkins' (1937) comprehensive study of all suicides and attempted suicides in Liverpool between 1932 and 1935 showed similar sex differences in method with women employing less violent means. Both sexes showed equal use of coal gas poisoning which had been widely introduced into domestic use between 1910 and 1920, and by the mid-1930s had become the method most frequently employed in both suicide and parasuicide. However Hopkins' series demonstrated a dramatic difference between the sexes in other methods, with 20.1% of the men using "cut throat" as opposed to only 6.7% of women, and "liquid and corrosive poisons" being chosen by 35.6% of women and only 18.9% of men (Table 4.3). It is interesting to note that even at that time—before the advent of the relatively safe benzodiazepine class of tranquillisers and their ready availability through the National Health Service—the use of "sedative poisons" was twice as common among women. Hopkins concluded (p.76):

> The reason for the disparity in methods of the two sexes is not far to seek. It may reasonably be assumed that an individual will use the means with which he or she is most familiar and which is near at hand. The razor is predominantly a male instrument; whereas the woman in the home has charge of disinfectants, cleaning materials, and medicines as a rule.

Thus, although poisoning became the predominant form of attempted suicide for both sexes in the early years of this century, gender differences in the poisons chosen are clearly evident and reflect the domestic focus of women's lives, and, in this sense, the influence of normative sex roles on this form of female deviance. The comments of early authors such as Lendrum and Hopkins are evidence of an early awareness of this, but this perspective was not developed by a later generation of psychiatrists even though many came to be concerned at the increasing use of medicinal agents in self-poisoning, and convinced of their "causal role". Erwin Stengel (1952, p.614), for example, categorically asserted that the increase in self-poisoning after World War Two was "obviously related to the increased availability of sedatives since the institution of the NHS in 1948", and Figs. 4.4 and 4.5 showing post-war trends in London and Edinburgh seem to support this, demonstrating a massive increase in self-poisoning with barbiturates in 1947–1950.

Medicinal Agents in Self-poisoning

The supremacy of coal gas as a method was short-lived and the first person suffering from barbiturate poisoning was admitted to the Edinburgh Poisons Unit in 1932. Such cases remained a rarity until after the Second World War, however, with about half-a-dozen cases a year until then (Kessel, 1965). It was not until this time that salicylate poisoning first appeared but by 1947 barbiturates had overtaken coal gas as the predominant method of self-poisoning and they were to retain that position until superceded by the benzodiazepines introduced in the late-1960s (Table 4.4).

An Office of Health Economics publication considering the decline in the importance of barbiturates among self-poisoners described the

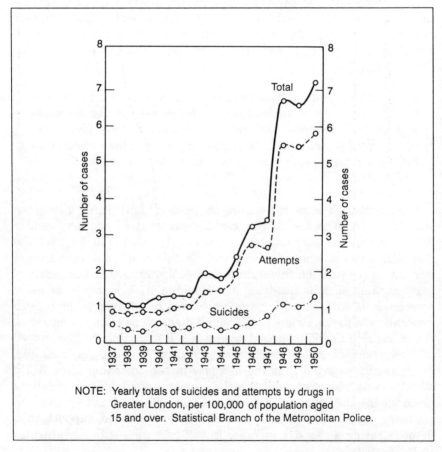

NOTE: Yearly totals of suicides and attempts by drugs in Greater London, per 100,000 of population aged 15 and over. Statistical Branch of the Metropolitan Police.

FIG. 4.4. Self-poisoning with medicinal agents, London 1937–1950 (Stengel 1952).

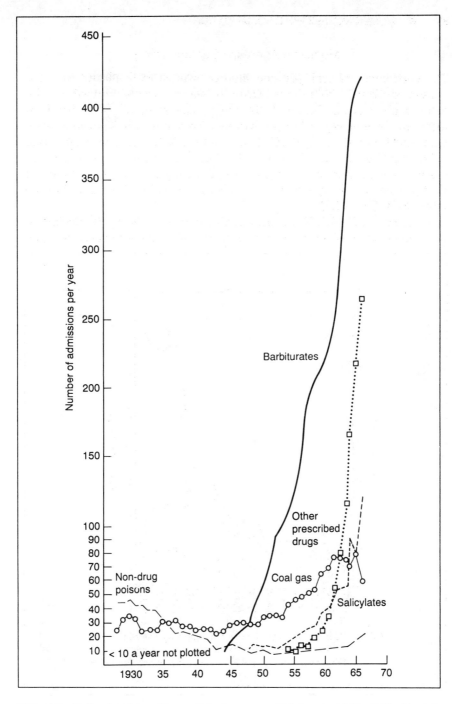

FIG. 4.5. Self-poisoning with medicinal agents, Edinburgh 1928–1966 (HMSO, 1968).

TABLE 4.4
Annual Numbers of Psychotropic Prescriptions Dispensed in England and Wales (in millions), 1961–1966 (HMSO, 1968)

	1961	1962	1963	1964	1965	1966
Barbiturates	15.2	15.8	15.9	16.1	17.2	16.8
Non-barbiturate hypnotics	3.4	2.6	2.5	2.6	2.7	3.0
Tranquillisers	6.2	6.6	7.1	9.0	10.9	13.0
Anti-depressants	1.4	2.0	2.4	2.8	3.5	3.9

NOTE: This table does not include drugs issued in hospitals. The amount prescribed per prescription has not decreased during the period.

TABLE 4.5
Annual Number of Psychotropic Prescriptions (in thousands)—Great Britain, 1966–1985 (DHSS, 1987)

	Hypnotics (Barbiturate)	Hypnotics (Non-barbiturate)	Tranquillisers	Anti-depressants
1966	18,705	3,940	13,677	4,252
1967	17,893	5,323	16,059	5,309
1968	17,020	6,480	17,480	5,770
1969	15,800	7,151	18,086	6,251
1970	14,695	8,048	18,945	6,887
1971	13,034	8,655	20,227	7,673
1972	11,686	9,552	21,486	7,949
1973	10,731	9,904	22,698	8,264
1974	9,619	10,700	23,674	8,906
1975	8,155	11,723	24,339	9,127

(Change in therapeutic classification)			
	Hypnotics	Sedatives and Tranquillisers	Anti-depressant and Sedative/ Tranquilliser Combinations	Anti-depressants
---	---	---	---	---
1975	16,810	24,707	1,740	8,049
1976	16,715	25,007	1,745	8,067
1977	16,967	24,816	1,680	7,759
1978	17,212	25,043	1,582	7,812
1979	17,460	24,390	1,493	7,582
1980	16,546	22,493	1,368	7,241
1981	16,605	21,920	1,259	7,539
1982	16,862	21,413	1,134	7,468
1983	16,406	17,604	1,039	7,351
1984	16,433	16,410	967	7,231
1985	15,979	14,326	721	7,329

NOTE: The data are estimates based on a sample of 1 in 200 prescriptions in England and Wales (1 in 100 in Scotland) which were dispensed by retail chemists and appliance contractors.

TABLE 4.6
Admissions to Hospital for Treatment of Poisoning by Type of Poison—England and Wales, 1957–1964 (HMSO, 1968)

	1957	1958	1959	1960	1961	1962	1963	1964
All poisoning								
Admissions to hospital	15,900	17,500	20,200	23,300	27,900	33,600	45,900	50,400
Percentage of all general medical and paediatric admissions	-	-	3.2	3.6	4.1	4.8	6.2	6.8
Deaths in hospital	523	563	477	445	541	649	887	952
Deaths per 1000 admissions	32.9	32.2	23.6	19.1	19.4	19.3	19.3	18.9
All analgesics and soporifics N970-N974								
Admissions to hospital	9,200	10,500	12,100	14,400	17,700	21,300	31,000	34,900
Deaths in hospital	-	-	218	290	322	449	570	451
Deaths per 1000 admissions	-	-	18.0	20.1	18.2	21.1	18.4	12.9
Barbituric acid and derivatives N971								
Admissions to hospital	6,100	6,600	7,500	8,800	10,500	12,100	16,500	16,300
Deaths in hospital	-	-	197	176	137	293	370	301
Deaths per 1000 admissions	-	-	26.3	20.0	17.8	24.2	22.4	18.5
Aspirin and salicylates N972								
Admissions to hospital	2,300	2,500	3,000	3,800	5,200	6,200	9,800	11,800
Deaths in hospital	-	-	21	93	125	125	106	97
Deaths per 1000 admissions	-	-	7.0	24.5	24.0	20.2	10.8	8.2
Carbon monoxide N968								
Admissions to hospital	1,900	2,300	2,200	2,200	2,400	2,700	3,700	2,900
Deaths in hospital	-	-	187	114	135	146	158	183
Deaths per 1000 admissions	-	-	85.0	51.8	56.3	54.1	42.7	63.1

NOTE: Hospital In-patient Enquiry for 1957–1964, based on a 10% sample of hospital discharges, including deaths.

importance of this change in these terms (Wells, 1981, p.48): "... modified GP prescribing habits do appear to have influenced trends in self-poisoning with barbiturates. The reduction in the number of scrips issued in England from 14.2m in 1968 to 5.1m in 1978 has been the major factor in the halving of the relative importance of sedatives and hypnotics in (hospital measured) deliberate self-harm". (See also Table 4.7)

However as the prescription rate of barbiturates declined, that of the benzodiazepines inexorably increased, and with it both the absolute numbers of cases of self-poisoning and the percentage of them which employed benzodiazepines. These parallel trends are clearly shown in Figs. 4.6 and 4.7: the latter juxtaposes the increasing rate of prescription of tranquillisers, the decreasing rate of barbiturate prescription and the contemporaneous change in the relative numbers of self-poisonings employing each over the period 1960-1975. By using data from two centres (Edinburgh and Bristol) the graph shows that in 1962, when barbiturate prescription was near its peak, 55% of self-poisonings in Edinburgh involved this class of drug, while only 23% employed other types of psychotropic. By 1972 the picture had reversed, in keeping with the reversal in relative numbers of prescriptions for these drugs, such that in Bristol in that year only 13% of episodes involved barbiturates whereas now 53% employed other psychotropics, mainly tranquillisers.

These trends were not only typical of Great Britain but were reflected throughout the western world, so much so that by 1973 an American

TABLE 4.7

Discharges and Deaths Due to Adverse Effects of Medicines by Type of Drug—England and Wales, 1968 and 1977 (Wells, 1981)

Agent	1968 (%)	1977 (%)
Antibiotics and other anti-infectives	1.4	1.7
Analgesics and antipyretics	25.6	23.1
Other sedatives and hypnotics	23.8	9.4
Psychotherapeutics	14.7	30.0
Agents primarily affecting the autonomic nervous system	2.2	1.0
Agents primarily affecting the cardiovascular system	1.1	1.6
Alcohol in combination with specified medicinal agents	1.8	3.7
Others	29.4	29.5
	100	100

Source: Hospital In-patient Enquiry.

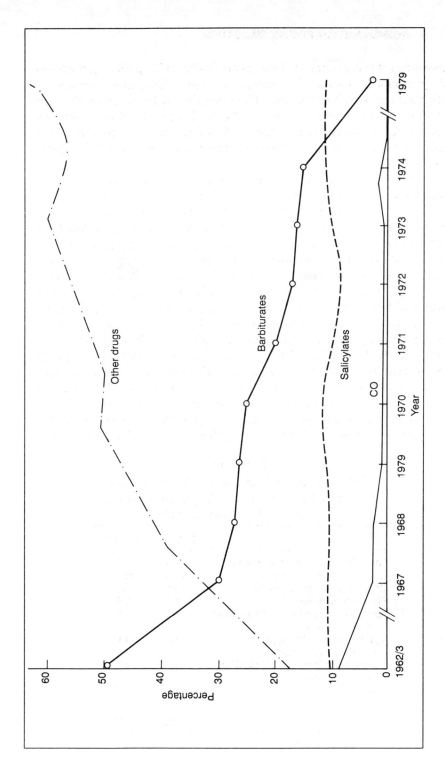

FIG. 4.6.   Changes in drugs used in self-poisoning—Edinburgh, 1962–1979 (WHO 1982).

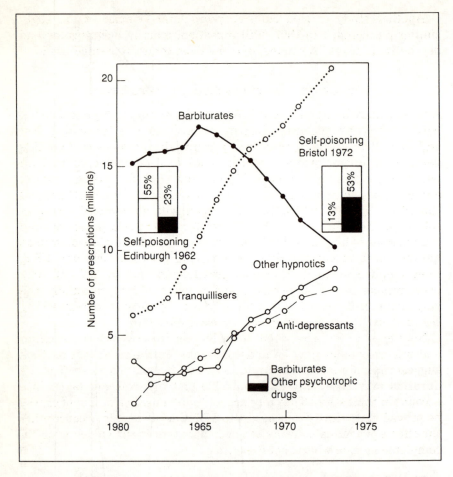

FIG. 4.7. Changes in drugs used in self-poisoning—Edinburgh 1962 and Bristol 1972 (Morgan, 1979).

review of national and international studies (Weisman et al., 1973, p.90) concluded that:

Every study noted that by far the most common method was by the ingestion of pills, often accounting for over 80% of the attempts. The frequency with which pills were used has led investigators to deplore the modern tendency to resort to drugs to solve problems in living. In this regard it is interesting to note if the low suicide attempt rate in 1955 is related to the unavailability of minor tranquillisers and psychotropic drugs.

Another study carried out five years later (Wexler et al., 1978) similarly concluded (p.180): "Pill ingestion, usually barbiturates and psychotropic drugs, continues to be the most common method used."

The Causal Role of Psychotropic Prescription

A recent study by Forster and Frost (1985) examined the relationship between psychotropic drug prescription levels and self-poisoning. Not only did these workers take into account the possible confounding variable of unemployment—which could lead to increases in both psychotropic prescription and self-poisoning—but also that of hospital admission capacity, because the availability of general medical beds and the efficiency with which they are used will influence the rate of self-poisoning admissions. They therefore employed inter-regional comparisons of health authorities in relation to these factors as well as national data to analyse changes occurring between 1968 and 1978. They found a mean psychotropic prescription rate in 1978 of 1021 prescriptions per 1000 persons, and when analysed regionally the variation in self-poisoning was "largely and significantly explained" by regional variations in psychotropic prescription rate.

Forster and Frost accept that the relationship between self-poisoning and unemployment may be underestimated in their analysis as they suggest that, if unemployment has a cumulative pathological effect, its duration may be a significant variable and this was not taken into account in their study. They also accept that "causality cannot of course be proved statistically" but assert (p.572) that uncertainty concerning the effects of available means has been apparent in the epidemiology of completed suicide where, none the less:

> The balance of evidence with respect to reductions in completed suicide in the 1960s is that measures such as the reduced toxicity of coal gas and prescribed medicines have been responsible for the fall in suicides.

The case of Holland where the replacement of coal gas with natural gas did not lead to a fall in suicides (often cited as evidence against this contention) is not accepted by Forster and Frost:

> ... coal gas poisoning was always an infrequent method of suicide in Holland and changes in it would be unlikely to affect the overall completed suicide rate to any significant extent.

The authors propose (p.571) that such evidence, in conjunction with that which indicates that psychotropics are often prescribed excessively and inappropriately, leads to the conclusion that: "It is clear that the psychotropic prescription rate is the major explanatory variable". The importance of this conclusion is emphasised in Hawton and Blackstock's (1977) findings that 60% of the episodes of self-poisoning employed psychotropic drugs, that the number of prescriptions written for tranquillisers had doubled between 1964 and 1974, reaching 21.5m, and that a great deal of the prescibing was "... unnecessary and positively harmful".

Morgan, one of the Bristol team which has regularly contributed to the debate on parasuicide, wrote in 1979 that if parasuicide was to be regarded as an epidemic then the "infective agent" must surely be psychotropic drugs. Presenting the graph shown in Fig. 4.7 which describes changes in the incidence of self-poisoning in Bristol and Edinburgh and national rates of psychotropic drug prescription, he asserts that: "... there is compelling evidence for an association between the incidence of deliberate self-harm and the availability of psychotropic drugs through medical prescription" (Morgan, 1979).

Again, Prescott—a consultant physician and reader in clinical pharmacology—commenting that the possible causal role of psychotropic prescription "does not seem to have been considered seriously", reported the results of a study of 230 adult patients (Prescott, 1985, p.1633) which showed that:

Psychotropic drugs may increase suicidal thoughts, cause depression and predispose to self-poisoning ... the prescribing of these drugs (was) strongly associated with repeated overdosage.

Brewer and Farmer (1985) in a letter to the *British Medical Journal*, asserted in relation to the decline in self-poisoning since 1976:

This fall in the incidence of overdoses is without peace time precedent ... we suggest that the most important and likely cause is that since 1976 the annual number of prescriptions for hypnotics and tranquillisers has also fallen steadily ... These findings add to the evidence that self-poisoning ... is influenced much more by external factors which are sometimes controllable, such as availability, than by internal, pathological ones such as "depressive illness".

These authors provided the graph shown below which illustrates these parallel trends.

There is much support, therefore, for the proposed relationship between psychotropic prescription rates and the prevalence of self-poisoning. However, it has become apparent in this review that, as

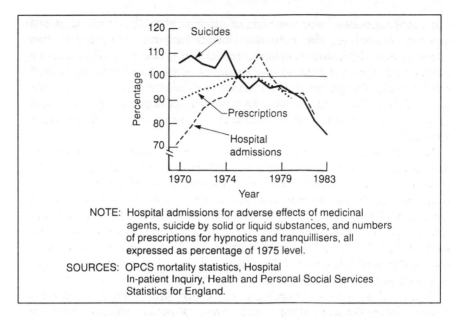

FIG. 4.8. Admission rate for self poisoning, prescription rate of psychotropic medication, and suicide rate, England 1970–1983 (Brewer & Farmer, 1985).

in other areas of the study of the phenomenon, little attention has been devoted in the modern literature to gender and its relationship to methods employed in self-poisoning. The only recent allusion to the possible relationship between gender and the employment of psychotropics in self-poisoning comes from the recent comparative study by Steven Platt and others of rates in Oxford and Edinburgh. It is suggested (Platt et al., 1988, p.19) that a possible reason for the observed decline in rates could be due to: "The fact that females have shown both the greatest decline in numbers of prescriptions for minor tranquillisers over recent years and have also shown the greatest fall in parasuicide rates".

The otherwise almost total neglect of gender differences is particularly puzzling in this context in view of the widely reported 2:1 predominance of women, not only among self-poisoners, but among the recipients of psychotropic medication (Cooperstock, 1978).

Sex Differences in Psychotropic Prescription

The first benzodiazepine marketed was Librium in 1960. This was soon followed by Valium—introduced in 1963 and by 1973 the most prescribed drug in the United States. It was estimated in 1975 that one in ten American adults used one or other of these in any three-month period (Koumjian, 1981). In the United Kingdom the same massive growth in prescription of benzodiazepines was observed, with a doubling of prescriptions for tranquillisers between 1964 and 1974, when 21.5m prescriptions were written (Hawton & Blackstock, 1977), and one in seven people in the UK reported taking these drugs during the previous year (Balter, Levine, & Manheimer, 1974). A study of prescribing among 19 Oxfordshire general practitioners confirmed this finding when it discovered that 19.3% of the population had received a psychotropic drug (which includes anti-depressants, tranquillisers and hypnotics) in the previous 12 months (Skegg, Doll, & Perry, 1977).

This trend has shown a marked differential according to sex of recipient. The study of Oxford GPs referred to above, which involved a population of 40,000, concluded that "9.7% of the males in the population and 21% of the females received at least one psychotropic drug during the year" (See Tables 4.8–4.11).

This finding has been replicated internationally and Cooperstock, reviewing 23 international studies of psychotropic use in 1982, noted that all found a predominance of women among recipients, and most described a sex ratio of 2:1 (Cooperstock, 1982). A French study of adolescent health carried out in 1983 found that among a sample of 400 16 year olds, more than 50% of young women took at least one kind of tranquilliser compared with only 20% of males (National Institute of Health and Medical Research, 1988).

These findings describe the disproportionate prescription of psychotropics to groups of women who it is known also predominate among self-poisoners. But what evidence is there that these drugs are actually used in self-poisoning?

TABLE 4.8
Frequency of Drug Prescription by Sex and Age—Oxford, 1974
(Skegg et al., 1977)

				% of People Prescribed				
						≥5		20
	Population		Any Drug		Prescriptions		Prescriptions	
Age	M	F	M	F	M	F	M	F
≤ 14	4776	4275	58.8	60.0	14.9	15.6	0.6	0.7
15–29	4072	4381	44.4	63.5	7.7	23.1	0.5	1.2
30–44	3543	3671	48.7	66.5	14.2	31.0	1.5	3.9
45–59	2984	3118	55.5	69.4	23.2	37.7	4.8	8.6
60–74	1992	2108	63.1	69.8	37.2	46.5	10.4	15.7
≥ 75	415	945	75.7	78.2	55.4	61.2	20.2	24.3
All Ages	17,782	18,498	53.8	65.7	17.9	30.0	3.0	5.7

TABLE 4.9
Major Classes of Drug Prescribed—Percentages of
People and Their Sex who had Prescriptions
Dispensed—Oxford, 1974 (Skegg et.al., 1977)

Therapeutic Class	% of all Prescriptions	% of Males	% of Females[a]
Psychotropic	17.4	9.7	21.0 (20.0)
Antimicrobial (excluding topical preparations)	14.3	25.5	30.6 (31.1)
Cardiovascular (including diuretics)	12.3	4.9	9.2 (8.2)
Respiratory	10.0	14.1	16.3 (16.4)
Nervous system (excluding psychotropic)	9.5	11.7	17.1 (16.3)
Dermatological	7.8	13.1	17.2 (17.1)
Alimentary	7.3	9.8	12.5 (11.8)
All others	21.3		

[a] Percentages standardised to age distribution of male population shown in parentheses.

TABLE 4.10
Percentages of People who Received Psychotropic Drugs According
to Age and Sex—Oxford, 1974 (Skegg et al., 1977)

	% of People Prescribed					
	Any Psychotropic Drug		≥ 5 Prescriptions		At least 1 Prescription Every 4 Months	
Age	M	F	M	F	M	F
≤ 14	3.7	4.0	0.1	0.3	0.1	0.3
15–29	4.9	15.5	0.6	2.0	0.5	1.3
30–44	11.5	27.2	2.7	7.6	2.7	6.8
45–59	15.3	33.0	4.7	12.9	4.3	12.1
60–74	18.2	31.5	6.6	14.7	6.6	14.6
≥ 75	27.2	37.7	13.3	20.2	13.3	21.2
All Ages	9.7	21.0	2.5	6.9	2.4	6.5

Self-poisoning with Prescribed Drugs

Several British studies of the help-seeking behaviour of male and female self-poisoners are interesting in this respect. An Oxford study (Bancroft et al., 1977b) carried out in 1972 among 130 self-poisoners found that women had a markedly higher rate of attendance at their GP surgery

TABLE 4.11
Percentages of People who Received Psychotropic Drugs by Type of
Drug and Age of Recipient—Oxford 1974 (Skegg et al., 1977)

| | % of People Prescribed | | | | | |
| | Sedatives or Hypnotics | | Anti-psychotic Tranquillisers | | Anti-depressants | |
Age	M	F	M	F	M	F
⩽ 14	2.8	2.9	0.7	0.6	1.0	0.7
15–29	3.6	10.8	1.2	2.7	1.2	5.0
30–44	8.8	20.3	2.5	4.8	3.2	8.9
45–59	11.6	24.9	3.1	7.5	4.4	11.2
60–74	14.3	24.7	4.4	6.9	4.4	8.7
⩾ 75	21.4	29.9	8.0	12.6	7.2	8.9
All Ages	7.4	15.8	2.2	4.4	2.6	6.5

than did men immediately before their overdose. Thus 41% of female
self-poisoners had attended their GP within the week preceding their
overdose compared with only 24% of the males.

Especially interesting is the age distribution of those in receipt of any
type of non-psychiatric treatment at the time of their self-poisoning.
Among males aged 16–20 none were receiving treatment, whereas
among females in this age group 33% were; among females aged 21–25
a similar stark disparity is evident, with 31% of females and only 9% of
males receiving treatment. These are of course the peak age groups for
self-poisoning among women. When one goes on to consider the
distribution of non-psychiatric treatment in the peak age group of
self-poisoning for men, the distribution of those receiving medical
treatment is reversed, with 33% of men between 26–35 receiving
treatment as opposed to only 14% of women in this age group.

The study also noted "unusually high rates of non-psychiatric
hospitalisation"—four times higher than the rate for the general
population as disclosed by the *General Household Survey*. This was
especially so among women, 34% of whom had been so admitted within
the previous 12 months, compared with 22.5% of men. Skegg also
reported a surprising rate of hospitalisation among females in his group
of self-poisoners—over 20% having had an admission for gynaecological
disorder within the previous 2 years (Skegg, Skegg, & Richards, 1983),
and Hawton and Blackstock (1976) similarly described high rates of GP
attendance among female self-poisoners.

An American study by Beck, Lester, and Kovacs (1973) comparing the
characteristics of 240 male and female self-poisoners similarly reported
that the sexes differed significantly on 16 variables, one of which was

that females had sought medical care more frequently in the 6 months preceding the episode. Similar findings were reported by Davis (1968). Such studies indicate that women self-poisoners more frequently seek medical assistance before their self-poisoning: they might be seen as supporting the notion that women are therefore more likely to receive psychotropic drugs with which to poison themselves, a contention we have been exploring. These studies do not, however, discuss the extent to which women who receive psychotropic drugs subsequently use them for this purpose. There are two British studies which have considered this question, exploring the use of such medication by self-poisoners and supporting the view that this class of drug is often prescribed inappropriately and may enhance the risk of self-poisoning to the recipient.

Prescott (1985) studied a series of 230 self-poisoners and the drugs they had recently been prescribed. He found that 61% of the patients poisoned themselves with psychotropics, that only a minority had a psychiatric illness for which drug treatment was indicated, and that most were disadvantaged, disappointed, frustrated, or unhappy because of personal and social problems. In addition it was found that patients who were taking these drugs regularly were more likely to take repeated overdoses than those who were not. Prescott states (at p.1633):

> Psychotropic drugs were prescribed for more than a third of patients with no psychiatric illness and a normal personality, nearly half of those with existing alcohol or drug abuse problems and for most of the unemployed. Fewer than a third of the depressed patients were prescribed anti-depressants but a half had been given benzodiazepines and other potentially depressing drugs.

An earlier study had explored the incidence of self-poisoning in a total population of 43,117 patients in Oxfordshire, to elucidate what percentage of those given psychotropics subsequently take them in overdose (Skegg et al., 1983). The researchers did so by linking records of prescriptions issued by GPs with the records of hospital admissions and deaths. Such methods would substantially underestimate the percentage of self-poisoners as it is known that a significant proportion are not admitted to hospital beds anyway and that as many as 30% are treated outside of hospital either by doctors or friends (Kennedy & Kreitman, 1973).

None the less 3 per 1000 people who received these drugs were found to have poisoned themselves with them within 12 months. Women were more likely to poison themselves with psychotropic drugs and, although the authors describe this difference as non-significant, the female rate

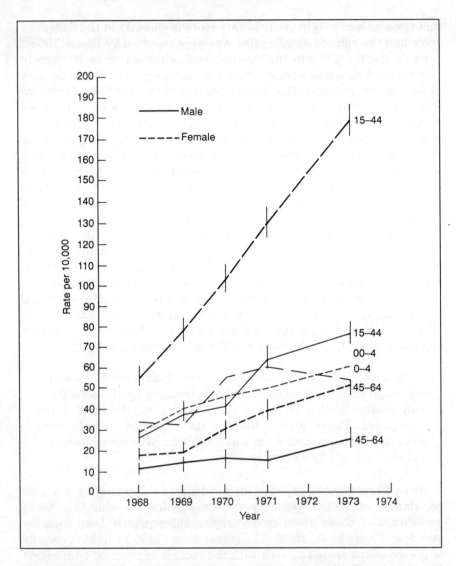

FIG. 4.9. Admission rates for self-poisoning with psychotropic drugs by age and sex—England and Wales 1968–1973 (Farmer & Hirsch, 1980).

of self-poisoning per 1000 recipients of psychotropics is 4.7 as opposed to the male rate of 1.8, with the highest rate in the 15–29 age group—a remarkable reflection of the age and sex distribution of self-poisoners (Skegg et al., 1983).

These findings seem amply supported by the report of Farmer and Hirsch (1980), one result of which is shown in Fig. 4.9. Here the much more rapid rate of increase in female self-poisoning with psychotropics is very evident and coincides with the period of the greatest growth in their rate of prescription between 1968 and 1974, which is recorded in Table 4.5 shown earlier.

In relation to the interaction of age and sex in the employment of psychotropic drugs in self-poisoning, a study of Oxford adolescent self-poisoners demonstrated distinct age grading effects, which are illustrated in the graph in Fig. 4.10 taken from the study (Hawton & Goldacre, 1982d). The authors summarise their results in this way (p.168):

The most striking differences between the sexes were the much greater increase in the use of analgesics and anti-pyretics with age by the younger females compared with the younger males; the persistent

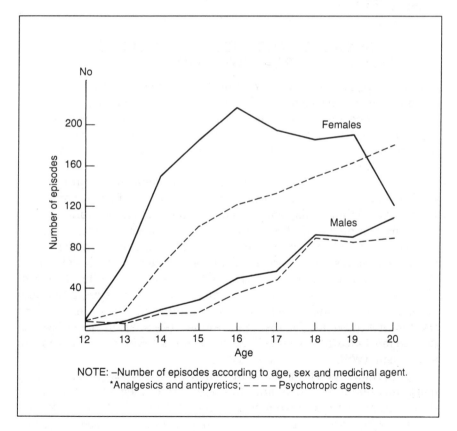

NOTE: –Number of episodes according to age, sex and medicinal agent.
*Analgesics and antipyretics; – – – – Psychotropic agents.

FIG. 4.10. Adolescent admissions for self-poisoning—by age, sex and type of drug—Oxford 1974–1979 (Hawton & Goldacre, 1982).

increase in their use with age by males as opposed to their decreasing use with age in females; and the fact that psychotropic drugs seemed to take over with increasing age as the drugs most frequently used by females but not by males.

They conclude with the assertion that by the age of 19 psychotropic medication is by far the most widely used class of drug among women self-poisoners.

There is considerable evidence, therefore, that the rate of prescription of psychotropic drugs has influenced the prevalence of self-poisoning, that twice as many women as men are prescribed such drugs, and that they are more likely to take them in subsequent self-poisoning. The question remains of why women should so clearly predominate among the recipients of such medication, and it is to an exploration of this that we must now turn.

SEX ROLES AND THE PRESCRIPTION OF PSYCHOTROPICS

It is not surprising in view of the facts in relation to the rate of psychotropic prescription that the use of their most common form—the benzodiazepine group of tranquillisers—has been described as: "... perhaps more than a medical practice, as it has probably reached the scale of a mass cultural phenomenon" (Bellantuono, Reggi, Tognoni, & Garattini, 1980).

In the absence of any known biological difference to account for the sex distribution of psychotropic prescription, cultural factors have been sought to explain the disparity. It has been suggested, for example, that reporting symptoms of personal distress is seen as non-masculine by men and more in keeping with the female role—leading more women to report symptoms and seek medical care (Phillips & Segal, 1969; Chevron, Quinlan, & Blatt, 1978). That there are similar levels of distress in both male and female populations but the symptoms take different forms and therefore invoke different help-seeking and treatment behaviour: for example, women are seen to have rates of depression twice that of men but the ratio is reversed in relation to alcoholism. (Williams & Spitzer, 1983).

Again, it has been proposed that women's roles expose them to stress more than do those of men, and that therefore women are in fact sicker than men and thus receive more treatment (Gove, 1978). Finally, that commonly held stereotypes about the more emotional nature of women influence the clinical decisions of doctors and lead to overdiagnosis and treatment of women for mental disorders (Broverman et al., 1972;

Warner, 1978) Proponents of this view argue that this stereotyping and overprescribing is promoted by the massive advertising of psychotropic medication by drug companies. This is aimed at doctors and emphasises women, specifically those who are younger with family and social problems such as poor housing, as potential beneficiaries, and by "defining everyday stress as a medical problem makes individual brain chemistry, rather than social conditions, the target for intervention" (Stimson, 1975; Prather & Fidell, 1975; King, 1980).

While all of these proposals have proven contentious and none may be said to have found universal support, a variety of empirical studies exist, the results of which endorse the view that the sex role system powerfully influences sex differences in psychotropic consumption.

Sex Differences in Psychic Distress and Sex Roles

An American survey of 2552 adults aged 18–74 published in 1978 considered the relationship between psychic distress, life crises and psychotherapeutic drug use (Mellinger, 1978). Although it found no significant sex difference in the incidence of life crises, for any given level of such crises (measured by the Holmes and Rahe Social Readjustment Rating scale) higher levels of psychic distress (as measured on a shortened version of the Hopkins symptom check list) were evident among women, more common among young women than young men (see Table 4.12), among divorced and separated women, and among women of lower economic status (Table 4.13). Women who had experienced high levels of either psychic distress or life crises were more likely than others to report using psychotropic medications during the previous year and more likely to have been regular users (Table 4.14). As we have earlier noted these groups are prevalent among self-poisoners.

The second study from America by Gail Cafferata and her colleagues employed a national sample of 14,000 randomly selected households who were interviewed 6 times over an 18 month period in 1977 (Cafferata, Kasper, & Bernstein, 1983). This study confirmed the finding of most previous studies that women exceeded men in use of these drugs by 2:1, and discovered that (p.132):

... women had a significantly higher likelihood of use than men under similar family circumstances (and) among women certain family role responsibilities, structures, and stressful events significantly affected the likelihood of obtaining psychotropic drugs even when socio-demographic and health status/access to care variables were controlled

TABLE 4.12
Psychic Distress and Life Crisis by Age and Sex—USA, 1978
(Mellinger, 1978)

	High Psychic Distress (%)			High Life Crisis(%)			No.		
Age	Men	Women	All	Men	Women	All	Men	Women	All
18–29	24	36	31	52	51	51	241	340	581
30–44	21	35	29	30	34	33	282	411	693
45–59	15	35	26	19	31	26	308	420	728
60–74	18	25	22	13	17	15	218	332	550
All	19	34	27	29	35	33	1049	1503	2552

TABLE 4.13
Relation of Psychic Distress and Life Crisis to Selected Demographic
Variables—USA, 1978 (Mellinger, 1978)

	High Psychic Distress (%)		High Life Crisis %		No.	
	Men	Women	Men	Women	Men	Women
Marital Status						
Never married	27	29	40	32	173	165
Married	17	33	26	35	780	976
Separated/ divorced	28	49	46	49	56	141
Widowed	25	32	21	25	41	220
Index of social position						
1–36 (high)	16	27	31	33	291	343
37–48	18	33	31	32	270	405
49–59	21	36	28	40	276	397
60–73 (low)	22	38	23	32	201	344
Race						
White	19	34	27	34	969	1370
Black	25	32	48	45	73	125
Region						
Northeast	15	30	24	31	255	368
North Central	17	34	26	35	342	456
South	19	34	30	33	306	473
West	32	38	41	43	146	206

(thus) ... While both women and men were affected by role responsibilities, women were affected more.

Men and women were found to be equally at risk of unsupportive family structure and stressful events, but among women the likelihood

TABLE 4.14

Relation of Psychic Distress and Life Crisis to Psychotherapeutic Drug[a] Use and Moderate to Heavy Use of Alcohol—USA, 1978 (Mellinger, 1978)

	Psychotherapeutic Drug Use (%)			
	Any Past Year	Regular	Alcohol Use (%)	No.
Women				
Psychic Distress				
Low	12	3	18	560
Medium	20	5	21	425
High	34	14	27	504
Life Crisis				
Low	15	4	16	352
Medium	21	7	21	627
High	26	9	27	510
Men				
Psychic Distress				
Low	6	3	51	566
Medium	10	2	53	263
High	23	10	60	210
Life Crisis				
Low	7	1	42	295
Medium	10	3	53	434
High	13	7	64	310

[a]Tranquilisers (minor and major), daytime sedatives, and anti-depressants. Figures refer to use of drugs obtained through conventional medical channels, excluding hospital use.

of obtaining a psychotropic drug was greatest in "non-intact" families where the woman had no spouse, was not working and had children under six years old; and in all circumstances of stress, apart from bereavement, psychotropic drug use was twice as likely for women as men. These results are summarised in Table 4.15. In addition to these main findings it was discovered that where men more closely approximated the female role with regard to work status or childcare, they too showed a higher incidence of drug use.

This is a finding both reminiscent and supportive of the conclusions of numerous workers described earlier in relation to historical changes in sex roles and various forms of psychopathology. In particular those reached by Showalter in relation to the changing forms of male and female psychopathology—particularly hysteria; by Gove in relation to the likely results of changing sex roles on male rates of psychopathology—particularly depression; and by Kessler and McRae on the "convergence of coping styles" in relation to the similar

TABLE 4.15
Receipt of Psychotropic Drugs by Sex and Selected
Family Characteristics—USA, 1977 (Cafferata et al., 1983)

Family Characteristics	Per Cent			Standard Error		
	Total	Men	Women	Total	Men	Women
Total	12.3	8.1	15.9	0.4	0.3	0.6
Family role responsibilities						
Employment status						
Never worked	18.7*	17.7**	18.9***	0.8	1.6	0.8
Worked part year	14.9*	11.6**	16.1	1.0	1.5	1.2
Worked all year	9.3*	6.7**	13.3***	0.3	0.3	0.7
Number of children						
None	15.2*	10.2**	19.6***	0.6	0.6	1.0
1	11.1	6.7**	14.7	0.6	0.6	0.9
2	10.4*	7.4	13.1***	0.6	0.8	0.9
3 or more	9.0*	5.7**	11.8***	0.7	0.6	1.0
Presence of child under						
5 years of age						
Yes	6.3*	4.4**	8.0***	0.4	0.5	0.6
No	13.7*	9.0	17.8***	0.4	0.4	0.6
Family structure						
Traditional	12.1	7.2**	16.5	0.4	0.3	0.6
Non-traditional	12.9	11.3**	14.2	0.7	0.9	0.9
Intact	11.9	8.1	15.4	0.4	0.3	0.6
Non-intact	18.1*	7.5****	19.4***	1.3	2.8	1.5
Nuclear	12.3	8.1	15.9	0.4	0.3	0.6
Extended	12.5	8.2	15.8	1.1	1.4	1.5
Traditional nuclear intact	11.6	7.2	16.0	0.4	0.4	0.6
Traditional extended intact	10.6	6.7	14.4	1.2	1.4	1.9
Traditional nuclear non-intact	19.1*	8.9****	20.3***	1.4	3.6	1.6
Traditional extended						
non-intact	18.0*	d	20.4	3.4	d	3.8
Non-traditional nuclear intact	12.7	11.1**	14.1	0.8	0.9	0.9
Non-traditional extended						
intact	15.6	14.5****	16.6	3.3	4.3	4.0
Non-traditional nuclear						
non-intact	14.8	d	15.3	3.2	d	3.5
Non-traditional extended						
non-intact	d	d	d	d	d	d

convergence of male and female rates of self-poisoning. All of which
seems to lend credence to our own view of the relationship between sex
roles, self-poisoning and psychotropic medication.

To recap: these studies together provide evidence that women make
more consultations than men, that they are more likely than men to
receive psychotropic drugs when experiencing stress, and that they are
more likely than men to experience high levels of stress in the face of

TABLE 4.15 (cont.)

Family Characteristics	Per Cent			Standard Error		
	Total	Men	Women	Total	Men	Women
Family stressors						
Death in family	27.0*	26.2**	27.7***	3.7	4.5	5.0
Family moved from one residence to another	11.9	7.5	15.6	0.6	0.6	0.7
Departure of family member[b]	12.5	6.5	17.5	0.9	0.9	1.4
Unemployment of spouse	NA	NA	22.8***	NA	NA	2.4
Hospitalisation in family	10.9	6.1**	17.3	0.7	0.6	1.3
Birth of child	7.2*	3.2**	10.8***	1.0	1.0	1.5
Spouse in poor health [c]	22.2*	14.0**	28.5***	1.8	2.6	2.4
Child in poor health	18.4*	12.6	22.2	2.4	3.3	3.4

[a] Excludes single, never married individuals.
[b] Head or spouse moved out of family: child over 17 moved out other than to attend college.
[c] Person appraised health as "poor" in response to question "Compared to other people your age, would you say your health is excellent, good, fair or poor."
[d] Fewer than 50 cases in the cell.

* Significantly different from estimate for total population at 0.05 level using Z-scores.
** Significantly different from estimate for all men at 0.05 level using Z-scores.
*** Significantly different from estimate for all women at 0.05 level using Z-scores.
**** Relative standard error 30 per cent.

severe life crises. Women in non-intact family structures are more likely to obtain such drugs than other women.

Sex Differences in Responses to Stress and Help-seeking Behaviour

Parry et al., (1974) suggest that men are more likely than women to become coping drinkers in response to anxiety and depression, while women are more likely to become users of psychotropic medication. In this connection the study by Mellinger (1978) referred to earlier proposed that cultural factors influenced whether relief from distress was sought within the medical system or elsewhere. Thus it considered patterns of alcohol use and found that in contrast to women, very few young men with high distress scores were using psychotherapeutic medications obtained from a physician although the great majority of them were moderate to heavy drinkers (Table 4.14). The study (Mellinger, 1978, p.1050) suggests therefore that:

Cultural factors, as evidenced in age and sex differences, are important in determining the extent to which people rely on the medical system for treatment, or whether they are more likely to go outside the medical system for the alleviation of symptoms ... the much greater prevalence of moderate to heavy alcohol use ... among men than among women ... reflects strong normative pressures that still remind us that in effect "nice women" do not drink too much. For young and middle aged men, however, society continues to "prescribe" alcohol as a culturally acceptable and masculine way of coping with life, frequent reliance on the physician may well be regarded as a sign of weakness by younger men. In short we suggest that use of medically prescribed drugs and use of alcohol are generally viewed as alternative ways of coping with emotional distress and life crisis.

A more recent study by Kessler, Brown, and Broman (1981) also addressed this question and reached similar conclusions. Employing data from four large scale American surveys, the study indicated that women had higher physician consulting rates and that:

... men are are less likely than women to interpret symptoms associated with depression and low general well-being as signs of emotional problems. As a consequence, men are considerably less likely than women to obtain professional help voluntarily for psychiatric problems.

This analysis of sex differences in culturally approved coping mechanisms is supported by Westbrook and Mitchell in another Australian study which asked 112 health professionals and 112 non-health professionals, half of whom were male and half female, to rate the personality characteristics of the average sick male or female on the Bem Sex Role Inventory. Both sexes were seen, when ill, as having less masculine and feminine characteristics, but there was a relatively greater loss of masculinity by males, supporting the hypothesis that men suffer a loss of sexual identity when ill (Westbrook & Mitchell, 1979).

An earlier study (Horwitz, 1977) of 120 patients at a community mental health centre also pointed to sex differences in coping behaviours, finding that (p.174):

Women are more than twice as likely as men to self-label their problem as a psychiatric one, providing support for the hypothesis that women are more responsive than men to defining problems as emotional ones. Women are also more likely to be labelled by kin, friends and professionals other than physicians, possibly because they more often discuss their problems with these members thus making the problem visible to them ... The labelling process for men is quite different. Since men rarely approach others for help, their problems are less visible to members of their network.

Horwitz concludes that this sex difference in help-seeking may be related to "a socialisation process that leads to self-definitions as helpless". However, not only is there evidence that women are socialised to a greater extent than are men to view themselves as being in need of psychological help—as "helpless"— but evidence exists that this view is shared by those whose help they seek.

SEX ROLES AND CLINICAL JUDGEMENTS

The often quoted, though not always supported, contentions of an early study by Broverman, Clarkson, Rosenkrantz, and Vogel (1970) were that the clinical judgement of doctors and other professionals of both sexes was influenced by sex role stereotypes. The study used a sample of 79 clinically trained psychologists, psychiatrists and social workers of both sexes who were given a Stereotype Questionnaire consisting of 122 bi-polar items such as "aggressive" ... "Not at all aggressive". One pole was characterised as typically female, the other as typically male. Three groups consisting of mixed male and female subjects were then asked to rate, using this questionnaire, which items were typical of healthy males, females and adults (gender unspecified). On the basis of the results, the authors concluded that (p.323):

... a double standard of health exists for men and women, that is, the general standard of health is actually applied only to men, while healthy women are perceived as significantly less healthy by adult standards.

In addition it was found that not only were these views held by physicians but also by their female patients who shared the negative stereotype of women as less independent, less competent, less objective and less logical than men, which led them to be more self-denigratory and to have a more negative self-concept.

This study was replicated by Nowacki and Poe (1973) who were concerned to test the generalisability of the Broverman findings and, employing a sample of 254 college students, found that there was indeed a different conception of mental health for males and females. The tendency found by these authors for women to hold negative stereotypes of their own mental competence might be expected, as the Kessler et al. (1981) findings suggest, to predispose women to interpret social problems as symptomatic of emotional disorder rather than as the cause of it.

Several other studies of physicians' attitudes to female patients providing corroborative support for these contentions are reviewed by Fidell (1980) in a discussion of sex role stereotypes and the American physician. An early paper by Mechanic (1965) described doctors as believing that women were less stoic during illness than men; Clingman and Musgrove (1977) found that physicians were more conservative than lawyers about the proper role of women; Cooperstock (1974) that doctors believe women to have more social problems and present with vaguer symptoms than men and that, when asked to describe the typical complaining patient, 72% of a sample of physicians spontaneously described a woman (Cooperstock, 1971).

Of particular importance in view of the working class origins of most self-poisoners, the social problems which disproportionately beset them, and the findings reported above that female patients are seen to be difficult and complain more frequently than men, are the findings that mood modifying drugs are more likely to be prescribed for patients to whom the doctor finds it less easy to talk (Cartwright, 1974); that physicians consistently underestimate the level of word comprehension of their working class female patients, (McKinlay, 1975); and that mood modifying drugs were also found to be more prescribed when the physician is pessimistic about the outcome of treatment or feels anger toward the patient (Shader, 1968).

Most recently Lopez (1989) described a comprehensive review and meta-analytic study of the results of 60 surveys of therapists judgements reported between 1973 and 1986. Finding only equivocal support for clinical bias in the reported results of the majority of these studies, Lopez suggested that conflicting results could be due to methodological problems. Thus many studies employ a definition of clinician bias limited to severity judgements whereby the severity of symptoms is overrated among certain groups, leading to overdiagnosis of disturbance among them. However Lopez points out that the minimisation of symptom severity similarly represents bias. Thus depressive symptomatology may be regarded as normative among mothers of young children. Secondly, most studies are concerned only with bias in the overdiagnosis of certain conditions among certain groups: Blake (1973) using case summaries found that cases identified as black were more often ascribed a schizophrenia diagnosis than identical ones labelled white. Equally biased ascriptions could occur in the underascription to certain groups of various conditions. Applying this broader definition of bias Lopez found twice as many studies had contained evidence of gender bias among clinician judgements.

Lopez also suggested that more attention should be given in bias studies to the particular disorders employed as clinical stimuli, as bias may be evident in relation to some disorders and not others and general measures of clinicians' gender attitudes would not reveal this. This assertion is in keeping with the earlier findings of Hamilton, Rothbart, and Dawes (1986) who found—using case studies—that among 65 clinical psychologists, females were rated significantly more histrionic than males exhibiting identical histrionic symptoms, but that there was no comparable bias in the diagnosis of anti-social pathology. Also Ford and Widiger (1989) reported on a survey using case studies with 381 psychologists that:

> There was a clear tendency of subjects to diagnose women with histrionic personality disorder and not with anti-social personality disorder, even when cases were more anti-social than histrionic. There was also a tendency not to diagnose men with histrionic personality disorder, but the sex biases were more evident for women …

The results of such analog studies on clinician judgements have continued to receive support from naturalistic studies of gender differences in treatment received by patients complaining of similar symptoms. An Australian study (Mant, Broom, & Duncan-Jones, 1983) surveyed 1301 consultations with Sydney GPs, data being collected from both patients and physicians. Patients filled out a self-report questionnaire (which included the 30-item Goldberg General Health Questionnaire), a psychiatric screening assessment, demographic details and details as to what symptoms or illness brought them to the surgery. The doctor filled out a questionnaire which asked for an opinion as to whether that day's main problem was primarily physical, a check up, primarily emotional, family or work situation and so on. In addition, information was sought on management (prescription, follow up etc.)

The two independent sets of data were then compared in terms of the doctors' assessment of and response to the problems brought by the patient. Not only did the study find that: "doctors are significantly more likely to diagnose a woman as psychiatrically disturbed, all other things being equal", but also that (p.190):

> There is some tendency to diagnose as emotionally disturbed patients who have normal GHQ scores and that tendency is slightly more pronounced for female patients than males … doctors are twice as likely to be aware of morbidity in women with high GHQ scores as they are to diagnose men with similar scores.

Other studies which have found sex differences in medical treatment received include that of Armitage, Schneiderman, and

Bass (1979) who examined the records of husband and wife pairs of patients in an American practice and found that, for the same complaints, men received systematically more extensive "work-ups" than did women. Lack (1980) found, in comparing males and females who both complained of chronic facial pain, that women received more psychotropic drugs and fewer surgical procedures than men.

A recent British work (Williams, Murray, & Clare, 1982) was a longitudinal study of 153 patients attending six GPs over a three-month period. Information was collected by questionnaires completed by both patient and doctor, dealing with the nature of the consultation, the prescription and past history, the mental and physical status of the patient and their socio-demographic characteristics and social problems. It was found that women presented more "psychological" problems, and were identified more often as psychiatric cases by the mental status questionnaire, "personal relationship problems" were identified by the doctors as more common among women, and the duration of drug use was significantly associated with number of social problems with women, but not among men. Depressed women were also far more likely to receive a tranquilliser than were depressed men. The study concluded (p.204) that: "... long-term use is more likely in those with severe psychological symptoms and, for women, in those with with marked social difficulties", and that: "Social problems were positively associated with the duration of drugs use for women and not for men, and there was no association between the presence of physical illness and duration".

These studies provide much support for the notion that women's social problems are indeed "medicalised" through the doctor/patient relationship more extensively than are those of men, the nature of this interaction is described in Helen Roberts' (1985) study of eight English GP practices where it was concluded that:

Not only did the doctors have highly stereotyped views of what a woman's role should be, but most of the women we spoke to were only too willing on one level to be slotted into such a role.

SEX ROLES, PSYCHOTROPICS, AND SELF-POISONING

Earlier, when discussing the possible causal role of psychotropic prescription in the increasing rate of self-poisoning since World War Two, we referred to Brewer and Farmer's (1985) contention that:

These findings add to the evidence that self-poisoning ... is influenced much more by external factors which are sometimes controllable, such as availability, than by internal, pathological ones such as "depressive illness".

It has become clear that these external factors—here the seeking and prescription of psychotropic drugs—emanate from normative cultural influences rooted in the sex role system. Ruth Cooperstock (1978), in concluding her review of the literature on sex differences in psychotropic prescription, affords credence to this assertion when she states (p.185):

Critical to our understanding of sex differences in drug use today, however, is an understanding of the expansion of the medical model to encompass increasing aspects of our lives. This, along with the development of the psychotropics, has had a profound effect on the medical profession, not least of which has been the sanctioning, within the medical model, of a variety of culture bound views of women as well as the provision of the "tools" with which to treat the "problems" seen.

Not only, therefore, has the expansion of the health care system and the development of psychotropics affected doctors' perceptions of female distress and their response to the social problems of women, but so too has it profoundly influenced women's perception of these problems, their origins, and the appropriate means of their resolution. Richard Cloward and Frances Piven, in their paper on the normative construction of female deviance (Cloward & Piven, 1979), describe these developments thus (p.666):

... the proportion of women being drawn into the health system, including the mental health system, is enlarging ... More and more women are being led to think of the tensions they experience as rooted in their health or mental health. Moreover, we think that the same process is occurring among the lower class. The point is not that either women or the poor are neccessarily experiencing more stress, although they may be, but increased stress or not, the form of response still requires explanation. To reach such an explanation we need to look at the rise of the health system ... (it) is the expansion of a system that helps to define for women the nature of the stresses they confront. Stresses are refracted through an ideology which encourages women to search within their psyches and their bodies for the sources of their problems ... Moreover, the health care industry also provides the resources for acting on the understanding of stress which it generates ... the utilisation of these resources helps set women on the path toward the privatised and self-destructive forms of deviance with which we began our enquiry.

We began our own enquiry by suggesting that any useful explanatory paradigm in relation to female self-poisoning must be capable of addressing three questions: Why women? Why self-poisoning? Why now? We discovered in the early chapters that existing paradigms were unable to provide convincing answers to these questions, and suggested that this inadequacy stemmed from their shared assumption of psychopathology as a causal factor and the neglect of social context inherent in such a perspective.

In the previous chapter we turned, therefore, to a consideration of normative socialisation, finding in the sex role socialisation of women the origins of that hopelessness and helplessness which some authors have identified as a distinctive characteristic of self-poisoning. This perspective proved to have explanatory power in relation to the predominance of women among such patients, and an historical account of the relationship between psychopathology and the sex role system proved of similar heuristic value in accounting for temporal shifts in the prevalence of, and sex ratio, within this phenomenon.

The continued application of this paradigm to the historical and contemporary relationship between poisons and parasuicide in the present chapter has furnished further empirical as well as theoretical support for its robustness. Thus, the demonstration of the influence of sex role socialisation on patterns of female help-seeking and psychotropic drug prescription has suggested the normative origins of this particular form of behaviour—self-poisoning—as an expression of female helplessness.

There seems ample justification, therefore, to move forward now to a detailed description of the most explicit account of the nature of helplessness—Martin Seligman's Theory of Learned Helplessness (Seligman, 1975), its most recent revisions and and an exploration of its particular relevance to female self-poisoning.

CHAPTER 5

Learned Helplessness and Causal Attribution

The literature we have reviewed offers much support for the contention that the sex role socialisation of women predisposes them in a variety of ways to especially salient adverse events, to experience helplessness in the face of them, and to self-poisoning as a method of their resolution. Although those works referred to earlier afford valuable theoretical justification to our proposal, none of the authors attempted any direct, empirical validation of their views with parasuicidal patients. Heshusius' paper suggested that Martin Seligman's concept of learned helplessness might provide a fruitful integrating paradigm through which to approach female self-injury, but she did not extend her analysis into a consideration of this theory and its implications for self-poisoning among women.

We have found support from within the literature on locus of control that working class women, who are over represented among self-poisoners, display fatalistic, helpless responses to adversity, which are characterised by beliefs that control is external and that such orientations adversely affect their coping behaviour. In addition direct evidence, although equivocal, has been found supporting this perspective in that parasuicides show predominantly external control orientations. The common emphasis shared by Beck's hopelessness theory and locus of control perspectives on self-poisoning is the perceived non-contingency between action and outcome, and this non-contingency provides the cornerstone of the theory of Learned

Helplessness. It could also be said, in Showalter's words, that it is the loss of the "sense of being an autonomous actor in a manipulable world" which underlies hopelessness and helplessness.

The theory of learned helplessness proposes that learning that outcomes are uncontrollable results in motivational, cognitive and emotional deficits. Martin Seligman originally developed the theory in animal experiments. He established that dogs who were subjected to electric shocks from which they could not escape, eventually responded with passive resignation to continued shocks, and furthermore failed to try to escape when they did have the opportunity. In addition animals subjected to unavoidable shock showed a lack of aggression, lost appetite and weight and showed sexual deficits—all symptoms of depression in humans.

Seligman (1975) hypothesised that learned helplessness:

1. Reduces the motivation to control the outcome because the organism has learned that outcomes are independent of responses, and expects that this will be the case in the future.
2. Interferes with learning that responding can control the outcome.
3. Produces fear for as long as the subject is uncertain of the uncontrollability of the outcome, and then produces depression.

Laboratory experiments subsequently provided supporting evidence for similar effects of uncontrollability in humans. An example is that of Hiroto (1974) who reported an experiment involving three groups of college students. The first group was subjected to loud noise which they could terminate by pushing a button four times, the second to uncontrollable noise which terminated independently of their efforts, and the third group received no noise. In the second stage of the experiment all groups were tested on a hand shuttle box, which gave all subjects control of the noise termination when they pushed a lever from one side of the box to the other. The group receiving prior controllable noise as well as that which had received no noise learned to shuttle; the group with prior uncontrollable noise did not do so and listened passively to the noise—a very similar result to the earlier animal experiments.

Miller and Norman (1979) reviewed numerous studies involving human subjects which had tested the Seligman hypotheses. They found 23 studies which had attempted to demonstrate the occurrence of changes in performance in humans due to such learned helplessness training and concluded that in the main such studies have found consistent support for "the conceptualisation of learned helplessness as a performance deficit". In addition they recounted the results of six studies investigating the affective aspects of learned helplessness and reported that these also supported his conclusions.

They described two studies employing the Multiple Affect Adjective Check List devised by Zuckerman, Lubin, and Robins, (1965) which administered the check list to subjects before and after exposure to contingent and non-contingent reinforcement, and both reported significant increases in feelings of depression, anxiety and hostility following non-contingent reinforcement (Miller & Seligman, 1975; Gatchel, Paulus, & Maples, 1975).

There is therefore considerable support from laboratory experiments for the negative expectancy, and the cognitive, behavioural and affective consequences of uncontrollablity. Outside the laboratory and in terms of a more general vulnerability, Seligman (1975, p.159) proposed that in the real world helplessness could be induced by poverty for "a child reared in poverty ... will be exposed to a vast amount of uncontrollability", and susceptibility to learned helplessness could therefore be offered as an explanation for the higher incidence of depression and psychological distress found among those groups whose actions might be imagined least effective in bringing about good or avoiding bad events or outcomes—groups such as the unemployed, the poorly educated, those in lower socio-economic groups and women.

Sex role socialisation is interpreted as promoting learned helplessness among women in the theoretical work of Heshusius and in the results of an empirical study by Baucom and Danker-Brown (1979), who were concerned to establish the relationship between sex, sex roles and the development of learned helplessness. One-hundred-and-sixty college students were allocated to groups according to sex type as masculine, feminine, androgynous and undifferentiated using Baucom's scale of masculinity/femininity (Baucom, 1976). Half the students in each group were given unsolvable concept formation problems (helplessness induction procedure), and the other half were given solvable ones. Masculine and feminine sex typed subjects showed cognitive and motivational deficits whereas androgynous subjects showed only dysphoric mood and undifferentiated subjects were unaffected by the helplessness condition. Differential susceptibility to the helplessness manipulation was solely a function of sex roles, not sex per se.

These results are related to those of Bem (1975) who found that androgynous subjects are more flexible and have a wider range of strategies for dealing with diverse situations than do either masculine or feminine sex typed individuals. However Baucom and Danker-Brown's findings seem to contradict our own hypothesis of greater vulnerablity of females to helplessness and self-poisoning, and they themselves are concerned that their results appear to be out of keeping with sex differences in the incidence of depression. Thus it is suggested that persons with different sex role types encounter situations involving loss of control with differential frequency (Baucom & Danker-Brown, 1979, p.934):

... through the socialisation process, males have more often than females become more masculine sex typed. Because of this sex typing, males may then have avoided uncontrollable situations more often than females. This avoidance of uncontrollable situations may account for the lower incidence of depression in males than females.

Thus these findings and the interpretation of them now may be seen as supportive of our own proposal that sex role socialisation promotes learned helplessness among females in two ways: females experience more non-contingency between response and outcome in diverse areas of their lives, and women are actively trained to comply with a female stereotype which emphasises passivity and helplessness. There are several additional sources of empirical support for these contentions.

Maccoby and Jacklin (1974) although finding few sex differences in socialisation, reported that parents consistently treated girls and boys differently in the way they reacted to their behaviour. Whereas boys' behaviour was praised or criticised accordingly, that of girls' was frequently ignored. Unresponsiveness to female behaviour, even when it involves aggression, was also described by Serbin, O'Leary, Kent, and Tonick (1973) in a study of nursery schools. Girls got fewer reactions than did boys overall, and even in cases of temper tantrums accompanied by physical aggression, their behaviour was more likely to be ignored completely—findings more recently confirmed in a report on infant classes in Northern Ireland from the Equal Opportunities Commission (EOC 1986). Olejnik (1980) in turn, found that the extent to which college students rewarded children was associated as much with their age and sex as it was with their actual achievements—with boys generally receiving more rewards for comparable success.

Dweck and Bush (1976) in their studies of classroom interaction found that boys' behaviour was much more frequently the object of criticism by teachers than was that of girls, and furthermore the nature of the feedback differed in that negative feedback from teachers to boys was couched in terms of their lack of discipline or effort (i.e. controllable aspects), whereas that to girls came less frequently and related more to work-related matters such as ability (which is an uncontrollable aspect). Not surprisingly in view of the learned helplessness hypothesis, boys feedback resulted in their improved performance and persistence, but girls' feedback resulted in performance deficits.

Studies of adults have reported similar findings, with observations of small group interactions finding that the contributions of women are more frequently ignored than those of men, more often interrupted, and have less influence on group decisions. Even when women are given the right answer to a group problem ahead of the rest of the group, they have still not been able to get the group to accept it (Altemeyer & Jones, 1974).

All these studies support the view that the actions of males more frequently have consequences—even if sometimes unfavourable—than do those of females, and the contention that females therefore have more experience of response outcome non-contingency and are rendered more susceptible to learned helplessness. These are socialisation experiences which indirectly lead to helplessness: however there is also empirical evidence for the view that women are literally trained to be helpless as part of their socialisation into the "helpful but helpless" female role.

Studies of parent-child interactions in the area of responses to help-seeking have shown that although direct reinforcement of dependent behaviour in girls may not be evident, mothers respond to requests for help from their daughters differently than they do to similar requests from their sons. Rothbart (1976) discovered that mothers more often reinforced girls' help-seeking behaviour by giving active support and encouragement, whereas help-seeking by boys was more likely to be ignored or denied. Other studies have shown that such differences in reinforcement and extinction, using adult attention as the reward, can readily alter the dependent and independent play behaviours of children (Serbin et al., 1978).

Adult women have more equivocal experiences around success than do men. Horner's "fear of success" hypothesis proposed that negative reinforcement is sometimes contingent on goal achievement, therefore achievement motivation in women may be undermined by the negative effects of the social rejection which meets women who fail to conform to the helpless female stereotype by being successful (Horner, 1972).

Further evidence of the conflictual aspects of female sex role socialisation is to be found in another study of factors influencing the selection of job applicants with the apposite title "When beauty is beastly". Heilman and Sarawatari (1979) found that although success in the female role (heightened femininity) is heavily dependent on physical attractiveness, attractiveness detracts from perceptions of the suitability of women for managerial positions—stereotypically a male preserve, whereas it enhances perceptions of male suitability. Physical attractiveness is however considered an advantage for "accessory", less influential jobs such as secretary. Thus achieving success in one sphere results inevitably in failure in another. This may be interpreted both as an experience of indirect reward for failure (or helplessness) and as an example of response outcome non-contingency—i.e. success leads to failure—a situation reminiscent of Phyllis Chesler's (1972) assertion that women "in order to win have to lose".

Further laboratory work with implications for the learning of helplessness in everyday female roles, is that of Langer and Benevento (1978). Their experiments established that individuals can erroneously infer incompetence from situational factors. Even though subjects had previously performed experimental tasks effectively, when told that they would continue to perform them but in the role of assistant to another person, their performance declined. They proposed that being assigned labels denoting inferiority, no longer performing a task now performed by another, and allowing someone else to do something for one can also lead to a sense of powerlessness and helplessness.

All of these are situations to which women are exposed in the occupational sphere, where as we have seen, women who most apparently fulfill the female stereotype are regarded as highly qualified for accessory jobs; and in the domestic role characterised by its major task of "nurturance" or serving the needs of others. The typical division of labour in the home, whereby women are regarded as unable to perform "technical" tasks which have to be completed by men is another example. Even driving a car is seen as a more typically male than female role: a study of sex role stereotypes in children's media indicated that women are far more frequently shown as passengers than as drivers (Women on Words and Images, 1972).

In a lengthy review of the literature on the social implications of helping behaviours, Piliavin and Unger (1985) describe a multitude of studies which have demonstrated in a variety of ways that the more a woman conforms to the stereotypic notion of femininity the more she will be perceived as requiring help. One of the less weighty examples of this, though none the less emphatic, is a study which showed that women who wore feminine attire are six times as likely to have a door opened for them as women who dress in a less conforming way.

Nolen-Hoeksema (1987) reports on numerous studies which indicate that girls are socialised to be less active and independent than boys and that in adult life women have reason to expect that their actions will be less successful in generating desired outcomes than those of men. For example in laboratory studies, men's performances were rated higher than comparable performances by women; and the achievements of women are rated as less valuable than those of men. Outside the laboratory, women are less likely to be promoted than are men of similar job performance.

Thus the learning of non-contingency and training in helplessness characterise female childhood socialisation and their everyday adult experience. There seems to be considerable support, both from within and outside the laboratory, for the contention that the female sex role affords women more frequent experiences of response outcome independence, and actively trains them to become helpless in order to conform to the stereotypical view of femininity. Women are therefore more susceptible to learned helplessness and its characteristic affective, cognitive and motivational deficits in the face of adverse events.

The potentially debilitating effects of sex role socialisation and its associated learned helplessness, may impinge particularly on those young working class women who are most frequently found among self-poisoners. Seligman pointed to the particular susceptibility of those raised in poverty to the experience of uncontrollability, and several studies have shown that distress among working class women is greater in the face of comparable adversity than that in middle class women (Brown & Harris, 1978; Westbrook & Mitchell, 1979). Experiences of early parent loss, either through death or marital disharmony and separation, and the breakdown of parent–child relationships are found to be common among self-poisoners and represent the type of uncontrollable outcomes which are central to the development of helplessness in Seligman's model. In addition those events known to precipitate self-poisoning are characterised by their perceived "uncontrollability" (Paykel, Prusoff, & Myers, 1975). Young, working class women with fatalistic orientations and passive coping styles who take overdoses may be seen as responding with learned helplessness due to their perceived and actual inability to control outcomes.

The accounts of women who had taken overdoses described by Sally O'Brien (1986) in her book *The Negative Scream* provide eloquent testimony of this contention, and especially to the importance of gender relations and sex role socialisation in the aetiology of learned helplessness and female self-poisoning:

My mother was always busy with her work, and her favourite was my brother. I never felt she loved or was interested in me. I used to keep trying to do things that I thought she would approve of, I suppose to try and make her love me. So I worked really hard, got my A levels, went to university. It never made any difference. I started looking for love with men, but the relationships never worked. I was too dependent and too demanding. Deep down I don't feel I can ever be loved. People say to me you are above average intelligence, looks and personality. I suppose it's true but it doesn't mean anything because I can't achieve the one thing I want. Love.

Before I was always trying to be what others thought I should be. Yes, I had plenty of friends, particularly men, but if I showed them my real side, my insecure side, they would leave me. That just reinforced my feelings I was nothing and that inside I was horrible. The only time people liked me was when I was being what they wanted me to be. I fluctuated between thinking I was really wicked, and thinking I didn't exist at all.

Sally O'Brien found in her interviews with women that the feeling of only existing by other people's approval was constantly expressed:

To be a good woman, wife, mother, you are meant to love and care for your man and children. But how do you know how to do it when you've never experienced it yourself?.

It's women who suffer from these emotional insecurities, not men. However career minded I or my friends are, we still cannot get away from the idea that our real measure of success is whether we have a man. Thus our feelings about ourselves are always dependent on another person. Women tend to blame themselves if things go wrong, whereas men tend to blame other people.

O'Brien states that most of the women saw themselves as failures, blaming themselves for being unlovable, and although frequently expressing anger to O'Brien in the interviews, feeling that they were incapable of directing it at the person who was making them angry:

Men control everything. They tell us we have to be the best wife, mother, whore, career woman, etc. I spent my whole time trying to be this ideal woman. Of course I felt a failure. No-one could be all that, but I never stopped to think what I wanted to be.

Despite the eloquence of these accounts, very few of these women felt strongly about feminism, although this research was carried out in the mid-1970s when feminist views and the women's movement were enjoying a resurgence. O'Brien (1986, pp.81–83) recalls that :

These women were leading independent lives, with their own jobs and friends, yet their lives were dominated by trying to find the "right" man. Their failure to find a good relationship eclipsed every other facet of their lives ... For these people it is difficult to take control of their lives when they have no models to follow.

This sense of no control, a lack of contingency and helplessness is also revealed in Bancroft's study of the reasons people give for taking overdoses (Bancroft et al., 1979). He administered a structured interview schedule to 41 patients which offered them a list of 11 reasons with which they were asked to explain their overdose. The most commonly chosen reasons were:

The situation was so unbearable that you had to do something and didn't know what else to do (56%).
Get relief from a terrible state of mind (44%).
Escape for a while from an impossible situation (32%).
You seemed to lose control of yourself and have no idea why you behaved in that way (27%).

The least frequently chosen reasons were:

Seek help from someone (15%).
Frighten or get your own back on someone/make people sorry for the way they have treated you (7%).
Try to influence some particular person to get them to change their mind (7%)

The implications of these responses, with the most common reasons clearly reflecting the feelings of helplessness and powerlessness described by O'Brien's respondents, are self-evident in terms of the learned helplessness perspective we have been exploring. The sense of a loss of control, a conviction in the futility of actively trying to alter external circumstances, and the adoption of a passive escape/avoidance resolution are strikingly similar to the proposed cognitive, affective and behavioural components of the learned helplessness model.

We have stressed the theoretical and empirical similarities between Beck's hopelessness theory of self-poisoning and Seligman's learned helplessness model as it might be applied to female self-poisoning: the points of convergence are "negative expectancy" in Beck's formulation and "non-contingency" in Seligman's model. This convergence was promoted with the subsequent reformulation of learned helplessness theory by Abramson, Seligman, and Teasdale (1978) which was designed to remedy inconsistencies in the findings when the original theory was applied to humans. As the centrality of cognitive elements was enhanced, so too was its value as a theoretical approach to female self-poisoning.

THE CRITIQUE OF LEARNED HELPLESSNESS

Inconsistent results were obtained when experiments attempted to transfer the learned helplessness construct from animals in the laboratory to humans—individuals responded differently from each other in face of what were apparently the same stimulii. Such findings suggested that it was the cognitive appraisal of their situation—the subjective meaning attached to it—that led some individuals to experience helplessness and others not to do so. No longer, therefore could it be viewed as an uncomplex conditioned response as it had been in animals. Thus, for example, in the studies referred to earlier of Miller and Seligman (1975) and Gatchel et al., (1975), which employed the Multiple Affect Adjective Check List, not only were the predicted feelings of depression and anxiety present in subjects confronted with uncontrollability, but also hostility featured prominently among some subjects' responses, which the theory neither predicts nor explains.

The importance subjects attach to the test task was also found to mitigate the effects of helplessness training in the laboratory. Several studies have shown that where subjects attribute importance to the task—such as college students being informed that the test tasks were measures of academic ability and intelligence—these subjects showed significantly greater helplessness than in those situations where they attached no such importance to test tasks (Roth & Kubal, 1975).

Not only is the subjective importance of the task influential in determining outcomes, but so too is its perceived difficulty. Tennen and Eller (1977) provided subjects with a "double helplessness" experience, whereby groups were told that each succeeding task was either easier or more difficult. Regardless of the non-contingency involved, the "easier" group displayed more helplessness than the "difficult" group, indicating that task difficulty affects the development of helplessness, which is not predicted in the theory. Again, some studies discovered that, rather than performance deficits resulting from non-contingency, improvements in performance occurred in later task performance. The study by Roth and Kubal found that exposure to minimal amounts of uncontrollability resulted in increased effort, whilst subjects exposed to greater degrees of uncontrollability showed the predicted deficits. The original model of learned helplessness as conceived by Seligman claimed to embrace the cognitive aspects of the phenomenon in as much as it proposed that it was expectancy changes in the face of uncontrollability which led to helplessness (i.e. the experience of current non-contingency led to the expectancy of future non-contingency and therefore to helplessness). However, possibly due to its origins in animal experimentation, the cognitive aspects of the model based on this expectancy construct have proven inadequate to explain certain experimental results, and also inconsistencies in the analogy with depression.

Thus, for example, the fact that depressed people experience acute guilt, feelings of responsibility for outcomes which were outside their control, and an associated diminution in self-esteem—none of which can be adequately explained in terms of the expectancy changes of helplessness alone. Neither can it explain why there are such evident individual differences in the depth of depression. Again, the theory predicts that people will experience helplessness or depression in response to good event occurrence over which they have no control—for which there is no evidence; and, finally, it has a problem with the fact that not all those who are exposed to uncontrollable events become depressed, or show cognitive/motivational deficits in the laboratory. None of these phenomena can be explained with this construct in its original form.

THE REFORMULATION

The nature of those experimental findings which were inconsistent with the predictions of the theory clearly suggested that it was the neglect of the cognitive dimension which was fundamental to the problems which arose in its application to humans. Thus in their attributional reformulation of learned helplessness, Abramson and her colleagues proposed that it is the individual's perception of what causes their helplessness which determines the nature of their reactions to non-contingency (Abramson et al., 1978).

It is asserted that there are three attributional dimensions: internal/external; global/specific; and stable/unstable. The attributions individuals make along these dimensions will determine the particular form of their reaction to non-contingency and helplessness. Thus, if an individual who is unable to solve an anagram attributes this to an internal cause (such as his lack of intelligence), this will result in a loss of self-esteem. Whereas if he attributes it to an external cause (such as the difficulty of the anagram) he will assume that others too will be unable to solve it and therefore his self-esteem will not suffer. It is important to note here that internal locus of cause is not synonymous with internal locus of control. An individual who makes an ability attribution (i.e. assumes that failure in a test is due to a lack of intelligence), is not assuming that he controls the cause of his failure because intelligence is not controllable. Thus it is possible to have internal, uncontrollable attributions.

The distinction between internal and external attributions for helplessness helps to explain the different responses of those subjects in the Tennen and Eller experiment mentioned earlier. Subjects who were told that the tasks were increasing in difficulty showed less deficits than those who were told the tasks were getting easier. This would be explained by assuming that the subjects with the "difficult" tasks could attribute their failure externally to task difficulty, assume that others would encounter similar difficulty and therefore not suffer reduced self-esteem and performance deficits.

This assumption is supported by the results of a study by Klein and Seligman, (1976) who reported that instructions that the task was difficult tended to increase attributions for failure to external causes and also minimised performance deficits, whereas the reverse was true when subjects were told tasks were easy, which encourages internal attributions for failure, lowers self-esteem, and increases performance deficits.

The second dimension in the attributional reformulation is that of global/specific. The attribution of failure to intelligence is a global attribution of causality in that the lack of intelligence is likely to affect performance on a range of tasks, whereas an attribution to task difficulty is specific in that there is an expectation that other tasks may not be difficult and therefore performance will be better.

Thirdly, Abramson and colleagues proposed that attributions may be to stable or unstable causes. Thus intelligence level is a stable characteristic and is not going to change in the future, so an attribution to lack of intelligence to account for failure in a test predicts future failure also, thereby promoting expectancy of future failure and associated performance deficits.

It is apparent from this single example of attributions involving lack of ability, that in fact an attribution to low intelligence in the face of failure is simultaneously internal, stable and global. The reformulated model suggested that this type of attribution for failure leads to the maximisation of deficits associated with learned helplessness in that self-esteem is reduced, expectancy for future failure is increased and performance deficits are therefore more likely to result in future tasks. In addition, internal attributions are more likely to also be stable as they are often associated with aspects of the individual's personality, intelligence or other dispositions, thus the low self-esteem generated by internal attributions for failure is liable to be compounded by the expectancy of future failure which the stability of the attribution generates. On the other hand external, specific and unstable attributions for failure—an example of which might be bad luck on the day of the test in question—would not result in generalised helplessness and its associated cognitive, motivational and affective consequences. Again, external attributions are more likely to be unstable as situations have the potential to change more than do the internal dispositions of individuals.

AN ATTRIBUTIONAL "STYLE"

Although the reformulation of learned helplessness, like the original model, was primarily concerned with depression, Abramson et al. (1978) concluded by suggesting that (p.68):

> Individual differences probably exist in attributional style. Those people who typically tend to attribute failure to global, stable and internal factors should be more prone to general and chronic helplessness depressions with low self esteem ... our model predicts that attributional style will produce depression proneness, perhaps the depressive personality. In the light of the finding that women are from 2 to 10 times more likely to have depression, it may be important that boys and girls have been found to differ in attributional styles, with girls attributing helplessness to lack of ability (global, stable) and boys to lack of effort (specific, unstable).

Thus the attributional reformulation of learned helplessness not only enabled some of the important anomalies to be resolved, but recast the original pathology oriented model into a theoretical framework capable of general application to human cognition, motivation and emotion. The attributional approach suggests that people are engaged in seeking explanations for events and behaviours and do so in "logical" ways, and having arrived at them, act in accordance with them equally logically. People who attribute their success to internal, stable causes understandably expect success to continue in the future and persist in their efforts to ensure such outcomes. People who attribute their helplessness in the face of failure to internal, stable and global causes, such as low intelligence, equally understandably—or "logically"—suffer lowered self-esteem, expect future failure and give up trying: they become depressed.

In other words, the maladaptive behaviours of the depressed person need not be viewed from within the confines of a pathology theory which speculates that something has gone wrong with the subject, and therefore has to propose an abnormal dynamic governing their behaviour—such as those of the psychoanalytic or biochemical schools of thought. No special mechanisms are necessary to explain depression as the mechanisms responsible for it are those which govern everyday cognition, motivation and emotion. Recalling Steve Taylor's words in Chapter Three, it becomes apparent that, unlike the pathology paradigm, this conception does not "turn society's influence off like a tap" to reach an explanation of deviant behaviour.

Not only does the attributional reformulation remove the divide between normal and abnormal, but also that between the internal and external, the psychological and the social. Depression is not described solely in terms of intrapsychic processes, nor solely in terms of environmental, social factors. Rather an attributional account is an interactive one which sees depression as a consequence of the interaction of the individual and the environment. The attributional style which characterises an individual is a social product, not a psychological disorder.

This renders the reformulated learned helplessness model particularly attractive as an explanatory paradigm for female self-poisoning, meeting as it does Nicholas Braucht's (1979) criteria referred to in Chapter Three for a truly interactive theory—namely:

1. That such real life behaviours cannot be adequately understood by recourse to either individual difference variables alone or environmental variables alone;
2. That neither individuals nor environments can be understood to be pathological in themselves; and that
3. behaviour is not viewed as sick or well, but is defined as transactional—an outcome of reciprocal interactions between specific social situations and the individual.

Thus an explanatory model is offered here which views self-poisoning, not as the aberrant response of the disordered mind or personality to random events, but as the logical, though undesirable, consequence of normative processes governing everyday female experience and behaviour.

It is proposed therefore that female sex role socialisation exposes women to the repeated experience of non-contingency or helplessness and also leads them to possess an attributional style which renders them less able to deal effectively with this experience. That is to say that in the face of adverse events which engender subjective helplessness, women make causal attributions which are more internal, stable and global for their helplessness than are those of men, and this results in the cognitive, motivational and emotional deficits predicted by the reformulation—i.e. expectancy of future failure and reduced capacity to recognise subsequent opportunities for response/outcome contingency, lowered self-esteem and the ultimate expression of passive resignation, self-poisoning.

Affective Implications—the "Depressogenic" Attributional Style

In the quotation above taken from their paper on the reformulation hypothesis, Abramson and her colleagues allude to the possibility that women acquire an attributional style which predisposes them to helplessness and depression. In a later work Seligman (1981) describes this depressive attributional style in this way (p.124):

> The individual possesses an insidious attributional style (which) consists of a tendency to make internal attributions for failure, but external attributions for success; stable attributions for failure, but unstable attributions for success; and global attributions for failure, but specific attributions for success.

Seligman supports this contention by describing two experiments with psychology students in which he employed the Attributional Style Questionnaire which consists of 12 questions, half of which relate to good events and half to bad. The subjects are asked to imagine themselves in each of the situations described and to state what would have been the major cause had the situation happened to them. They then rate the internality, stability, and globality of the cause. The experimenters then correlated these results with those scores achieved by the subjects on another questionnaire—the Beck Depression Inventory. Seligman (1981, p.124) describes the results in these unequivocal terms:

> We found a clear depressive attributional style ... For bad outcomes, depression ... correlated with internality ($p < 0.0001$), stability ($p < 0.0001$) and globality ($p < 0.0001$). As for good outcomes, depression correlated with externality ($p < 0.01$), instability ($p < 0.002$), but not significantly with specificity.

This is taken as lending substantial support to the notion of a depressive attributional style, but obviously leaves unanswered the question of whether this style is the product of the depression or its cause. In order to more closely approach this problem Seligman goes on to describe a further experiment in which students with various attributional styles were asked to rate what grade they would consider a failure in their forthcoming psychology examinations (Seligman, Abramson, Semmel, & Von Baeyer, 1979). Retested after the examination, those students who had previously made stable and global attributions for failure tended to become depressed on receiving disappointing results significantly more often than those who had a different style.

A later study set out to further test the hypothesis with larger numbers of students. It was again found that the more internal or global students' attributional styles for negative events were at the first testing, the more severe were their depressive reactions in the face of negative life events—in this case, receiving a low grade in examinations. Furthermore, students who were extremely external or specific in their attributional style at first test were invulnerable to depression upon receipt of low grades (Metalsky et al., 1982).

In addition it was again emphasised that the attributional reformulation of depression is a personality theory as well as a clinical theory. Thus (Metalsky et al., 1982, p.613):

> Its predictions apply to the development of transient depressive effect in response to negative daily life events as well as to the development of the clinical syndrome of depression in response to major or cumulative life stressors.

These are important points in relation to our concern to apply this model to self-poisoning where precipitant life events are a major characteristic of the phenomenon, and many subjects do not demonstrate clinical depression, although transient affective states of anxiety and depression are frequently noted. However the most important aspect of attribution theory in relation to self-poisoning is not the affective deficits, which it suggests accompany dysfunctional attributional styles, but the cognitive and motivational deficits and their consequences for coping skills in the face of adverse events.

Towards the end of Chapter Three, a vulnerability–stress model of coping deficits among self-poisoners was beginning to emerge from cognitive theory such as Neuringer's notion of dichotomous thinking and cognitive rigidity and Beck's Hopelessness Theory. It was suggested there that empirical support for the importance of each of these constructs was convincing but that a theoretical framework is still awaited which is capable of integrating these disparate elements and offering a comprehensive theory of coping skills deficits in self-poisoners.

D'Zurrilla and Goldfried (1971) in developing a model of problem solving suggested a typology of problem solving deficits with five elements:

1. An inappropriate general set or orientation to problems.
2. Deficits in problem identification and specification.
3. Deficits in the generation of potential alternative solutions.
4. Deficits in evaluation and selection of generated alternatives.
5. Deficits in implementation or verification, or both, of the chosen alternative.

The remainder of this chapter will be concerned to demonstrate that attribution theory provides such a comprehensive account of deficits in coping skills and their relationship to the known facts of self-poisoning—in particular the female predominance.

SEX DIFFERENCES IN ATTRIBUTIONS AND COPING BEHAVIOUR

There is much support for the existence of a dysfunctional attributional style which predisposes people when confronted with uncontrollable negative events to react with helplessness. This style may result in clinical depression for which hypothesis there is considerable though by no means unequivocal support in the literature (Coyne & Gotlib, 1983; Parry & Brewin, 1988). Rather than occupying a causal role in clinical depression, dysfunctional attributions are now more commonly felt to be implicated in the persistence of depressive episodes once they have begun (Lewinsohn, Steinmetz, Larson, & Franklin, 1981; Dent and Teasdale, 1988). There is more widely shared agreement however on the effects of dysfunctional attributions on coping behaviour.

Attributional research in both naturalistic and laboratory settings has produced results which, broadly speaking, share the view that internal, stable, and global attributions for failure result in motivational and behavioural deficits which inhibit performance. In most studies this is explained by the negative expectancy associated with stable, global attributions—for example to a lack of ability or personality factors—which suggest that there is little likelihood of improvement regardless of the effort expended. Thus individuals with this dysfunctional style are less successful and less persistent following uncontrollable (i.e. non-contingent) failure.

There is some disagreement, as in the literature relating to the affective consequences of dysfunctional attributions, on the role of the locus dimension. Some results suggest that non-helpless individuals are those who make external, unstable, specific attributions for failure—for example to luck or task difficulty. Other findings have indicated that internal, unstable, and specific attributions for failure—to effort or other behavioural factors—avoid helplessness deficits. It has been suggested that this apparent anomaly may be accounted for by the well documented tendency for expected outcomes to be attributed to internal, stable, and unexpected ones to external, unstable factors such as luck (Feather & Simon, 1971; Deaux & Farris, 1978). Furthermore, internality has been shown to be multifactorial in that such attributions can involve stable, global factors (intelligence or personality), but also could relate to unstable, specific factors such as effort or behaviour. Unless all three dimensions are assessed, apparently conflicting results may occur.

In general, however, there is agreement that helplessness deficits are most marked in those who make internal, stable, global attributions for failure—i.e. to ability or character.

One of the most convincing demonstrations of all these aspects of this debate is Craig Anderson's (1983) study, carried out in a naturalistic setting, of the attributions and performance shown by individuals involved in a blood donor recruitment drive. While much of the research into the performance deficits associated with dysfunctional attributions has employed academic tasks in school or college settings, Anderson's work has the added advantage from our own point of view of demonstrating that such deficits also occur in interpersonal situations. As we have seen in an earlier chapter, failure in interpersonal situations most commonly precipitates female self-poisoning.

Subjects were preselected according to their attributional style: in this case whether they more commonly attributed interpersonal failures to character (stable, global) or behaviour (unstable, specific). The test task of trying to persuade people over the telephone to donate blood ensured that all subjects experienced some success and some failure. Prior to the task, which continued over a one-week period, subjects were randomly assigned to three groups each receiving different attributional manipulations. In one it was suggested that success on the imminent interpersonal persuasion task would be due to abilities and personality traits; in another that success would depend on the correct strategies and effort; and the third group received no prior attributional manipulation.

Anderson found that subjects who made strategy/effort attributions (internal, unstable, specific) whether by manipulation or by preselection expected more success, expected more improvement with practice, displayed higher levels of motivation, and performed better at the task than did subjects who made ability/trait attributions. He concluded (p.1144): " Of particular importance in the present results is the finding of attributional effects, both predispositional and experimental, on motivation and performance measures in a highly complex interpersonal setting".

Although Anderson did not discuss his results in terms of sex differences in attributions and performance there is a wealth of empirical support for his findings in relation to the motivational and behavioural consequences of dysfunctional attributions and for the existence of sex differences.

One of the earliest of these studies was that of Dweck and Repucci (1973) who explored attributions and classroom behaviour among young children. There were attributional differences between those who gave up in the face of failure—whom the authors described in terms of

Seligman's early model as "helpless"—and those who persisted. The persistent children demonstrated "effort" attributions for both success and failure. Effort is an internal, unstable factor which is controllable and as such maintains the expectation of improvement and success in future tasks. The children who were helpless—who did not persist—attributed failure more frequently to lack of ability. This being a stable factor is dysfunctional in the face of failure as it reduces expectations of improvement and thus inhibits persistence. The dysfunctional style was most common among girls.

In a second study Dweck and Gilliard (1975) again found boys attributing failure to internal, unstable factors such as lack of effort more than girls, and girls attributing failure to a lack of ability. Boys demonstrated increased persistence in the face of failure whereas girls showed a decrease. An additional finding of this study was that attributions of failure to stable factors such as ability are associated with larger drops in expectancy following failure than are attributions to unstable factors such as effort and luck.

Nicholls (1975) reported similar results showing that girls more readily revised their expectancies downward than did boys when failure followed previous success, and that satisfaction with test success was greater when success was attributed to ability (as with boys) but not when it was attributed to effort (as with girls).

Ickes and Layden (1978) separated 40 males and females into groups according to whether or not they possessed dysfunctional attributional styles (i.e. internal attributions for failure, external for success). Initially all subjects completed an attributional style measure following which they were given solvable anagrams to be completed against the clock in order that a baseline of performance could be set for each individual (pre-test). This was then followed by a series of 13 anagrams of which only 2 of the first 9 were solvable (the failure test), but of which the last 4 were all solvable (the post-test performance measure). There were pronounced differences in performance according to attributional style with those subjects who had an internal style for failure becoming significantly slower and less accurate following failure. No impairment occurred among those making external attributions for failure. The performance of the female subjects was definitely impaired by the failure experience, becoming slower and less accurate; that of males was unimpaired. The conclusion was reached therefore (p.142) that: "The disruption of performance by a failure experience is least evident for males who externalise failure and most evident for females who internalise it".

In one of the more recent studies Stipek (1984) showed that girls were more likely to attribute failure on maths tests to lack of ability and less likely to attribute success to ability than were boys, even when there was no difference in actual performance. Boys and girls who rated their performance as excellent or good made the same number of errors, as did those who rated their performance as very bad or not good. Indeed, where boys' performance was objectively poorer (on spelling tests), boys who failed still made less self-derogatory attributions than girls who failed, boys being more likely to attribute failure to an unstable cause—bad mood—than girls.

Stipek, in discussing the likely consequences of such sex differences in attributional style, comes to conclusions reminiscent of Nicholls' a decade before to the effect that (p.979):

> ... girls' attributions have serious implications for their achievement in maths. Despite the fact that actual performance was the same for boys and girls who claimed to have succeeded in the maths test, boys probably benefited more from their success by attributing it more often to ability. The girls greater tendency to attribute their failure to lack of ability ... has further negative implications for their self-perceptions and achievement behaviour. A comparison of boys and girls in the failure group revealed that girls had lower expectations than boys for their performance on the next maths test. The ability attributions for failure and the resulting low expectations for future success ... are logically associated with feelings of hopelessness and with helpless behaviour which inhibits learning.

These findings suggest not only that dysfunctional attributions do indeed have motivational and behavioural deficits and that females more commonly demonstrate them, but that as a result their coping behaviour suffers more following failure than does that of males and is enhanced less by success. Over the past decade there has been repeated empirical support for these findings including: Bond and Deming (1982); Levine, Gillman, and Reis (1982); Erkut (1983); Bell and Schaffer (1984); Stipek (1984); Williams and Brewin (1984); Gannon, Heiser, and Knight (1985); and Martin and Nivens (1987).

GENDER DIFFERENCES IN ATTRIBUTIONS AND COPING

Although there is, therefore, convincing evidence of sex differences in attributions and coping, this does not in fact establish that sex role socialisation is the source of the dysfunctional attributions which more commonly are found among women. Such differences could be due to biological factors rather than socialisation. There are several studies which have explored the relationship between aspects of sex role stereotypes and attributions. Aspects of individual personality, such as sex role identity (the extent to which individuals identify with stereotypically masculine or feminine attributes), are acquired through social learning not biology and therefore any relationship between such variables and attributions would implicate sex role socialisation. Several studies have succeeded in demonstrating these relationships.

Gannon, Heiser, and Knight (1985) proposed that the degree of sex role stereotypy—as measured on the Bem Sex Role Inventory (Bem, 1974)—rather than sex *per se*, would influence the relationship between uncontrollability and subsequent performance. Subjects completed the Bem Sex Role Inventory and following non-contingent feedback on a test task were subsequently given anagrams and maths problems. They then completed an attributional questionnaire. The results suggested that high masculinity subjects (whether men or women) more commonly made effort attributions, performed best and were invulnerable to the debilitating effects of non-contingency. Low masculinity subjects demonstrated the predicted increase in performance deficits as a function of non-contingency.

Again using the BSRI, Erkut (1983) set out to "directly test whether sex differences in expectancy and attribution are a by-product of stereotypical sex role orientations". Before a mid-term exam male and female students completed the sex role inventory, a questionnaire eliciting their expected results and the basis of this expectation in terms of attributions to ability, effort, task difficulty, and luck. Following the results being received subjects again completed the attributional measure in relation to their results. Initial expectancy of success was higher in men, and men made more ability attributions and women more effort attributions.

The results showed that sex differences in expectancy and attribution patterns are related to sex role orientation. All sex differences turned out to be related to feminine sex role orientation especially among women—feminine women expect lower grades, claim not to have the ability to do well, expect the exam to be difficult and, performing less well, attribute poor performance to lack of ability or task difficulty. Erkut points out that ability and task difficulty are stable attributions, unlikely to change over time. She concludes (p.228) that:

These attributions coupled with poor performance would seem to trap feminine women in the low expectation cycle. Initial low expectancy followed by failure and the attribution of this failure to internal and stable causes, reinforces the likelihood of future failure.

Whilst feminine men shared some of these characteristics—achieving poor grades and claiming this to be due to task difficulty—their attributions are not so debilitating as they are not ability attributions, and therefore allow the expectation of future higher achievement. In addition femininity is not associated with low initial expctancy among men. Thus high feminine orientation among women is associated with a more debilitating pattern of attributions and expectancy than it is amongst men.

Erkut (1983) proposes that, in the light of these results, those studies which have not found sex differences in attributions (McHugh, Frieze, & Hanusa, 1982) and expectancy have not done so because they have ignored the distribution of sex role identity among their subjects. Where a sample contains few feminine women and/or many feminine men, sex differences will be obscured.

Numerous other studies have found similar relationships between aspects of sex role identity, expectancy, and attributions. Welch, Gerrard, and Huston (1986) tested the hypothesis that sex typed personality attributes as measured on the BSRI (Bem, 1974) would predict women's responses to success and failure and established that for feminine subjects failure depressed performance and success had no effect, whereas for androgynous subjects performance was unaffected by failure and enhanced by success. As findings we have reported earlier would lead one to expect, androgynous subjects attributed their success to ability whereas they attributed failure to task difficulty—what the authors describe as an "egotistical attribution profile". Feminine women in contrast were less likely to make ability attributions for success and less likely to attribute their failures externally to task difficulty. Welch and Huston point out that, because both groups of women scored equally highly on the femininity scale of the BSRI, the major difference between them is their masculinity attributes and therefore their results suggest a correlation between masculinity and achievement behaviour.

These results find support in other attributional studies linking gender-related personality characteristics—such as levels of achievement motivation, self-esteem, and instrumentality/expressiveness—with particular patterns of attribution.

High self-esteem has been shown to be associated with high masculinity (Spence, Helmreich, & Stapp, 1975; Lamke, 1982) and numerous studies have demonstrated that individuals with low self-esteem internally attribute failure and externally attribute success. In an early study Fitch (1970) showed that males with low self-esteem were more likely to attribute failure internally while those with high self-esteem attributed success more to internal causes. The attributions of women more closely resemble those of low self-esteem individuals whereas men's resemble those with high self-esteem (Ickes and Layden, 1978). More recently Brewin and Shapiro (1984) found that high self-esteem subjects felt significantly less responsible for negative outcomes, whereas women felt significantly more responsible for them.

High achievement motivation is typically associated with high masculinity (Spence & Helmreich, 1978) and Levine et al. (1982) established that high need for achievement (as measured by Mehrabian's n-achievement scale (Mehrabian, 1968), contributed most to sex differences in patterns of attribution - whereby males attributed outcomes to ability and were less likely than females to attribute outcomes to effort or luck. Gail Crombie (1983) found that women who are androgynous and high in achievement level attribute their academic success more to ability than effort.

Instrumentality and expressiveness refer to constellations of personality characteristics identified as stereotypically masculine and feminine (i.e. task oriented or emotion focussed respectively). Vollmer (1986) demonstrated that men score higher on instrumentality and women on expressiveness as measured on the Personal Attributes Questionnaire (Spence & Helmreich, 1978), and in an American study of college women (Welch, Gerrard, & Huston, 1986) it was found that high instrumental women attributed their success primarily to internal factors and their failures to external ones, whereas low instrumental women did the opposite. There were marked correlations between these styles and performance: for the high instrumental group, success facilitated task performance whereas failure had no debilitating effect. However, for those low on instrumentality, success had no effect on subsequent performance but failure interfered with it. When there was no feedback on the concept discrimination tasks there was no difference in performance. The authors summarise their findings in this way (p.231):

> Thus high instrumental women improve their performance after success, do not deteriorate after failure, and exhibit an ego-enhancing pattern of attributions by attributing success to ability and failure to external causes. Women who perceive themselves as low on instrumental attributes do not respond to success with improved performance but do respond to failure with declining performance. They tend to attribute failure to ability and success to external causes.

They conclude that (p.232):

> The study does have some strong implications for women in achievement settings. The pattern of performance and attributions exhibited by low

instrumental women is not adaptive ... These women appear to lack confidence in their abilities and to respond quickly to failure by assuming they cannot perform a task. Such a pattern of task performance could significantly impede their achievement in educational and career arenas.

These conclusions are borne out in the real world of career achievement in an aptly titled study *On the Importance of Being Masculine* (Wong, Kettlewell, & Sproule, 1985) which dealt with the relationship between sex role identity, career achievement and attribution. It was found that women classified as feminine on the BSRI achieved less in their careers and attributed their career performance less to ability and effort than women classed as masculine.

In view of this weight of evidence implicating sex role socialisation in dysfunctional female attributions, there seems little reason to differ now with the conclusions reached by Ickes and Layden (1978, p.143) in the study reported earlier which was carried out over a decade ago:

> This leaves us in the unhappy position, however, of having to propose that females in general ... may be socialised to react to failure or frustration in an achievement situation by essentially giving up. If this explanation is correct, it is hardly surprising that women in this culture are generally less productive than men, because society has burdened them with an internalised motivational handicap that they must somehow learn to overcome if they are to succeed.

The credibility of these findings on the motivational and behavioural deficits of dysfunctional attributions and of the sex and gender differences which characterise them is enhanced by several experimental studies involving attributional retraining (Dweck, 1975; Chapin & Dyck, 1976; Andrews & Debus, 1978; LaNoue & Curtis, 1985). In these studies individuals with dysfunctional attributions and marked performance deficits in the face of failure are identified and retrained to employ more functional effort attributions. Their attributions and subsequent performance following failure are then monitored and it has been shown that dysfunctional attributions can be altered and performance following failure improved.

We shall return in the final chapter to discuss attributional retraining and its therapeutic potential. Now, however, it is more important to relate the sex differences in attributions and coping we have observed, to the results of those studies described in Chapter Three in which Neuringer, Beck, Schotte and Clum and others established distinct cognitive characteristics of self-poisoners. In doing so the requirements of D'Zurrilla and Goldfried for a comprehensive model of problem solving deficits will be addressed by integrating these disparate cognitive characteristics within an attributional model of self-poisoning.

DYSFUNCTIONAL ATTRIBUTIONS, COPING DEFICITS, AND SELF-POISONING

We began this discussion of sex differences in attributions and coping behaviour by describing Craig Anderson's study of attributions for success and failure in recruiting blood donors by telephone. While most of the studies we have reported rely on the negative expectancy associated with internal, stable and global failure attributions to explain performance deficits, other cognitive factors may also be involved. Thus Anderson (1983) accounted for the performance deficits shown by those making character attributions for failure in this way (p.1144):

> Viewing one's failures as the result of a poor strategy should lead one to attend to strategic features of the task, to expect improvement as one learns effective strategies, and to actually perform better. This analysis may not apply though to many of the simple, algorithmic tasks commonly seen in the psychological literature. In tasks such as ... anagram solving and simple maths problems, strategy plays a considerably weakened role due to the more limited range of possible strategies. But in most everyday situations of importance, particularly in complex interpersonal situations, strategy plays a major role in determining one's performance.

Anderson's paper and his conclusions about why strategy attributions lead to enhanced coping point to additional ways in which dysfunctional attributions might inhibit coping. He suggests that strategy attributions are beneficial because they direct the subject's attention to strategy and the need to constantly improve it in response to feedback. On the other hand, internal, global attributions direct attention away from task to self. These speculations as to the adverse attentional consequences of internal, global attributions for negative events had earlier been voiced by Ickes and Layden (1978, p.142–143) who suggested that those who internalise failure may make negative self-attributions to factors such as incompetence or stupidity which interfere with the attentional aspect of task performance by generating states of anxiety and increased self-concern.

Mikulincer and Nizan (1988) carried these speculations forward by exploring the effects of global attributions for failure on cognitive interference and the generalisation of learned helplessness deficits. The authors began by reviewing that literature which has demonstrated that those who make global attributions following failure suffer more impaired performance subsequently than do those who make specific attributions (Pasahow, 1980; Anderson, 1983; Mikulincer, 1986). They also point to Alloy's results which showed that performance deficits generalise from the unsolvable situation to a new dissimilar task only among those who make global attributions (Alloy, Peterson, Abramson, & Seligman, 1984). However, Mikulincer and Nizan (1988) disagree with the emphasis placed on negative expectancy as the sole mediator of the performance deficits associated with global attributions for negative events.

Instead they propose that "off-task cognitions" have an important and neglected role whereby globally attributed failure, because it emphasises the actor's negative characteristics, produces more task irrelevant self-preoccupation than a specifically attributed failure. This process may also promote the generalisation of helplessness deficits by (p.471):

> ... drawing the subject's attention away from task performance and from situational cues that indicate that the new, solvable problem is different from the old, unsolvable one. This attentional block to situational information may prevent subjects from discriminating between dissimilar ... tasks and thereby may facilitate the generalisation of performance deficits.

The authors employed the Attributional Style Questionnaire (Peterson et al., 1982), and a measure of off-task cognitions called the Cognitive Interference Questionnaire (Sarason et al., 1986). This consists of 21 items each of which presents a particular type of intrusive thought—half consisting of task related thoughts (e.g. about competency) and half task irrelevant (e.g. family and friends). Subjects rate the frequency with which each type of thought occurs. Subjects then undertook a series of quite dissimilar tasks upon which failure and feedback were manipulated with a view to assessing the generalisation of any helplessness deficits.

The results of three related experiments supported the authors' views in that performance deficits following failure feedback occurred only among those who made global attributions, and those who made such attributions engaged in more task irrelevant cognitions which interfere with performance—the more frequent the task irrelevant thoughts the worse the performance was on a new and different task. In a second related experiment, subjects who were induced to make global attributions for failure showed more task irrelevant thoughts and greater performance deficits following failure. In a third experiment the authors employed instructions given during the tests to discourage off-task cognitions. This procedure succeeded in discouraging subjects from making off-task cognitions while working on unsolvable anagrams and eliminated the performance deficits produced by globally attributed failure.

As is so often the case, Mikulincer and Nizan did not report results by sex of subject. However there is, as we have seen, ample evidence that women (and high femininity males) more frequently than men make internal, stable, global attributions for failure and would therefore be more prone to the attentional deficits described in this study. In addition there is support from the literature dealing with sex differences in depressive illness which suggests that the predominance of women among the clinically depressed is due their greater tendency to ruminate about their depressed state—in Mikulincer's terms to indulge in task irrelevant self-preoccupation.

Nolen-Hoeksema (1987) presents findings which show that men are more likely to engage in distracting behaviours that dampen their mood when depressed, but women are more likely to amplify their moods by ruminating about their depressed state. Rumination, because it interferes with attention, concentration, and the initiation of instrumental behaviours may lead to more failure and greater helplessness. She suggests that the males' more adaptive response may originate in sex role socialisation in that their activity may result from conformity to the sanctions against emotionality carried within this socialisation. Referring to the work we have reported by Dweck and Goetz (1978) which deals with differences in the type of feedback received by boys and girls from parents and teachers, Nolen-Hoeksema (1987, p.276) reminds us that:

Although parents and teachers may not directly reward girls for passivity and contemplation—they simply do not reward them as much for activity as they do boys. In addition, because women are told they are naturally emotional, they may come to believe that depressed moods are unavoidable and cannot be easily dismissed when present. Such an attitude would decrease the probability of women taking simple actions to distract themselves from their moods.

How, then, do these findings on sex differences in attributions and coping behaviour relate to those described in Chapter Three on the cognitive characteristics of self-poisoners? Charles Neuringer proposed that "suicidal" individuals think dichotomously. Seeing external events in terms of extreme polarities (good or bad) they lack the cognitive ability

to discriminate between alternative courses of action and experience the
world as an ever decreasing set of options. He asserted:

> All people think dichotomously but most individuals have the capacity
> to moderate or even ignore the dichotomies ... suicidal individuals lack
> this flexibility and cling to extreme polarised views. (This) precludes the
> possibilities for moderation, compromise and shifting of perspectives ...
> (which) leads to diminished problem solving and adaptation.

As we have discovered, people who make internal, stable and global
attributions   for   failure   are   making   causal   attributions   to
characterological factors which are uncontrollable and are assumed to
be unchangeable. Therefore such attributions preclude opportunities for
moderation and compromise. The self-preoccupation which results leads
both to a neglect of strategy—as this is felt not to affect outcomes—and
to attentional deficits such that alternative courses of action which may
present themselves are not perceived. These factors preclude shifts of
perspective and lead to diminished problem solving and adaptation and
in this way Neuringer's cognitive rigidity hypothesis can be subsumed
within an attributional model of "suicidal behaviour".

Beck's theory of hopelessness requires little interpretation as there
is such commonality between his theory and Seligman's attributional
reformulation of learned helplessness—such commonality that in fact
the theory has recently been renamed the learned hopelessness theory
(Alloy et al., 1988). Beck et al. (1975b) asserts that (p.1147):

> ... suicidal behaviour is derived from specific cognitive distortions: the
> patient systematically misconstrues his experience in a negative way
> and, without objective basis, anticipates a negative outcome to any
> attempts to attain his major objectives or goals.

An attributional account simply states that hopelessness is the
consequence of making internal, stable, global attributions for failure
and that the possession of such a dysfunctional attributional style leads
to   the   negative   expectancy   and   hopelessness   associated   with
self-poisoning.

The problem-solving deficits identified by Patsiokas et al. (1979), who
found that "suicide attempters" were less able to generate alternative
uses for well known objects, are described thus:

> ... an inability to display diversity in coping with their stressors. The
> cognitively rigid person has difficulty conceiving and following through

suggestions of new behaviour options and may be deterred from contemplating anything other than his stressful situation.

Anderson's interpretation of the consequences of global attributions in terms of the attentional deficits that prevent the perception of alternative strategies offers a convincing attributional account of Patsiokas' findings of decrements in the conceiving of alternative behaviours. The motivational deficits associated with a dysfunctional style account for the lack of persistence in following through suggestions, and Mikulincer's well supported hypotheses in relation to the self-preoccupation associated with global attributions for failure suggest an explanation for the inability of the self-poisoner to contemplate "anything other than his stressful situation".

The Alternative Uses Test employed by Patsiokas, upon which he based his proposals about the coping skills deficits of self-poisoners, was at best an indirect measure of the skills required in a naturalistic setting involving interpersonal events. In recognition of this Asarnow (1987) employed a Coping Strategies Test which involved subjects being asked to generate solutions to hypothetical stressful situations. Suicidal ideators were less likely to generate active coping strategies—including self-comforting statements and instrumental problem solving—as opposed to those involving physical or verbal aggression or running away. Asarnow concluded that this was because of their inability to generate cognitive mediational strategies to regulate their affective and behavioural responses.

An attributional account of Asarnow's findings would invoke Anderson's assertions on the dysfunctional consequences of ability attributions in terms of diverting attention from strategy and thereby discouraging that continuous monitoring of behaviour and efficacy which would promote instrumental coping. Additionally Ickes and Layden's proposal that dysfunctional attributional responses to failure may encourage characterological self-preoccupation, and hence result in increased anxiety, offers some insight into the flight or fight response found among Asarnow's subjects.

Finally it will be recalled from Chapter Three that Schotte and Clum (1982) found that suicidal ideators generated less than half as many potential solutions to interpersonal problems selected from their own lives as did depressed subjects; they focussed to a greater extent on the potential negative effects of implemention and they were less likely to implement these once generated. The authors concluded that the hopelessness of suicidal subjects stems as much from a "maladaptive general orientation towards problems" as to specific deficits in interpersonal problem solving skills.

Again, internal, stable, global attributions encourage self-preoccupation and divert attention from situational clues which might suggest alternative courses of action are possible as situations change. If characterological factors are perceived to be the cause of interpersonal failure then few alternatives would in fact present themselves, there would be limited expectancy of improvement if any were implemented, and this negative expectancy would undermine persistence. The maladaptive general orientation towards problems which Schotte and Clum suggest might be most important, but are not able to identify specifically, could therefore be the dysfunctional attributional style from which the various problem-solving deficits identified among self-poisoners could emanate.

Thus we may conclude that not only is there considerable empirical support for the cognitive and behavioural deficits associated with a dysfunctional attributional style, but that this style and the helplessness resulting from it is more commonly found among women, and those men who possess feminine personality attributes. Furthermore the coping deficits which have been shown to arise in the face of adversity among those possessing a dysfunctional style are remarkably similar to those known to characterise self-poisoners.

Certainly an attributional approach to problem-solving deficits could meet the requirements of D'Zurrilla and Goldfried's typology:

1. The dysfunctional attributional style represents an inappropriate general set or orientation to problems.
2. Such a style could result in difficulty in problem identification and specification due to its cognitive sequelae. Thus the individual who possesses a dysfunctional attributional style may generally attribute the cause of negative events to internal, stable, personal factors when their origin may lie in external circumstances.
3. The generation of potential alternative solutions to negative events could follow from the self-preoccupation and attentional deficits resulting from internal, global attributions for failure.
4. Where alternatives are generated their evaluation and selection will be impeded by the cognitive deficits associated with a dysfunctional style. Thus, for example, the inaccurate attribution of cause of failure to internal factors will lead to the positive evaluation and subsequent selection of solutions targeting internal causes.
5. Deficits in implementation and verification of chosen alternatives will result respectively from the motivational deficits associated with the negative expectancy inherent in a

dysfunctional style and the generalised tendency to attribute negative outcomes to internal, stable and global causes and positive ones to external, unstable and specific ones.

Thus the cognitive and motivational sequelae of a dysfunctional attributional style adequately account for the deficits in problem-solving skills described in D'Zurrilla's typology and implicated in parasuicide by Schotte, Clum and others. Furthermore the attributional theory of hopelessness closes the explanatory circle in relation to the definitive characteristics of self-poisoning by providing a model of the mediating role of attributions between negative events, problem-solving deficits and hopelessness.

It was suggested in the Introduction to this work that there were three questions for which any comprehensive theory of self-poisoning should be able to provide answers. These were:

Why women? More explicitly phrased as why has there been such a predominance of women among self-poisoners?

Why self-poisoning? The most common form of parasuicide involves the deliberate ingestion of drugs in excess of the recommended dose. Why have medicinal agents become the most frequently used?

Why now? The remarkable increase in the incidence of self-poisoning between 1960 and 1976 is still largely unexplained. What explanation could there be for the chronology of this epidemic?

In Chapter Four, which discussed sex role socialisation, its relationship to medicine and the prescription of psychotropic drugs, an account was given of why self-poisoning with drugs should have become the most common form of parasuicide. This account was placed within an historical context which suggested an explanation for the historical fluctuations in this phenomenon. The question of the female predominance has been a thread passing through each stage of our discussion and in this fifth chapter we have approached a model of female self-poisoning based on sex and gender differences in attributions and coping skills. As the model has developed the importance of gender has become apparent and with it the realisation that an attributional approach is capable of providing a comprehensive account of the phenomenon—including the presence of men among self-poisoners.

There remains one further aspect of the sex differences in self-poisoning which requires discussion before a comprehensive theory based on causal attribution can finally be stated. Perhaps there should have been a fourth question in our Introduction—Why sex differences in precipitant events?

Female self-poisoning is most commonly precipitated by events in the "private realm" such as the breakdown of interpersonal relationships, usually with men. Events precipitating male self-poisoning however are more commonly those occurring in the "public realm" such as financial difficulties or problems with the police. If an attributional model of self-poisoning is to be comprehensive then it must address this issue for, as we have seen, the strength of the model is that it promises to provide a mechanism linking adverse events, helplessness and self-poisoning. In order to do so it must, therefore, offer an account of the specific vulnerability of women to helplessness in the face of adverse events in the private or "affiliative" realm.

In Chapter Six such an account will be offered beginning with a consideration of the several different functions which causal attribution fulfils. It has become apparent from the discussion thus far that adaptive causal attribution serves at least two functions—"cognitive mastery" or the rapid processing of information to promote understanding and action, and the "egotistical" function, that of maintaining self-esteem. These are indeed the two most commonly recognised ones and they are important in understanding female patterns of attribution within an interpersonal context. But another function, that of "self-presentation", is also important, as is the possibility of conflict between these various functions such that a particular attributional style which is adaptive in some circumstances may be maladaptive or dysfunctional in others.

CHAPTER 6

Causal Attribution and Female Self-poisoning

THE FUNCTIONS OF ATTRIBUTION

Information Processing and Expectancy

Central to the information processing perspective on causal attribution has been the assumption that a primary motive in humans is the need to develop an organised and meaningful view of the world in order to promote control of events within it. Establishing the causes of events is essential to their subsequent control and causal attribution is fundamental to the "cognitive mastery of the causal structure of the environment" (Kelley, 1967, p.193). Humans according to this perspective are seen as intuitive scientists processing information according to certain logical principles which "resemble formal procedures of statistical inference" (Tetlock & Levi, 1982, p.68). Expectancy has been seen by many attribution theorists as forming the basis of this inferential process.

It has been repeatedly observed that expected outcomes tend to be attributed to dispositional factors—internal, stable, global (Deaux & Farris, 1976)—and unexpected outcomes to situational factors—external, unstable (Feather & Simon, 1971). If, for example, success is expected, this expectation is based upon the dispositional assumption of high ability. If the outcome is success then it is attributed to the internal, stable factor upon which the expectation was based. If the outcome is failure, an internal attribution is discounted because of the initial assumption of high ability, and therefore an external attribution to luck or task difficulty follows logically from the initial expectation. Expected outcomes, because they do not challenge established causal beliefs, are most likely to be met with this automatic processing and individuals remain largely unaware of the causal schemata underlying their judgements.

The implications of this information processing view of attribution for patterns of female attribution are important because women are commonly found to have lower expectations of success than are men. Thus Crandall (1969) found that females generally had lower expectancies for success in a variety of tasks and that in all age groups from elementary school to college, males had higher initial expectancies and tended to overestimate their future successes relative to their ability level, whereas females tended to underestimate their future performances. In addition, when information is mixed or inconsistent, girls tend to weight the negative aspects and boys the positive. Numerous other studies have confirmed the finding of higher male expectancies for success (Deaux & Emswiller, 1974; Deaux, White, & Farris, 1975; Vollmer, 1986).

Thus the tendency of women to make internal, stable attributions for failure and external, unstable ones for success may be explained in terms of their lower initial expectancies and is here seen as an inevitable outcome of the inferential principles guiding information processing.

A more recent English account of reactions to failure in the driving test supports these assertions, finding marked and consistent sex differences in expectancy and subsequent goal oriented behaviour. Women had lower initial expectancies of success and when they did succeed they thought it less to do with basic competence. In addition, when they failed they were less likely to reapply for another test (Williams & Brewin, 1984).

These consistent findings led Bond and Deming (1982), linking sex role stereotypes, expectancy and attribution, to conclude that (p.1205): "In our society failure itself may be stereotypically more sex appropriate for females ... females' failure may function as a relatively anticipated outcome eliciting more stable, internal attributions".

Thus, females' tendency to have lower initial expectancies for success than men is both reinforced by and contributes to the pattern of attributions women typically display towards success and failure.

Motivation and Egotistical Attribution

An alternative approach to causal attribution suggests that its function is to maintain self-esteem. This has been called the "self-serving bias"

(Bradley, 1978). Here causal attribution serves the function of enhancing the individual's self-image by making self-protective attributions which enhance self-esteem (i.e. internal attributions for success and external ones for failure) and it has been demonstrated that levels of self-esteem and self-serving or egotistical attributional style are indeed related.

Gordon Fitch (1970) described an experiment whereby 135 undergraduate business students were given a dot estimation test in which the subjects viewed slides projected on to a screen for three seconds. Each slide contained a number of randomly distributed dots and the subjects had to estimate their number on ten slides. Success and failure feedback were manipulated by the experimenter. Levels of self-esteem were measured using a standard scale which had been administered to the subjects a month before the experiment. Attributional style was determined by a questionnaire which offered subjects two internal attributions (ability and effort), and two external attributions (luck and the person's physical or mental condition during the test).

Fitch unfortunately did not report the results by sex but found that although subjects generally made more internal attributions for success than for failure, low self-esteem subjects who received failure feedback made more internal attributions than did high self-esteem subjects who received the same feedback.

The pattern of attribution for success and failure commonly found among women has been described as "self-derogatory" in that attributing success externally will not enhance self-esteem whereas failure attributed internally will diminish it. Ickes and Layden (1978, pp.131–132) reported that:

> High self-esteem subjects are inclined to take credit for positive outcomes by ascribing them to internal causes. In contrast low self-esteem subjects tended to take less credit for positive outcomes by attributing them relatively more often to external causes. For negative outcomes, high self-esteem subjects either make external attributions or else rate all causal factors ... as improbable, whereas low self-esteem subjects tend to "blame" themselves for such outcomes by making relatively more internal attributions ... With regard to sex differences ... males at each level of self-esteem exhibit attributional tendencies resembling those of high self-esteem subjects, whereas the attributional tendencies of females at each level resemble those of low self-esteem subjects.

More recently Elfriede Lochel (1983) has been concerned to discover how early self-derogatory attributional patterns become evident among girls. She found that among four year olds the attributions of girls were consistently self-derogatory—attributing success to luck and failure to lack of ability. This undermined persistence and the development of self-confidence, actively promoting helplessness in the face of failure. Boy's attributions on the other hand were ego-enhancing and promoted persistence and self-confidence.

Lochel also found that girls more frequently made no attributions for their successes, claiming not to know what caused them, and she suggested that this represents a female technique for cognitively distancing oneself from one's successes. Thus self-derogatory attributions may be adaptive in minimising role conflict in a society where females are socialised to have lower expectations for success. Lochel states (p.218):

> ... there already exist sex differences in achievement attributions at the age of four years. The direction of the sex differences is the same as in adults and can be linked to prevailing sex role stereotypes which ascribe higher competence to males than to females ... girls show a pattern of attributions which is clearly self-derogatory in its consequences ... there are indications of an attitude of learned helplessness ... girls seem to use attributions in such a way as to diminish ... the ambivalence of success which is rooted in the incompatibility of the female stereotype with successful achievements.

Lochel's results and the conclusions based upon them point to further functions which causal attribution may fulfil in that it may serve to reduce role conflict potentially aroused by non-conformity to stereotypical patterns of sex appropriate success and failure. Although this interpretation refers to the management of self-image and intrapersonal conflict, others have suggested that causal attribution also has a function related to self-presentation in interpersonal situations and interpersonal conflict.

Self-presentation and Interpersonal Relations

Forsyth (1980) succinctly summarises the self-presentational function of attributions as facilitating the communication of social identity information to others. Consequently, attributions for one's outcomes may be communicated to others in such a way as to promote approval. Thus he proposes (p.186):

> Although attributions are not typically conceptualised as interpersonal communications, this interpretation is consistent with a symbolic

interactionist conception of social identity negotiation ... in its emphasis on exchanged interpersonal information. Goffman's dramaturgical notions suggest that individuals trade identity-establishing and maintaining information through their self-presentations (Goffman, 1971). In attributional terms, actors in a social encounter can potentially control the perceptions of others by selectively manipulating their symbolic descriptions of causality ... From the actor's point of view, observers should be guided in the direction of internal attributions that will yield increases in social esteem".

Stryker and Gottleib (1981) share this view, suggesting (p.446) that the main attribution theory has concerned itself with the assignment of meaning, but that this might not be the central issue:

The central issue is not to assign but to communicate meaning. Interaction proceeds on the basis of shared systems of meaning; consequently, the achievement of a sufficient consensus is the major problem. The critical problem for the actor does not occur in the observation of an event or in its initial representation; it occurs when it becomes evident that others implicated with one in a social act do not share its meaning.

In a society where strongly held stereotypic notions of femininity endorse expressiveness rather than instrumentality and where the female role is that of the "helpful but helpless" woman, a self-derogatory attributional style may indeed be adaptive within interpersonal relationships, especially, it may be assumed, those between men and women. If within such relationships women—to be recognised as feminine—must conform to the helpless but helpful female stereotype, then self-derogatory attributions for success and failure would promote this recognition and signal conformity to the shared meaning of the interaction.

Returning to Forsyth's remarks, from the female actors' point of view making internal attributions for failure and external ones for success (thereby not only promoting helplessness but communicating it) is, ironically, likely to yield increases in social esteem in as much as their femininity is enhanced. It will be recalled that LaNoue and Curtis (1985) found in their experiments with attributional retraining described earlier that women were more likely to make self-derogatory attributions for success and failure when in the presence of men. When alone or in same sex situations, women's attributions were similar to those of men. Those studies which show that successful women are often rated as less acceptable and likeable than unsuccessful ones support these contentions (Feather & Simon, 1975), and that of Costrich, Feinstein, Kidder, Maracek, and Pascale (1975) in which assertive women were rated as more unattractive and in need of psychotherapy than were assertive men suggests further consequences of female non-conformity.

Attribution as Communication

It has been demonstrated that women, through the process of sex role socialisation, acquire an attributional style which perpetuates and reinforces the stereotypic view of themselves as instrumentally ineffectual, as helpless. This helplessness is an integral part of being "feminine", of the woman's social identity, and the characteristic self-derogatory attributional style of women enhances this view, and therefore enhances their femininity, thereby promoting their self-esteem and, in Forsyth's terms, and from the perspective of symbolic interactionism, has the function of communicating their femininity to others.

In stable heterosexual relationships this style will be adaptive in maintaining the woman's self-concept within the identity reinforcing role relationship, and in maintaining the consensual mutuality of meaning essential to social interaction. However, when breakdown occurs in such relationships, and mutuality is therefore lost, this attributional pattern inhibits effective coping in that it undermines self-esteem and persistence in the search for resolution, which may be conceived as the re-establishment of consensual meaning in social interaction.

The breakdown of interpersonal relationships is frequently instrumental in precipitating self-poisoning in women, and such behaviour may therefore be viewed as the "dramaturgical" communication of the extreme helplessness such events evoke.

The view of self-poisoning as communication has been promoted by several authors. Erwin Stengel and Nancy Cook's paper on the social significance of self-poisoning is an early example (Stengel & Cook, 1958), although a more explicit statement of this conception was made by Norman Kreitman (1977), who suggested as we saw in Chapter Two, that self-poisoning represents a signalling process, and sought to establish (p.66) that there is a "sub-culture of parasuicide" characterised by:

... a relative lack of emphasis on verbal communication with greater value attached to the immediate discharge of emotion and the use of physical methods to convey meanings. There is also likely to be an emphasis on the short-term relief of feelings as against long-term planning.

Kreitman found that self-poisoners had four times as many contacts with other self-poisoners as would be expected on a chance basis, and that this was particularly evident among young women. Although Platt (1985) failed to replicate these epidemiological findings, and we earlier criticised Kreitman's model on the additional grounds of its relative neglect of class and gender as sub-cultural influences, none the less it remains of theoretical interest here. This is especially so as he draws an analogy between hysteria and self-poisoning, asserting (Kreitman, 1977, p.73): "… these findings are in accord with what is known of other forms of communicated psychopathology, such as epidemic hysteria and *folie à deux*".

This is an analogy which we found informative in Chapter Four when, during the development of our own model of female self-poisoning, the relationship between socio-economic class, gender and mental health was considered. These are relationships to which we shall return, but for the moment suffice it to note that Kreitman felt the element of communication was a most important aspect of his study of the contacts of 135 parasuicides, which supported his contention (p.66) of the possibility that:

> … clusters of individuals exist for whom the act has a well recognised social meaning, and that an individual in this group need only engage in quasi-institutionalised parasuicidal behaviour in order to convey a preformed message to other members, that is to say, to perform a ritual.

That this preformed, ritualised message both emanates from and signals (or communicates) the existence of extreme female helplessness is also eloquently asserted by Phyllis Chesler (1972, p.47) in this way:

> Female suicide attempts are not so much realistic "calls for help" or hostile inconveniencing of others, as the assigned baring of the powerless throat, signals of ritual readiness for self-sacrifice. Like female tears, female suicide attempts constitute an essential act of resignation and helplessness—which alone can command temporary relief or secondary rewards. Suicide attempts are the grand rites of femininity—i.e. women are supposed to "lose" in order to "win".

Chesler's assertion that women are supposed to lose in order to win describes the contradiction inherent in female sex role socialisation, and loses nothing in its translation to "women are supposed to be helpless in order to be feminine". In attributional terms this contradiction is evident in the conflict between the adaptive function of a helpless attributional style in maintaining and communicating a woman's feminine self-concept within stable role relationships, and its maladaptive consequences in the face of their breakdown. The poignant reports of self-poisoning women recorded by O'Brien and described earlier are evocative of this conflict.

The following quotation taken from a recent discussion (Alloy et al., 1988, p.10) of the attributional reformulation of learned helplessness—now retitled learned hopelessness—suggests a dynamic relationship between an individual's attributional style and those events considered to be important by that individual:

> ... some individuals exhibit a general tendency to attribute negative events to internal, stable, global factors and to view these events as very important whereas other individuals do not. Thus the particular attributions people make for the specific negative events they experience are hypothesised to be a joint function of the situational information surrounding these events and their generalised attributional styles ... The logic of the diathesis-stress component implies that a depressogenic attributional style in a particular content domain (e.g. for interpersonal events) provides "specific vulnerability" ... to hopelessness depression when an individual is confronted with negative life events in that same content domain (e.g. social rejection).

In our attributional approach to female self-poisoning it has been suggested that those normative socio-structural factors which lead to the development of a negative attributional style and hopelessness in women not only expose them to greater adversity but also determine the nature of those adverse events which women consider important and which have been shown to be associated with their self-poisoning. The most recent attributional account of learned hopelessness offers new insights which are entirely in keeping with these propositions, and which provide the opportunity for a more detailed theoretical exploration of those aspects of our own model dealing with the importance of life events and female self-poisoning.

LIFE EVENTS—NORMATIVE AND NON-NORMATIVE INFLUENCES

There is considerable evidence that those who are predominant among self-poisoners (the young, working class and female) are more exposed to adverse events as a result of their socio-structural position. Brown and Harris (1978) surveyed 458 randomly selected women aged between 18 and 65 living in Camberwell. They studied the relationship between the incidence of severe life events ("provoking agents") and difficulties, the presence of certain "vulnerability factors", and the onset of depression. They discovered that "working class women have a three times greater chance of having at least one severe household event". These results are shown in Tables 6.1 and 6.2.

Masuda and Holmes (1978) reviewed 19 studies carried out in a variety of cultures with varied groups of subjects, all of which employed their Social Readjustment Rating Scale to measure the amount of change subjects feel certain events demand, and their Schedule of Recent Events, measuring the frequency of events. They assert (p.237) that:

> Peoples of different characteristics and cultures not only perceive differently the significance of life events, but also report a difference in the quality and quantity of life event occurrences ... life events that happen to people, as well as how they are perceived, are a reflection of their life style and culture.

Their review, some of the results of which are summarised in Table 6.3, discovered that people below the age of 30 experienced raised frequencies of life events, that certain events—such as serious illness and loss of spouse—occurred more frequently among women, whereas

TABLE 6.1

Life Events Occurrence to Camberwell (London) Women by Type of Event, Social Class and Presence of Child at Home (Brown & Harris, 1978)

			With Child %		Without Child %		Total %
Household	Middle	24	(29/120)	12	(12/98)	19	(41/218)
	Working	41	(63/154)	21	(18/86)	34	(81/240)
		p <0.001		n.s.		p <0.001	
Health	Middle	15	(18/120)	23	(23/98)	19	(41/218)
	Working	29	(45/154)	34	(29/86)	31	(74/240)
		p <0.001		n.s.		p <0.001	
Other	Middle	3	(3/120)	13	(13/98)	7	(16/218)
	Working	4	(6/154)	12	(10/86)	7	(16/240)
		n.s.		n.s.		n.s.	
Total	Middle	36	(43/120)	41	(40/98)	38	(83/218)
	Working	59	(91/154)	48	(41/86)	61	(132/240)
		p <0.001		n.s.		p <0.001	

TABLE 6.2

Proportion of Camberwell Women Having at Least One Severe Event or
Major Difficulty by Class and Life Stage (Brown & Harris, 1978)

	Younger %	-6 %	6–14 %	15 + %	Older %	Total %
Middle class	40 (17/42)	29 (15/51)	42 (16/38)	39 (12/31)	45 (25/56)	39 (85/218)
Working class	76 (13/17) p <0.01	59 (34/58) p <0.001	58 (32/55) n.s.	54 (22/41) n.s.	52 (36/69) n.s.	57 (137/240) p <0.001
			p <0.001			

males more frequently experienced changes in working conditions,
minor law violations and troubles with the boss, and that members of
lower social classes are exposed to more unfavourable—though not more
favourable—events. "Age had the most significant effect, with the young
adult incurring greater amounts of life events ... There was also a
tendency for women ... and single individuals to incur more life events".

One of the methodological problems with many life events studies is
that they are retrospective and therefore there is the possibility that
event reporting is influenced by memory effects. A very large study from
New Zealand (Ferguson & Horwood, 1987) is not open to this criticism

TABLE 6.3

Variables Affecting Social Readjustment Rating Scale Item Scores [a]
(Masuda & Holmes, 1978)

Variable	Group Comparison	Items Scored Differently [b]	Direction of Higher Scores
Age	Young (N = 206) vs. middle-aged (N = 137)	8	5, young: 3, middle-aged
	Middle-aged vs. old (N = 51)	23	23, middle-aged
	Young vs. old	23	23, young
Sex	Male (N = 179) vs. female (N = 215)	16	16, female
Education	< College (N = 182) vs. ≥ college degree (N = 212)	25	24, < college: 1, ≥ college degree
Marital status	Ever-married (N = 223) vs. single (N = 171)	15	15, single

[a] N = 394.
[b] Mann-Whitney U Tests at <0.05 probability.

as it studied 1018 women prospectively over a 6 year period to explore vulnerability to life events exposure. Using a four-fold classification of social disadvantage, including education and family socio-economic status, the study (p.745) found that "life event exposure was highest among women from socially disadvantaged backgrounds".

Normative social–structural factors therefore are clearly implicated in the raised exposure to adverse events of those groups who predominate among self-poisoners, and it is well documented that self-poisoning is precipitated by an accumulation of adverse events in the months preceding it.

The paper most commonly referred to in the context of life events and self-poisoning is that of Paykel et al.(1975). They found that in the six months prior to their attempt, patients had experienced four times as many events as the general population sample and one-and-a-half times as many as a group of depressed patients. These results are shown in Table 6.4 taken from Paykel's paper. Among the "attempters" a peak of events occurred in the month before the attempt, which is a result found later by many others including Katschnig (1980) who achieved the same result when he simultaneously employed two different life event measures, both of which corroborated Paykel's findings. Figure 6.1 is taken from Katschnig's work and clearly demonstrates the peaking effect.

In addition to this discovery, Paykel and his colleagues offered one of the first classifications of events, suggesting that particularly important to parasuicides were "entrances and exits in the social field", events with "threatening implications" which are not defined, and undesirable and uncontrolled events—the latter being those such as "death of a close family member" and "serious physical illness". The single most reported event by attempters was argument with spouse, followed by having a new person in the home, serious illness of family member, serious personal physical illness, and having to appear in court for an offence.

The "intensity of upset" of events was found to be higher among attempters than either of the other groups. In this respect the summary of the study (Paykel et al., 1975, p.331) is concise and will be seen to have important implications to our later discussion: "It was the more threatening categories of uncontrolled events and events rated as upsetting that were reported more by suicide attempters than depressives".

Sex Differences in Precipitant Events

Paykel did not discuss gender differences in precipitant events: however there is ample evidence that such differences exist and that they have

TABLE 6.4
Frequency and Type of Event Preceding Self-poisoning (Paykel et al., 1975)

Event	Frequencies of Individual Events[a] Groups			Significances[b]		
	Suicide Attempters	Depressives	General Population	Suicide Attempters vs General Population	Suicide Attempters vs Depressives	Depressives vs General Population
Serious arguments with spouse	19	8	0	<0.001	<0.05	<0.001
New person in home	11	4	0	<0.001	NS	NS
Serious illness of close family member (spouse, child, parent, sibling, or fiance)	17	7	4	<0.01	<0.05	NS
Serious personal physical illness (in hospital or 1 mo off work)	15	5	1	<0.01	NS	NS
Court appearance for offence	10	4	2	<0.05	NS	NS
Lawsuit	7	1	1	NS	NS	NS
Moving house	15	16	7	NS	NS	NS
Engagement	7	0	4	NS	<0.05	<0.05
Marital separation due to discord	6	9	2	NS	NS	NS
Start new type of work	5	8	1	NS	NS	NS
Pregnancy	4	3	1	NS	NS	NS
Unemployed for 1 mo	5	3	3	NS	NS	NS
Divorce	3	1	0	NS	NS	NS
Major financial problems (very heavy debt or bankruptcy)	3	3	1	NS	NS	NS
Death of close family member	2	2	0	NS	NS	NS
Family member leaves home	2	1	0	NS	NS	NS
Birth of child (for father)	2	1	0	NS	NS	NS
Stillbirth	2	2	1	NS	NS	NS
Birth of child (for mother)	2	2	1	NS	NS	NS

TABLE 6.4 (cont.)

Event	Frequencies of Individual Events[a] Groups			Significances[b]		
	Suicide Attempters	Depressives	General Population	Suicide Attempters vs General Population	Suicide Attempters vs Suicide Depressives	Depressives vs General Population
Son drafted into armed forces	1	0	0	NS	NS	NS
Marriage	1	1	1	NS	NS	NS
Child engaged	0	1	0	NS	NS	NS
Child married	0	1	0	NS	NS	NS
Change of school, college or university	0	2	0	NS	NS	NS
Retirement	0	0	0	NS	NS	NS
Demotion	0	0	0	NS	NS	NS
Jail sentence	0	0	0	NS	NS	NS
Business failure	0	0	0	NS	NS	NS
Fired	0	1	1	NS	NS	NS
Promotion	0	1	1	NS	NS	NS
Finish full-time education	0	0	3	NS	NS	NS
Major change in work conditions (new department or boss or big reorganisation)	2	11	7	NS	<0.05	NS

[a]Number of subjects reporting each event at least once.
[b]By x2 analysis with Yates' correction.

159

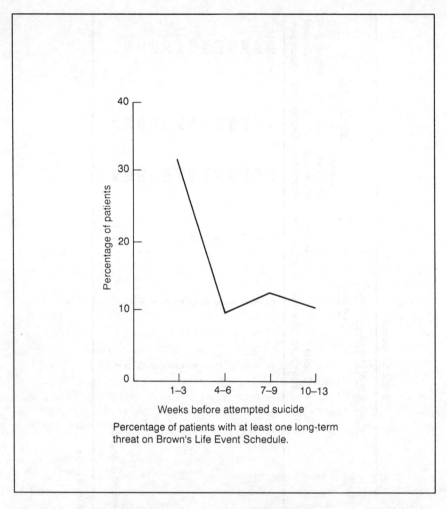

FIG. 6.1. Self-poisoning and life events—time and frequency of occurrence (Katschnig, 1980).

been a consistent feature of self-poisoning behaviour through the generations. Commentary from the late-19th and early-20th centuries, which we have already considered in other contexts, clearly noted this sex difference in precipitants and Tables 6.5 and 6.6, taken from two such accounts, illustrate them well. Those events associated with female self-poisoning are usually of a familial or relational type, and those with men of an extrafamilial type such as unemployment, criminal behaviour, and financial.

The different types of concern have more recently been described as "expressive" and "affiliative" in relation to women, and "instrumental"

TABLE 6.5
Precipitating Causes of Suicidal Attempts—Liverpool 1932–1935
(Hopkins, 1937)

Cause	Females	Males
Mental disorder	12	20
Domestic stress	18	12
Business or economic stress	8	12
Physical ill-health	8	5
Alcohol	5	8
Unemployment	none	6
Amatory disturbances	9	none
Old age and loneliness	1	1
Impending police charge, or fear of	1	2
Pregnancy, or fear of	2	..
Bravado	..	1

or "achievement oriented" in relation to men, and, turning to contemporary accounts the enduring nature of this gender division becomes apparent.

Aaron Beck et al. (1973) studied a series of 240 attempted suicides in Philadelphia and found that most were female. Unlike many of their contemporaries they specifically note that this fact renders sex differences worth exploring, and compared them on 58 variables finding that there was a sex difference on 16 of them—notably, the males were more often never married, had sought medical care less frequently in the previous six months, had more legal problems and job changes, and they reported less interpersonal friction than females. The authors concluded (p.966) that:

(The female) suicidal acts were more frequently attributed to interpersonal problems than were the males. The findings lend support to the notion that male attempts stem from performance motives (Failure to achieve particular goals) ...

Similar findings are reported by Weissman (1974) who found that unemployment and disappointment with work were related to male attempts; Bancroft et al. (1977, see Table 6.7) and Morgan (1980). In a study of completed and attempted suicides referred to the Los Angeles Suicide Prevention Centre, Wold (1971) identified two groups of suicidal women, one of which he refers to as "the discarded woman". These women had experienced repeated rejection by men, for example through divorce, had felt rejected by their parents and felt failures as women.

In Scotland, Fraser and Lawson (1975) reported on a survey of female self-poisoners seen between 1965 and 1973, establishing that 83.9% had

TABLE 6.6
Precipitating Causes of Suicidal Attempts—Detroit 1927–1930 (Lendrum, 1933)

Motives	Male		Female	
Reasons not given	86		107	
Denied		2		7
Refused to tell		6		13
Died before reason could be obtained		15		18
Released before reason could be obtained		18		44
No reason except mental condition		45		25
Motives				
Economic	119		93	
Unemployment		66		28
Unemployment of mate		0		11
Financial difficulties		25		41
Failure of business		2		2
Robbed		1		3
Debts		10		4
Gambling losses		8		0
Loss in stock crash		2		0
Eviction		1		3
Other economic reasons		4		1
Marital	98		244	
Quarrel with mate		48		148
Drunkenness of mate		1		20
Infidelity of mate		7		15
Sexual incompatibility		0		2
Jealousy		4		16
Beaten by mate		0		11
Deserted		19		22
Separation and divorce		19		10
Love	23		57	
Quarrel with lover		12		42
Jilted		7		12
Unrequited love		4		3
Domestic discord	14		61	
Friction with parent		4		25
Friction with child		3		3
Trouble with in-laws		2		14
Other quarrels with family or friends		5		17
Fear of whipping		0		2
Legal difficulties	31		18	
In jail on narcotic charge		10		3
In jail for forgery		5		1
In jail for other charge		12		3

TABLE 6.7
Precipitating Causes of Self-Poisoning—Oxford, 1977 (Bancroft et al., 1977)

		Marital	Boy/ girlfriend	Sex	Children	Religious	Financial	Work self	Work spouse	Accident operation	Other
Male	% of total	(n=39)	38	26	15	8	0	25.5	54	0	2.5	20.5
	% of those applicable	(n=18)	83	77	—	17	—	—	—	—	—	—
Female	% of total	(n=91)	43	26	14	15	2	16.5	16.5	5.5	19	15
	% applicable	(n=57)	68	70.5	—	26	—	—	—	—	—	—
Combined	% total	(n=130)	41.5	26	14.5	13	1.5	19	28	4	14	17
	% applicable	(n=75)	72	72	—	26	—	—	—	—	—	—

163

experienced marital disharmony, and that 11.8% of their sample of under 25 year olds were already divorced.

Slater and Depue's (1981) study of self-poisoners draws together the strands of uncontrollable events, affiliation, social support and hopelessness. They discovered that significantly more attempters than controls lacked confidant support, i.e. were living alone or only with children under the age of sixteen. Seventy-five per cent of this subgroup of attempters who were without confidant support were so because of an exit event that occurred during the study period. The authors conclude (p.248):

... we believe that the attempt-event association found in the study is a robust finding ... The role of social support as a moderating variable in suicidal risk ... is further suggested by its relative absence in the attempter group and by the fact that a high percentage of controls who suffered losses had other important sources of support with whom they lived. If events do increase the risk of suicide, our data further suggest that exit events, where an important social support is lost to the patient, may play a particularly significant role in initiating an attempt ... (and) may be a powerful contributor to the feelings of hopelessness that are frequently associated with suicidal behaviour.

Paykel et al. (1975) concluded the study referred to above in this way (p.333):

... events (cannot) be postulated as the sole cause of the suicide attempt. The same events are often experienced by others without any suicidal acts eventuating. It must be the interaction between event and personality, or the manner in which the stress is dealt with, that is ultimately crucial in determining the self-destructive consequence.

This suggestion of an interaction between personality and event echoes Alloy's assertion in our opening paragraph of an interaction between specific types of event and the attributional style of the individual, leading to "hopelessness", and a "specific vulnerability" in certain content areas. There seems little doubt that women are specifically vulnerable in relation to adverse events in the affiliative domain, and the possibility of a relationship between this content area and the commonly observed female attributional style is not without support from other sources.

Early Life Events and the Origins of Helplessness

In England in 1982 a study of 50 adolescent self-poisoners found that 48% were from broken homes as opposed to only 16% in a sample of the general population—and, although a series of consecutive admissions to a hospital, they were 90% female (Hawton, O'Grady, Osborne, & Cole, 1982c). Those events most frequently categorised by researchers as "uncontrollable" involve death and separation and it has repeatedly been found that early parental loss characterises parasuicides. Thus Goldney (1981b) reported an Australian series of 110 women self-poisoners aged 18–30 who were compared with a control group of women attending a community health centre. The self-poisoners experienced significantly more childhood loss through separation or divorce (though not loss through death) had more childhood stress due to broken homes, quarrelling parents or frequent disagreements between themselves and their parents, and they also had negative perceptions of their parents.

Goldney's findings are supported by those of numerous other studies in America (Crook & Raskin, 1975), New Zealand (Werry & Pedder, 1976), and Scotland (Birtchnell, 1970). Greer (1966) found that such patients had experienced parental loss through death, divorce or separation four times as commonly as had non-suicidal patients. Batchelor and Napier (1953) reported that 100% of male and female parasuicides aged 10–19 came from broken homes, and they also found sex differences in the experiences of loss, such that between the ages of 20–39 women had experienced this 20% more frequently than had men. Batchelor and Napier, unlike many other commentators, sought to draw theoretical connections between this early experience of parent loss and those current difficulties in relationships which precipitated self-poisoning, suggesting that (p.106):

> We may suppose that a broken home tends to render the individual less adaptable and, therefore, more vulnerable to the stresses of adult life and in particular less able to deal satisfactorily with personal relationships.

Martin Seligman (1975) in an early account of his theory of learned helplessness succinctly described such a dynamic in this way:

> Absence of mother, stimulus deprivation, and non-responsive mothering all contribute to the learning of uncontrollability ... Since, however, helplessness in an infant is the foundational motivational attitude which

later motivational learning must crystallize, its debilitating consequences will be more catastrophic.

Brown and Harris draw on Seligman's early model when discussing the implications of early loss events and their uncontrollable nature for current coping (Brown & Harris, 1978, p.256). They describe early parent loss as a "vulnerability factor" in relation to the onset of depression following the occurrence of adverse events, and particularly noted its incidence among attempted suicides in their patient sample. They found that those of their subjects who had attempted suicide had a higher incidence of such experience. The early experience of the uncontrollability of such outcomes, they propose, leads to a sense of powerlessness and helplessness in the face of adverse events in adulthood, a proposal evocative of Beck's hopelessness theory of self-poisoning.

Family and relational problems—particularly those perceived as uncontrollable—have therefore been found to characterise the events which occur immediately prior to self-poisoning in women. Our earlier attributional analysis of female self-poisoning provided a theoretical account of the attributional basis of this perceived uncontrollability and that analysis emphasised the normative origins of the negative female attributional style in the sex role system. The studies described above point to the exacerbation of the sense of non-contingency from which such a style may originate by non-normative loss experiences particularly prevalent among this population. Although slender sex differences have been found in the incidence of such early loss experiences, this alone cannot account for the significant excess of women among self-poisoners and the particular "threatfulness" of adverse affiliative events to them. Other sources of this "specific vulnerability" must therefore be sought and the relationship between adverse events in this sphere and the negative attributional style of female self-poisoners explored further.

AFFILIATION, GENDER, AND SEX ROLE STEREOTYPES

Masuda and Holmes (1978, p.250) assert:

> The individual's perceptions of the significance and impact of life events are clearly tempered by the uniqueness of his nature and environmental experience ...

They continue:

> ... culture ... ascribes an inferior role to the female in the whole of their development as to their reasoning performance capacity, but allowing for a separate role as a person acting more from "heart" than from "mind". If it is accepted that society has imposed a negative streotypic role on women, and if they, in general, have accepted it, then women are perceived to be freer to be more feeling than thinking. Such a psychological set might allow life events to be perceived by women as having greater emotional impact, whereas in men this might be inhibited as less congruent to the masculine stereotype.

There is considerable evidence of widely held stereotypic views of the female role. The extent of such stereotyping was described in the work of Broverman and her colleagues during the early-1970s. It was found that consistent results were obtained with a variety of subjects ranging from nuns to college students, to the effect that a strong consensus existed as to how men and women are different; characteristics ascribed to men are positively valued more often than those ascribed to women; positively valued masculine traits entail competence, rationality and assertion; positively valued female traits reflect warmth and expressiveness; both males and females incorporated these definitions into their own self-concepts.

Sandra Bem a few years later furthered this work with the development of her Sex Role Inventory, a measure subsequently used by herself and others to determine the relationship between sex role stereotypes and a variety of psychological states and behaviours, such as self-esteem, performance on ability tests, and levels of emotional well-being. Bem asserted that males and females potentially possessed both masculine and feminine qualities and that high levels of "androgeny" (i.e. the capability to display both masculine and feminine traits in appropriate situations) are psychologically healthy. However women, under the influence of cultural expectations to display qualities of nurturance, compassion and submission, supress the masculine facets of their character in order to maintain their femininity and are therefore at a disadvantage in competitive situations and those calling for assertiveness or appropriate aggression (Bem, 1975).

This was a theme discussed earlier by Horner (1972) in her Fear of Success model of female achievement whereby success in stereotypic male activities is felt to threaten femininity, thus motivating women to avoid success. More recently Williams and Best (1982) found similar clusters of characteristics identified as more frequently associated with women and men respectively. These clusters corresponded to the male "instrumental", female "expressive" distinction noted in earlier research. Susan Keyes (1984) has produced evidence of the ubiquity of such stereotypes, not only within cultures, but across them. Earlier American studies on commonly held sex role stereotypes were repeated with English subjects and (p.178) : "Results ... indicate the general, though not perfect, similarity of gender stereotypes in the United States and Britain".

It seems that to regard herself as "feminine", and be so regarded by others, a woman must show herself competent in relationships with others—especially children and men. Sex role stereotypes are the product of socialisation, not biology, and a review of the literature on this process of socialisation by Hoffman (1975) offers the following explanation for the emergence of affiliation as a major motivating force in women (p.136):

> It is our theory that the female child is given inadequate parental encouragement in early independence strivings. Furthermore, the separation of the self from the mother is more delayed or incomplete for the girl because she is the same sex with the same sex role expectations, and because girls have fewer conflicts with their parents. As a result she does not develop confidence in her ability to cope independently with the environment. She retains her infantile fears of abandonment; safety and effectiveness lie in her affective ties.

Convincing support for Hoffman's contentions comes from the extensive longitudinal study of 700 British children carried out by John and Elizabeth Newson (Newson & Newson, 1976). They referred to the importance of differences in "chaperonage" and stated (p.100):

> ... by the age of seven, and in a whole variety of ways, the daily experience of little boys in terms of where they are allowed to go, how they spend their time and to what extent they are kept under adult surveillance is already markedly different from that of little girls.

Hoffman (1975) suggests (p.135) on the basis of such evidence that when little boys are:

> ... expanding their mastery strivings, learning instrumental independence, developing skills in coping with their environment and confidence in this ability, little girls are learning that effectiveness—and even safety—lie in their affectional relationships.

A review by Lewis (1986) of the most recent literature in this field, has conclusions broadly similar to those of Hoffman who wrote 10 years earlier. Lewis in fact concludes (p.111):

... many studies show that parents, especially fathers, treat boys and girls differently, even in the first two years of life ... Behavioural differences between boys and girls are apparent, even within the first year of life ... girls seem more person oriented ... boys tend to explore more.

An interesting developmental perspective comes from Helen Weinreich (1978) in her discussion of these potential consistencies and conflicts in sex role socialisation and its relationship to achievement motivation. This is particularly apposite to age patterns we have earlier noted in self-poisoning, with late adolescence being one peak in the incidence of self-poisoning for women, and the peak for men being in their early–mid twenties.

Weinreich proposes that conflicts arise for girls at puberty when it has been observed that the tolerance of cross gender behaviour—tomboyishness—until this age more acceptable in girls than boys, becomes no longer acceptable. Whereas parents, particularly fathers, actively prohibit "cissy" behaviour in boys at an early age, such prohibitions come at adolescence for girls, leading to sharp role discontinuity. Her socialisation into the stereotypic female traits of tenderness, nurturance and dependence may then conflict with those required in her entry to the work role. The discontinuity for males comes later with their entry to the family role when they find that the "instrumental" masculine traits they have received through their socialisation conflict with the more feminine traits of expressiveness and nurturance required in the family role. Weinreich (1978, p.26) refers to the work of Broverman described earlier to extend this analysis, asserting that girls approaching adulthood are placed in the:

... conflictual position of having to decide whether to exhibit those positive characteristics considered desirable for men and adults, and thus have their "femininity" questioned, that is be deviant in terms of being a woman, or to behave in the prescribed female manner, accept second class adult status and possibly live a lie to boot.

This evocation of the conflicts surrounding the entry of young girls to adult female status is reminiscent of Phyllis Chesler's (1972, pp.46–47) typically dramatic description of the meaning of female self-poisoning:

Female suicide attempts are not so much realistic calls for help or hostile inconveniencing of others, as the assigned baring of the powerless throat, signals of ritual readiness for self-sacrifice. Like female tears, female suicide attempts constitute an essential act of resignation and helplessness—which alone can command temporary relief or secondary rewards. Suicide attempts are the grand rites of "femininity"—i.e. ideally women are supposed to "lose" in order to "win".

Weinreich's analysis provides us with a dynamic model of sex role socialisation and achievement motivation in terms of the changing significance of this socialisation for males and females through the years of their development to adult status, and has explanatory power in relation to the age structure of the self-poisoning phenomenon, it also lends added significance to Hoffman's (1975, p.144) concluding assertion that: "The anticipation of being alone and unloved, then, may have a particularly desperate quality in women".

SELF-CONCEPT, ROLES, AND ATTRIBUTIONS

Brown and Harris developed a theoretical model which brought together the various facets of social class, gender, coping style and the importance of affiliative factors. They suggested that working class women, due to their more frequent experience of early parental loss and contemporary exposure to higher levels of adverse events and difficulties, were possessed of a cognitive set characterised by feelings of powerlessness and a lack of control. This undermined their self-esteem and resulted in their higher incidence of clinical depression, although such feelings, as we have noted, were so ubiquitous among working class women as to lead the authors to wonder as to the legitimacy of describing it as an illness, and when Beck and his colleagues discovered analogous feelings of hopelessness among self-poisoners it was frequently in the absence of clinical depression (Beck et al., 1975b).

In their concluding chapter, Brown and Harris (1978) emphatically point to the implications of sex role socialisation in their model when describing the importance, as the crucial vulnerability factor, of the unsupportive relationships experienced by these women, when they face accumulated adverse events. The low levels of "intimacy" which they showed was characteristic of what others have described as the "especially oppressive" nature of working class marriage, and is said to critically undermine the self esteem of working class women whose husband they assert (p.287):

... is usually the main source of a woman's sense of achievement ... It will be remembered that the risk of depression was greatest among working class women with children at home, for whom a sense of achievement would be most closely related to their roles as mother and wife. She needs to be told she is doing well to refurbish her sense of self-worth ... His acceptance that there are difficulties and frustrations legitimises the experiences of pervasive irritation and unhappiness felt by many women about the routine care of children and helps them to accept that this does not reflect on themselves. In general his support helps a woman to create a rewarding idea of herself.

This contention that women's sense of self-worth and personal identity is derived from her relationship with men is afforded considerable empirical support in the literature of sex role socialisation, and in the accounts of female self-poisoners quoted in an earlier chapter derived from O'Brien's (1986) work. That self-poisoning women lack alternative roles from which to reinforce their self-concept is convincingly demonstrated in a recent Dutch study by Bille-Brahe and Wang (1985) from Odense University in Denmark. They assessed levels of social integration among parasuicides in terms of involvement with family, with community activities and occupational integration in terms of employment activity and work satisfaction. Their conclusions included the following (p.168):

Integration in the community was poor for 72% of the men and 85% of the women in the suicide attempter sample, as opposed to only 12% of the men and 25% of the women in the normal population.

They had earlier noted that:

More than half the men (55%) and 62% of the women in the suicide attempter sample were below the average level of occupational integration, while only 11% of the men but 50% of the women in the normal population were below the average level ... in the normal population, then, women were more poorly integrated than men, while in the suicide attempter sample there was no significant difference between sexes for degree of integration.

Very young women in the attempter sample showed very low levels of integration, whereas in the normal population they were particularly highly integrated. In addition they found that (p.169):

... even those of the suicide attempters who were occupationally active were poorly integrated in their work environment ... 80% of the working suicide attempters felt they had little or no influence at their place of work. In the normal population the figure was 50%.

The importance of the threatened self-concept to the instigation of psychological distress is elaborated in a recent paper by Oatley and Bolton (1985) who seek to further Brown and Harris's (1978) model of depression as being a result of the combination of provoking agents and vulnerability factors. This theoretical discussion has many points of relevance to our own interests in that Oatley and Bolton propose that the type of events identified as provoking agents in Brown and Harris, as well as in Paykel's work with parasuicides, are those which involve threats to the "sense of self"—frequently social exit events. The vulnerability factors, as we have seen in our earlier discussion, include the lack of an intimate and confiding relationship with husband or boyfriend. They propose that the individual builds a self-concept upon the mutual interactions and exchanges involved in key roles. When the continuance or veridicality of this role or roles is threatened by events or the breakdown of mutuality with others involved in the performance of the role, then the valuation of self that the role supports collapses. If, however, the individual has several roles, all of which contribute to this self-definition then this threat can be warded off. The authors elaborate in this way (Oatley & Bolton, 1985, p.377):

> Brown and Harris supposed that a woman's idea of herself is dependent on her role as, for instance, a mother. Seeing herself as a good mother may therefore be threatened by events such as her only child becoming a drug addict or getting into serious trouble with the police. In such circumstances, being without an alternative role of being a loved wife or having a job outside the home, for example, would make the woman vulnerable to the threatening event. It might make her feel like a failure in all aspects of her life and thus feel completely hopeless.

It is evident that what Bille-Brahe and Wang term "social integration" equates with the occupation of disparate, alternative roles through which individuals may maintain their self-concept. This equation is made by Oatley and Bolton who refer to several prospective studies of psychological distress in relation to life events which demonstrate that lack of social interaction, which they equate with alternative sources of roles which conceivably provide "a sense of self-hood", predicts raised levels of distress in the face of adversity. They relate the provisional results of their own prospective study of the relationship between social interaction outside work and levels of depression after redundancy in a sample of 49 men whom they compared over a 6-month period, with a matched control group of 49 employed men. They discovered (p.376) that, although there was no significant relationship between depression and levels of social interaction outside work among the employed men, in the unemployed: "... depression was significantly predicted by small amounts of social interaction outside working hours in the month before the first interview".

This is interpreted by Oatley and Bolton as supporting their theory of depressive onset in the face of adverse events in that males without alternative sources of self-validation, whose identity and self-hood was bound up entirely in their work role, literally suffered a loss of the sense of self and became depressed as a result when they lost this primary role. Of particular relevance to our own attributional approach to self-poisoning is their description of those vulnerability factors which, following a provoking agent, expose the subject to the full syndrome of depression. This occurs (p.382) if he or she:

... lacks (a) at least one secondary role relationship that gives a convincing sense of a worthwhile self; (b) strategies and circumstances conducive to generating new role relationships; and (c) the ability to take part in activities felt to be satisfying irrespective of the presence of a satisfactory role other.

This may be restated in attributional terms to equate with the lack of alternative sources of self-esteem, negative attributional style and its associated affective, cognitive and performance deficits, and the dependence of the female self-image on heterosexual relationships which we have suggested are characteristic vulnerability factors in female self-poisoners. The relevance of this model to our own is further reinforced by the following assertion (by Antonovsky, 1985, p.385) on the nature of vulnerability to psychological distress—in this context depression—quoted by Oatley and Bolton:

Antonovsky argued that pathogens and life events are ubiquitous. They can be reduced but not prevented. The real question of epidemiology is not how such factors cause illness, but how, amid them, many people achieve health. His answer is that people who achieve psychological and physical health are those who have a sense of coherence in that (a) they find their own reactions and the reactions of those with whom they interact to be relatively predictable, and (b) they find their lives meaningful.

This, it is our contention, constitutes the vulnerability of certain groups of women to self-poisoning. These are women who, because of their learned helplessness and negative attributional style, do not experience that sense of contingency which is necessary in Antonovsky's view to psychological well-being, and have invariably suffered the loss of a relationship through which they attributed meaning to their lives.

Elsewhere the authors, alluding to the similarities between their conceptions and those of the reformulated model of learned helplessness, suggest that there is an issue of "control" in their approach, although they are concerned to point out that control is here used in the sense of the "control of the stability of relationships". They assert that (Oatley & Bolton, 1985, p.384):

> More important than control is the achievement of a degree of predictability that allows mutual plans that satisfy self-definition goals to be carried through, and that allows a person to build a life of meaning within mutually generated rules and understandings. The sense of meaningfulness and coherence that Antonovsky argued is essential for long-term health, requires that people can make sense of their lives.

This is reminiscent of the work by Adrian Parker (1981) who described a repertory grid study of suicidal behaviour, and suggested (p.307) that a personal construct perspective on suicidal behaviour indicates that it is: "... a response to unpredictability, chaos and sudden loss of understanding of one's world".

Also similar are Landfield's earlier assertions from the same personal construct perspective when he proposes (Landfield, 1976, pp.94–95):

> The central units of meaning with personal construct theory are defined by the contrasting ways of understanding life events employed by the individual as he tries to make sense of his experience ... A personal construct interpretation of suicidal behaviour points to an individual's anticipation of chaos and potential breakdown of the system he employs for encompassing, interpreting and relating to events which are primarily social in nature. The imminence of breakdown in one's construct system is the instigating context of suicidal behaviour ... Suicidal behaviour will occur in the context of a decreasing ability to make sense of, interpret or react to one's personal world, most importantly, a personal world of people.

We have proposed that, in relation to female self-poisoning, attribution theory provides a particularly fruitful way of conceptualising what Landfield describes as the "... ability to make sense of, interpret or react to one's personal world". The theoretical model of the importance of alternative roles to the cognitive process involved in the development of psychological distress offered by Oatley and Bolton may be interpreted in attributional terms.

Harold Kelley, in an early exposition of attribution theory, proposed that the individual employs three types of information in arriving at causal attributions about whether internal or external attributions for behaviour and events are made. Information about how often the actor had done the action in similar circumstances elsewhere in the past, which is termed "consistency information"; how often the actor performed the same sort of action in different circumstances, termed "distinctiveness information"; and how many other people did that sort of thing in those sort of circumstances, which Kelley called "consensus information" (Kelley, 1967).

In his principle of covariation, Kelley suggested that all this information was brought logically to bear on one question—did the behaviour covary with the actor? That is, did the events occur if and only if that actor was there to perform them? If the result of this search for information was that the actor was frequently present when such events occurred in different settings then an internal attribution to a disposition of the actor is more likely than an external attribution to that actor's circumstances.

In the case of the woman in Oatley and Bolton's example, if the woman had alternative roles in which she might experience success, then it would be less likely that she would make internal attributions relating to her own inadequacy as a housewife and mother to explain the behaviour of her son. This is because, although her alleged dispositional tendency to be an inadequate person should always be present, no such outcomes had occurred to her in other situations. Whereas, if she only has the one key role from which to derive attributional information, it is likely that the information would tell her that similar failure outcomes had occurred in relation to her son previously (consistency), that she had reacted similarly to them (distinctiveness), and that other people probably reacted differently, as such outcomes are not the norm (a lack of consensus). Given this information an internal attribution is inevitable, and therefore such an outcome might indeed - "... make her feel like a failure in all aspects of her life and thus feel completely hopeless".

CAUSES OF CAUSAL ATTRIBUTION

Returning to Alloy's concern to match attributional style and situational cues in the specific vulnerability hypothesis of learned hopelessness, it was suggested that (Alloy et al., 1988, p.9):

Over the past 20 years, social psychologists have conducted studies showing that people's causal attributions for events are, in part, a function of the situational information they confront ... people would be predicted to make internal, stable and global attributions for an event when they are confronted with situational information suggesting that the event is low in consensus (e.g. typically failing a maths exam when others do well), high in consistency (e.g. typically failing exams in maths), and low in distinctiveness (e.g. typically failing exams in other subjects as well as maths). Thus informational cues present in a particular situation constrain the attribution process by making some attributions for particular life events more plausible than others and some not plausible at all ... Social psychologists have identified a number of additional factors that may also guide the causal attribution process including ... the motivation to protect or enhance one's self-esteem, focus of attention, salience of a potential causal factor and self-presentational concerns.

We have addressed the significance of the ego-enhancing and self-presentational functions of attributions and suggested that these may conflict with their "information processing", or "mastery" function. Our discussion of the particular importance of affiliative events to women has emphasised their salience—all these influences may be seen as constraining the attribution process in self-poisoning women, increasing the probability of helplessness and hopelessness in the face of adverse affiliative events, and promoting their specific vulnerability in this content domain. However, there are still other factors, not included in Alloy's paper, which exacerbate this vulnerability and also support the notion of a match between negative attributional style and adverse affiliative events.

These factors relate first to the nature of events which have been shown to instigate causal search; and secondly to the possibility that the possession of a particular attributional style itself encourages the individual to engage in such search.

Paul Wong and Bernard Weiner (1981) remind the reader that most authors in the field of attribution theory have not suggested that individuals are constantly engaged in attributional search, but that individuals carry with them sets of beliefs, or causal schemata, as to how various causes and effects are related. Thus if our experiences conform to our beliefs, or schemata, then there is no need to engage in causal search. The authors give the example that "aptitude" is regarded as a relatively stable attribute in our culture and that students with proven aptitude, say in maths, are expected to do well in that subject. If they then do well, if the causal schemata of the relationship between aptitude and success, cause and effect, is not challenged by experience, then there would be no need for attributional search. On the contrary, however, if a student with a demonstrable aptitude did fail, then there would be a disjunction between the causal schemata and the experience which would demand explanation and instigate causal search.

Wong and Weiner therefore propose that "expectancy disconfirmation instigates attribution processes". They suggest (p.651) that causal search may be considered as one aspect of the more general exploratory behaviours known to be instigated by novel or unexpected events, and that in addition to expectancy disconfirmation:

"... frustration (failure) is hypothesised to be a ... potent instigator of the attribution process. The law of effect dictates that organisms are motivated to terminate or prevent a negative state of affairs. But effective coping importantly depends on locating the cause(s) of failure. In this case, attribution serves an adaptive function. In support of this line of reasoning there is evidence that rejection in an affiliative context is more likely to elicit attributional search and information seeking than is acceptance.

In a series of experiments involving students, subjects were asked to imagine themselves in several different failure and success situations, which might be expected or unexpected given the information with which they were furnished, and then asked to write down what questions, if any, they would most likely ask themselves in such a situation. They were told not to write anything if such enquiries would not characterise their thinking. It was found that subjects did engage in attributional search and that failure and unexpected outcomes generated more attributional questions than did success and expected outcomes.

Wong and Weiner in their conclusions suggest that there is therefore ample reason to believe that people spontaneously engage in attributional search, that this is more likely after failure and unexpected outcomes, but also that such search is likely after "personal tragedy, interpersonal conflict etc.", with "novel and unknown effects having a similar instigating effect". They refer to Hastie's findings in support of this—Hastie (1984) having discovered that "incongruent" acts were more likely to lead to attributional search by an observer than were acts which were congruent with an individual's perceived traits. Very important from our point of view is their assertion from this (Wong & Weiner, 1981, p.661) that: "Events of great personal importance may also be an effective antecedent for attribution".

Later, in a 1985 review of the literature pertaining to spontaneous causal thinking, Weiner (1985, p.75), finding 17 studies, proposed that: "The findings allow rather unequivocal conclusions and lay to rest the uncertainty about the prevalence of attributional thinking in everyday life. In addition, there is agreement on the conditions which promote attributional search".

Pointing out that much of the experimental work involved hypothesised situations pertaining to marital problems, job loss and ineffectiveness and other important outcomes, Weiner returns to his earlier suggestion in stating (p.83): "One might hypothesise, for example, that information pertinent to the self is especially prone to engage attributional processes".

It has become apparent that Weiner's conclusions about the nature of those events which are most likely to instigate causal search, and those of Parker and Landfield in relation to the precipitants of parasuicide, point convincingly to those events which have been shown to be associated with female self-poisoning—unexpected, uncontrollable events in the affiliative realm, often involving incongruent behaviour of a loved one, and being particularly important to the self definition of the woman concerned. Several studies have demonstrated that the effects of a dysfunctional (or what Alloy refers to as a "depressogenic") attributional style are similar in relation to affiliative events as to those in the achievement domain, with which most of the empirical work has been concerned. Thus, in a recent paper, Bernard Weiner (1986) reported and reviewed the results of several studies of attributions in the affiliative sphere among adults, involving attributions for social rejection and for loneliness, and concluded (p.197): "... the findings in the achievement area replicated perfectly in the affiliative domain ... the causes of social failure (are) found to be similar to the dimensions uncovered in achievement contexts".

AFFILIATION AND THE "SPECIFIC VULNERABILITY" HYPOTHESIS

Empirical support for the adverse effects of a dysfunctional attributional style in females coping with interpersonal situations comes from the findings of several studies reported by Dweck and Goetz.

Noting that a great deal of the study of learned helplessness and attribution had focussed on failure in achievement situations, such as academic success and failure, Dweck and Goetz suggest that in the same way that intellectual failures can be met with a variety of responses, so too can social rejection. Thus they propose that such rejection may be met with a variety of strategies designed to reverse the rejection, or, on the contrary, with behaviour that represents a marked deterioration from the previous circumstances. They pose the question (Dweck & Goetz, 1978, p.173): do attributions guide the selection of coping patterns in social situations as well as in academic ones, and propose that helplessness resulting from non-contingency may indeed be demonstrated in interpersonal relationships: "For instance some popular children may interpret their few experiences with social rebuff as indications of permanent rejection not open to change by their actions".

Dweck and Goetz suggest that just as a failure attribution to some factors (such as effort) implies surmountability, so too do rejection attributions to misunderstanding. In addition it is proposed that blaming the rejector for interpersonal rejection is the same as blaming the evaluator for academic failure—as we have seen male children tend to do—whereas attributing the rejection to some enduring characteristic of oneself implies a relatively enduring outcome. They continue (p.174):

> Given the parallel implications for interpersonal and academic attributions, one would expect also parallel reactions and generalisation effects ... The data from over 100 children tested thus far indicate that individuals differ in consistent ways from one another in the causes to which they ascribe social rejection ... the data thus far indicate that there are striking differences in strategies for coping with interpersonal rejection. Responses range from mastery oriented patterns, with more and different strategies used after rejection, to complete withdrawal.

Unfortunately the results of this research were not reported according to sex of subject. These results, however, reward more detailed consideration because they gave rise to a further study which illuminates a match between the helpless attributional style of certain children and their propensity to engage in attributional activity.

The study involved children applying for a pen pal club by writing a letter which had to describe "what sort of person you are". Following this the children then received the club organiser's decision through the experimenter, in this case a rejection. The responses to rejection were then noted as the child is told he has a second chance to write to the club. It was found that about 10% of the rejected children could not come up with a second message to the club—not, that is, until the experimenter explicitly attributed the rejection to the club organiser, rather than to the personal qualities the child had described in the application letter, and told the children that the application would be processed by a different organiser. Those children who were initially helpless in the face of rejection favoured attributions that emphasised the insurmountability of rejection, whereas those children who were self-confident in their responses to the rejection emphasised the role of surmountable factors such as misunderstandings. The authors conclude (Dweck & Goetz, 1978, p.175): "... analysis of the attribution and coping measures suggests that individual differences in attribution are indeed systematically related to responses following rejection".

It will be recalled that in an earlier chapter the work of Lochel (1983) was described which dealt with the attributional process in four year old nursery school children. Lochel unequivocally concluded that girls demonstrated a helpless attributional style consistently more than did boys, which conclusion has important implications in relation to the second study by Dweck, this time in collaboration with Diener (Diener & Dweck, 1978).

This involved intellectual achievement and failure, and is interesting not only because it confirmed the existence of helpless versus mastery-oriented differences in attribution and task persistence, but also because, using an unstructured methodology designed to elicit spontaneous attributional activity, Diener and Dweck discovered that such attributional activity was far more prevalent among helpless rather than among mastery-oriented children. Thus, if it is permissible to apply these findings to the field of interpersonal relations, it seems that those children with the attributional style which least equips them to deal with rejection may be the ones who most frequently engage in attributional search following such rejection, thereby further exposing themselves to the affective, cognitive and motivational consequences of the possession of such a negative attributional style.

This contention finds support in Diener and Dweck's work which reported that helpless children showed a steady decline in the strategies they applied in the face of failure, whereas mastery-oriented ones demonstrated increased sophistication in their strategies. Prior to the failure experience the spontaneous verbalisations of all children tended to be similar—concentrating mainly on task strategy—but after failure experiences marked differences emerged. Whereas the helpless children quickly began to make attributions for their failures, attributing them to a lack or loss of ability and demonstrating negative affect in relation to the task, mastery-oriented children did not make attributions for failure, but rather engaged in "self-instruction and self-monitoring designed to bring about success", continuing to express positive beliefs about future outcomes, and to show positive affect. The succinct conclusions reached by the workers is:

It would appear that despite the feedback of the experimenter, the mastery-oriented children did not consider themselves to have failed.

They were making mistakes, to be sure, but they seemed certain that with the proper concentration and strategy they could get back on the track. Thus they dwelled on prescription rather than diagnosis, remedy rather than cause.

Although the suggestion that females who possess a helpless attributional style are more likely to engage in attributional search comes from studies based on children, similar findings have been described in adults. While not employing an attributional perspective this work may be seen as supporting this assertion, dealing, as it does, with gender differences in coping strategies.

Fleishman (1984) reviewed the literature on coping styles and reported several studies demonstrating that "problem focussed coping" reduces stress whereas "avoidance coping" actually increases it. These categories broadly conform to what Westbrook described as "instrumental" and "fatalistic" styles and, as we have seen, fatalism has strong conceptual links with helplessness. Fleishman found that those from higher socio-economic classes demonstrate greater mastery orientation, expecting their efforts to be effective in changing situations, they are more likely to engage in active problem focussed coping behaviour. Alternatively, those from less advantaged positions, believing their efforts to be potentially futile to alter events outside their control, demonstrate emotion focussed coping acts geared to reduce the anxiety evoked by the problem, for example by "looking on the bright side"—i.e. avoidance type behaviour, rather than confronting the problem itself. Fleishman describes passive acceptance and resignation as emotion focussed behaviours and states that people who are high in mastery eschew coping by denial or "reinterpretation".

In his own study, 2299 American adults completed scales measuring: mastery, which used 7 items such as "I have little control over the things that happen to me", as opposed to "I can do just about anything I set my mind to"; the Rosenberg Self Esteem Scale, whereby respondents expressed agreement or disagreement with items such as "I feel I have a number of good qualities" compared with "At times I think I am no good at all"; and a variety of other measures of denial, stress and coping syles, the latter identifying particular behaviours favoured by respondents when confronted with problems in different role situations such as marital and parental. His results included the finding that (p.239):

> ... compared with men, women more frequently use selective ignoring to deal with work and financial stress. In marriage and parenthood they seek advice more often and use other forms of passive coping, such as resignation and passive acceptance.

Fleishman draws support for his findings from the work of Billings and Moos (1981) as showing in particular that avoidance coping especially among women increases stress. Fleishman's proposals seem very close to those coping styles described in working class women by Westbrook and Mitchell (1979) and their effects in increasing, rather than diminishing, anxiety about childbirth. Although he established class differences in coping styles, Fleishman found that class had weaker effects than did sex in this respect. Of particular relevance to our earlier findings in relation to the different type of events associated with self-poisoning in males and females, and to Alloy's notion of a match between event and attributional style, is the author's assertion of the "specificity of influence" whereby different styles are evoked by different situations. Thus he proposed that people may have different perceptions of their ability to control the social (interpersonal) and non-social (work/finance) environments, and therefore coping styles will differ accordingly.

Richard Lazarus (1981), who extensively developed the concepts of emotion focussed and problem focussed coping, offers confirmation of this view in his proposal that (p.150):

> They represent two of the most important functions of coping, namely, that of changing a damaging or threatening relationship between person and environment (problem focussed) and regulating the emotional distress produced by that relationship (emotion focussed) ... in every complex stressful encounter people use a mixture of both kinds of coping. Moreover, when an encounter is appraised as permitting little or nothing to be done, there is a pull toward emotion focussed coping; and when it is appraised as permitting constructive actions, the shift is to problem focussed modes.

The work described earlier of Craig Anderson (1983) and Mario Mikulincer (1986) relating the adverse effects of internal, global attributions in the face of failure to attentional deficits and the neglect of strategy, and to off-task cognitions and self-preoccupation, clearly reinforces the findings of Fleishman and Lazarus and integrates them within our attributional model of coping skills deficits.

AFFILIATION, ATTRIBUTION, AND FEMALE SELF-POISONING

In view of the normative socialisation of women and the everyday experiences they encounter which promote a sense of non-contingency and powerlessness, and the non-normative loss experiences in early life which we have suggested further exacerbate this, it would be expected that female self-poisoners would display an emotion focussed coping style in Lazarus's terms. Such, indeed, were the findings of a study by Kreitman and Chowdhury (1973) from the Edinburgh Regional Posioning Treatment Centre.

Although gender divisions are by no means a central concern of the work, these authors reported a comparative study of the coping styles of those who rang the Samaritans as opposed to that of those who engaged in parasuicide. Their analysis of 121 help-seekers who rang the Samaritans, and 93 parasuicides admitted to the RPTC showed that almost 50% more males than females rang the Samaritans, whereas the ratio was reversed among those who self-poisoned. Reflecting the consistent finding of gender differences in problems presented, the study showed that 40% of female self-poisoners reported problems in relationships, compared with 22% of males, whereas 31% of males described employment problems compared with only 18% of females. This is not discussed but the authors concluded that there are significant sex differences in "distress behaviour" (pp.6–7):

... the apparently rational procedure of help-seeking is found to be resorted to more often among men ... while parasuicide is represented preponderantly by women. It might ... reflect a sex-linked preference for principally "instrumental" as against principally "expressive" activity, i.e. a desire to solve an objectifiable problem, in this case, by seeking advice and guidance, rather than by emotional appeal or attempting to intermit an intolerable state of mind.

The implications of these findings for our concern with gender variables in self-poisoning again become explicit. We have established that the hopelessness shown to be a definitive characteristic of self-poisoning is closely allied to helplessness in that both are based on the experience and expectancy of non-contingency. The recent reconsideration of the attributional model of learned helplessness by Alloy and others confirms this conceptual link in its argument, and, indeed, in its redesignation as the learned hopelessness theory. In this it is proposed that (Alloy et al., 1988, p.9):

... informational cues present in a particular situation constrain the attribution process by making some attributions for particular life events more plausible than others and some not plausible at all.

We have established considerable empirical support for the contention that a helpless, negative attributional style more commonly characterises females. If, therefore, helpless subjects do indeed engage in more attributional search—specifically in the face of failure in the affiliative realm as Weiner suggested, and as seems likely from the work of Oatley and Bolton, Parker, and Landfield—this would make females who have few alternative roles outside the affiliative realm particularly vulnerable to the hopelessness known to be associated with self-poisoning. They would engage in more attributional activity in the face of adverse affiliative events than males and the attributions resulting from their search would be, as we have seen from Kelley, Dweck and others, less favourable to adequate and persistent coping following failure. In this sense, therefore, the situational cues—adverse affiliative events in the absence of a diversity of alternative roles—and the possession of the characteristically female, helpless attributional style, would render internal, stable and global attributions for affiliative failure "more plausible than others".

Alloy et al. (1988) continue to elucidate the specific vulnerability hypothesis and the importance of "style based information processing" in this way (pp.16–17):

> Research in cognitive and social psychology offers some support for the view that a person's mode of thinking can differ across situations as a function of cognitive priming or activation ... This would be most likely in a situation in which the person has recently experienced a life event that is in some way analogous to depressogenic style-engendering situations of the past.

Thus the proposal in relation to female self-poisoning is that normative sex role socialisation engenders a helpless attributional style in women. Individuals with helpless attributional styles have been shown to engage in more causal search than others and women may therefore be more prone to the affective, motivational and performance deficits consequent on the possession of such a style. Those young, working class women with a non-normative history of family breakdown or losses who predominate among self-poisoners develop an extreme form of this style as a result of the uncontrollable non-contingency inherent in these experiences.

Not only, therefore, are such women in jeopardy because of their potential extreme helplessness, but they are in double jeopardy because those situations which have been shown most powerful in instigating the attribution process in women—due to the threat they pose to the self-concept—are those most analogous to the "depressogenic style-engendering situations" typical of the past of female self-poisoners. These are precisely those situations with which the helpless attributional style of women is least able to cope effectively. While the helplessness such a style promotes is functional in maintaining sex appropriate role relationships and the female self-concept based upon them within conventional, stable relationships, and in coping with failure in the achievement domain where failure and helplessness may even enhance their femininity, it is dysfunctional in defending and restoring the self-esteem and self-concept of the woman in the face of breakdown in those relationships.

In this sense, therefore, the attributional approach to female self-poisoning in the face of adverse affiliative events conforms to Alloy's contention quoted earlier to the effect that the:

> ... particular attributions people make for the specific negative events they experience are hypothesised to be a joint function of the situational information surrounding these events and their generalised attributional styles.

It may be fitting to conclude this theoretical account of the relationship between affiliation, attribution and female self-poisoning by recalling the words of one of the women patients interviewed by Sally O'Brien (1986, p.83):

> However career minded I or my friends are, we still cannot get away from the idea that our real measure of success is whether we have a man. Thus our feelings about ourselves are always dependent on another person. Women tend to blame themselves if things go wrong, whereas men tend to blame other people.

CHAPTER 7

An Attributional Model of Female Self-poisoning

Self-poisoning has an historical continuity which has been documented and, specifically since the late-19th century, there is convincing evidence that it has become a form of deviant behaviour more commonly engaged in by women. From the end of the Second World War until the late-1970s, in every western society, its prevalence increased dramatically and so too did the preponderance of women among its perpetrators. Despite this, gender has been a relatively neglected facet of the phenomenon, receiving little more than a passing reference in most of the voluminous literature devoted to its study during the past 30 years.

THE THEORY RESTATED
Gender Differences in Self-poisoning

There is ample reason to suppose that gender is an important variable, deserving of detailed consideration, not only because of the massive predominance of women among this population—amounting to a sex ratio of at least 3 to 1 in younger age groups and 9 to 1 in the very youngest—but also because there are gender differences in the demographic and social characteristics of self-poisoners, in the poisons used, the diagnoses applied, and the events which precipitate the behaviour. Furthermore, self-poisoning is not an historically static phenomenon. As rates of self-poisoning have varied so too have other social/historical phenomenon, such as changes in the age structure of the population, the level of female employment, the age of marriage and divorce rates. Changes in the availability of medical consultation and drug prescription to women have been implicated in changing patterns of self-poisoning.

The Pathology Paradigm

The moral and legalistic perspective which characterised early discourse on "attempted suicide", as with many other forms of deviant behaviour, has increasingly been replaced in our own century by the pathology paradigm, and the assessment and treatment of such patients, and much of the research into self-poisoning, has been undertaken by psychiatrists. Sociologists, in contrast to their interest in completed suicide, have largely ignored self-poisoning. Consequently a pathology oriented approach has been dominant, which has sought to establish differences in the mental state or personality between those who have deliberately poisoned themselves and those who have not. Where this has extended beyond the search for evidence of mental or personality disorder, it has instead consisted of epidemiological surveys accumulating a plethora of statistical correlations, the meaning of which has frequently lacked theoretical illumination.

The pathology paradigm has lacked explanatory power in that it is unable to account for the socio-demographic distribution of self-poisoning—i.e that it is perpetrated most frequently by young, working class women. In addition it has been unable to establish evidence of enduring mental or personality disorder in any but a minority of subjects. Furthermore the importance of specific adverse life events in precipitating female self-poisoning remains unexplained by the pathology paradigm. Finally, the ubiquity of self-poisoning questions the relevance of a paradigm which seeks to explain it by invoking the presence of psychopathology—the implication that 1 in 100 teenage women are in any meaningful sense "mentally ill" stretches credibility beyond the bounds of common sense.

There is a need, therefore, for a paradigm based on everyday, "normal" social–psychological processes, which is capable of integrating the social and the psychological dimensions of the phenomenon and addressing it within its social context. The theory of causal attribution, it is proposed, provides such a paradigm.

Attribution Theory

Attribution theory is a theory of cognition, motivation and emotion. It suggests that people seek to understand and hence control their environment by attributing causes to events occurring within it. The nature of the causal explanations people make (a cognitive process) has consequences for their level of motivation, performance, and affective state. Causal attributions typically fall along several dimensions: internal/external, whereby causes are perceived as being either within individuals or external to them in their environment; stable/unstable, where causes are either enduring or transient; and global/specific, such that causes either have global effects, which exist across situations, or are limited, specific, to the situation in question.

An Adaptive Attributional Style. The effects of attributions along these dimensions differ according to whether the events which instigate the attributional process represent success or failure. Thus in the case of success, internal attributions, for example to effort or ability, lead to positive affective states such as pride and the enhancement of self-esteem. Internal attributions also lead to the expectation that success will be enduring, as internal dispositions, such as ability, are enduring. Stable attributions suggest that the cause will continue to be present and therefore also lead to an expectation of future and continued success; and global attributions lead to the expectation that the cause will affect other situations as well as the immediately relevant one. Not only will this pattern of attributions have positive affective consequences, but, because it sets up expectations for future success, it enhances motivation and persistence, thereby promoting the probability, as well as the expectation, of future success. Additionally, in that reinforcement in the form of success is perceived as being contingent upon one's own ability or effort, it enhances perceptions of control over outcomes and directs attention to aspects of strategy conducive to further improvements in performance.

In the case of success, therefore, an internal, stable, and global pattern of attribution may be considered adaptive in its affective, motivational and behavioural consequences.

In the case of failure, however, the reverse is true. Here an adaptive attributional style would attribute the cause of failure to external, unstable and specific causes, such as bad luck or task difficulty. Thus, the individual with such an attributional pattern would not feel responsible for the occurrence, because its cause was seen as external to himself, as outside his control. There would consequently be limited affective implications and self-esteem would not suffer. The unstable nature imputed to the cause implies that it is not enduring and that therefore neither would the failure be expected to continue. The specific nature of the cause suggests that it only affects this particular situation and therefore would not be expected to lead to failure in other situations.

Finally, although the externality of the causal attribution implies uncontrollability, its unstable, specific nature suggests that the expectancy of control and success in other situations is not threatened and therefore persistence and a sense of contingency is maintained, thus enhancing the probability as well as the expectation of future success.

A Dysfunctional Attributional Style. If an external, unstable, and specific attributional pattern in the face of failure is regarded as adaptive, logically a dysfunctional style of causal attribution in the face of success and failure would be as follows. In the face of success an external, unstable, and specific attribution (for example to luck) would not enhance pride or self-esteem; it would not lead to an expectancy of future success and therefore neither would it promote persistence; and it would not promote a sense of contingency between one's actions and their outcomes, failing therefore to enhance a sense of control.

In the face of failure an internal, stable, and global causal attribution (for example to a lack of ability) would be similarly dysfunctional in that its internality would lead to a sense of guilt or shame and thereby undermine self-esteem; it would also imply the durability of cause. The stability attributed to the cause would imply its enduring nature, thereby promoting an expectation of continuing failure and thus engendering a lack of persistence; and its globality would result in expectation of failure in other situations also. In addition, internal, global attributions for failure have other negative cognitive consequences in that they divert attention from problem-solving strategy, and encourage off-task cognitions thereby inhibiting instrumental task centred behaviour and diminishing problem-solving ability. The attribution of failure to an internal, stable cause (such as a lack of ability) which is not controllable, leads to a sense of non-contingency and uncontrollability—i.e. that whatever one does the outcome will be unaffected.

Certain groups of individuals may possess an enduring attributional style: people prone to depression have been shown to exhibit a dysfunctional (depressogenic) attributional style in the face of success and failure such as we have described above. By contrast, those who demonstrate high levels of achievement orientation and high self-esteem possess an adaptive style which enhances self-esteem and positive expectation in the face of success, and defends self-esteem and enhances persistence in the face of failure.

Gender Differences in Attributional Style. Gender differences in attributional style have been demonstrated whereby women display the dysfunctional style characteristic of those low in achievement motivation and self-esteem. Thus, women are more likely to account for success with external, unstable, and specific attributions, and for failure with internal, stable, and global attributions. Consequently such women may experience the negative affective, motivational, and performance deficits associated with this style when confronted with success and failure. Success in women is less likely to lead to enhanced pride, self-esteem, persistence, or a sense of contingency and control. Failure is more likely to lead to shame, a lack of persistence and task centredness and a diminished sense of contingency and control—in brief, to helplessness.

Attributional style is conceived as a social construction and has been shown to be subject to the influence of particular patterns of social expectations and interactions. The self-derogatory attributional style more commonly held by women is said to originate from the particular nature of their socialisation into stereotypical sex roles and the every- day experiences contingent upon them. Attributions both influence and are influenced by expectations, and the sex role system promotes widely shared social expectations based on a pejorative stereotype of the "helpless but helpful" woman—passive, emotional, nurturant, and expressive rather than instrumental. Stereotypically male characteristics of dominance, objectivity and instrumentality are more highly valued in society and the distribution of influence and rewards reflects this. Thus women are disadvantaged in traditionally male-appropriate fields, and have a narrower range of sex-appropriate roles to provide the experience of, and opportunity for a sense of control and contingency between their actions and outcomes.

Attribution and the Sex Role System. Success for women is traditionally defined in terms of achievement in a narrow range of sex-appropriate roles centring on heterosexual relationships and the family. Feminine social identity and the female's self-concept are therefore crucially dependent on the assumption and maintenance of these sex-appropriate roles, and there is limited opportunity for the development of alternative sources of social and self-concept. Success in the domestic domain is, however, socially undervalued in comparison with success in the male dominated "public" domain—and thus women "have to lose in order to win". The constraints of the sex role system, with its narrow definition of female sex-appropriate roles and behaviours, limits access to traditionally male roles and, if achieved, success within them carries with it the threatened loss of femininity. It has been suggested that women therefore have a fear of success, and it has been demonstrated that failure in women is less socially disapproved than it is in men, and reinforces rather than undermines their social identity.

The dysfunctional, self-derogatory attributional style characteristic of women therefore represents the internalisation of this system of social expectations, both maintaining and being maintained by it. It has been demonstrated that gender based expectations are present in parents even before the child is born, and that the effects of sex role socialisation are evident in the expectations and behaviour of children as young as four years old. This pattern of expectations is promoted by interactions within the school setting and the limited access women have to achievement in male dominated, socially valued spheres in the adult world means that women have fewer role models on which to base expectancies of success.

Stereotypic views of women, and limited successful role models, encourage them to have lower initial expectations of success and in attributional theory, unexpected outcomes are most commonly attributed to external, unstable factors. The attribution of success to external, unstable factors does not enhance self-esteem, expectancy of future success or a sense of contingency and control. Such an attributional style thereby undermines persistence and the probability of future success. Women anticipate failure more than do men and expected outcomes are commonly attributed to internal, stable factors. The attribution of failure to internal, stable factors reduces self-esteem, promotes expectations of future failure, inhibits persistence and reduces the sense of contingency and control. The expectation of continued failure and the diminution of persistence in the face of it increases the probability of its continued occurrence, and in this way the characteristic female attributional style is both perpetuated by and itself perpetuates sex role stereotypes and the pattern of expectation associated with them.

If, as the literature suggests, attributional style is the product of social learning and in particular sex role socialisation, it is entirely feasible that biologically male individuals with certain learning histories could come to possess the dysfunctional style associated with a feminine socialisation. Such men would be more likely, therefore, in the face of severe adversity to exhibit the affective, motivational and behavioural deficits stemming from dysfunctional attributions.

Attribution and the Female Self-image.   The dysfunctional attributional style and its related affective and coping deficits has been characterised as "learned helplessness".

Causal attribution has been conceived as having several functions including those of mastery, adaptation ego-enhancement, and the communication of social identity. Identifying the causes of events in the environment—causal attribution—facilitates understanding and offers the possibility of adaptation and mastery, either through redefining their significance or acting upon the causes giving rise to events. In addition, attributions may serve an ego-enhancing function in that attributing the causes of success to internal, stable factors promotes self-esteem and self-concept, whereas external, unstable attributions for failure diminish the sense of personal responsibility thereby protecting self-esteem and self-concept. In social interaction, consistent, shared patterns of causal attribution lead to consensus as to the meaning and significance of events and behaviours, promoting mutuality and reciprocity in the performance of those role relationships which are the source of self-concept and social identity. It is possible therefore that an attributional style can be adaptive while serving one function but not another, and adaptive in one situation but maladaptive in another.

The effects of attributions are influenced therefore by the social context, and situations also influence the instigation of the process. Familiar situations, where expectations are not disconfirmed, especially those involving expected success instigate little in the way of attributional search. However those situations which are unexpected, particularly those involving failure, and which are highly salient to the individual, involving threat to the self-concept, have been suggested to be powerful instigators of the attribution process. It has also been proposed that individuals possessed of a "helpless" attributional style more commonly engage in attributional search, and are therefore more likely to expose themselves to the negative affective and motivational consequences of such a style.

An attributional approach to female self-poisoning based on these assertions would be constituted in the following manner.

Causal Attribution and Female Self-poisoning. Those people most commonly represented among self-poisoners are predominantly young, working class women. They are particularly likely to possess the helpless attributional style commonly found in women due to the relative powerlessness of their social and economic position, a lack of female models of success in the public domain and limited access to a diversity of role alternatives. This offers few opportunities for control over their environment and for the development of a sense of contingency between their actions and outcomes. Even within the sex-appropriate domestic domain, success is heavily dependent on the achievement and maintenance of mutuality with others—usually another male adult—and reinforcement is thus not necessarily dependent upon one's own efforts, which, again, fosters the sense of non-contingency and uncontrollability.

Lacking the alternative sources of self-concept and social identity which educational and professional opportunity provides for males and those of middle class origin, young, working class women are crucially dependent for the development and maintenance of their self-concept and social identity on those roles and relationships traditionally identified as appropriately female in the sex role system. In the domestic domain this promotes early involvement in courtship, marriage and childbearing; in the public domain it encourages participation in caring and service industries which are characterised by extensive part-time, low paid employment with limited opportunities for autonomy and career development. The exigencies of participation in both spheres further limits the possibilities for the development of social roles and identities alternative to those approved by the sex role system and renders success in the domestic domain even more salient to the maintenance of their self-concept.

Life Events and Specific Vulnerability.   Self-poisoning is precipitated by an accumulation of adverse life events and it is known that working class people are exposed to an increased incidence of adverse life events with the highest rates of physical and mental disorder, divorce, the reception into care of children, poverty and unemployment. This is true not only of the current experience of many self-poisoners, but also of their families of origin, and parental loss through parental separation and death is particularly common among them.

These experiences of uncontrollable adversity have been associated with the fatalistic approach to life events found among working class women, and to render them particularly vulnerable to the sense of non-contingency which promotes the helpless attributional style common among women in general. The adverse events particularly implicated in female self-poisoning involve the breakdown of personal relationships, and it is apparent that such events are particularly threatening to their narrowly based self-concept and social identity. It is in the presence of such threat and among people characterised by such "helplessness" that attributional search is most likely to be instigated, and hence its adverse effects encountered.

Conflicting Functions of Attributions.   The "helpless" attributional style common among women, and to which young, working class women may be seen as particularly prone, when present within stable heterosexual and family relationships serves the function of enhancing the stereotypical female self-concept, communicating social identity and promoting adaptation to the role relationships involved in their maintenance. However, in the face of breakdown in these relationships the same attributional style, while still serving the function of communicating the social identity of female helplessness, undermines self-esteem and self-concept and fails to promote adaptation and mastery. The result is the extreme hopelessness which is a definitive characteristic of self-poisoning.

Thus, attribution theory promises to illuminate the process by which women are particularly vulnerable to the helplessness and hopelessness associated with self-poisoning and why it is the breakdown in interpersonal relationship which precipitates this state. It does so without invoking pathology; rather it asserts that such an outcome is to be expected given the normative socialisation of women in general and the particular life experiences and adverse events confronting those women who ultimately engage in this behaviour.

AN EMPIRICAL INVESTIGATION

We have proposed on theoretical grounds that the attributional style of those who self-poison will differ in certain ways from that of those who have not done so. A study was designed involving 60 self-poisoning patients and a large number of patient and non-patient control subjects to test 5 specific hypotheses derived from the attributional model.

The first is that the attributional style of self-poisoners will be more internal, stable and global for negative events, and more external, unstable and specific for positive events than that of a non-patient comparison group.

We have suggested that the attributional style of women is characteristically more helpless or hopeless than that of men, and that this might constitute a vulnerability factor which could account for the preponderance of women among self-poisoners. The second contention is therefore that the attributional style of female non-patients will be more internal, stable and global for negative events, and more external, unstable and specific for positive events than that of male non-patients.

While these hypotheses are simply stated, a recent paper by Alloy et al., 1988 dealing with developments in attribution theory and research methodology cautions against the expectation of significant findings based on the proposal of such direct relationships. Instead the authors reiterate the need for interactive models capable of embracing the central role afforded to negative life events in the attributional reformulation of learned helplessness. Thus, when comparing two sample populations as we shall be doing in our study (i.e. self-poisoners and non-patient comparison subjects), differences should not be expected in attributional style between groups in the absence of negative life events. Alloy, using the newly coined terminology of "learned hopelessness", points out that (p.15):

> ... if the hopelessness theory is correct, the magnitude of differences in attributional style between depressed vs. non-depressed subjects would be influenced by the base rates of the hypothesised depressogenic attributional style, negative life events and subtypes of depression other than hopelessness depression.

Alloy continues to acknowledge that such a research design is not entirely feasible at present due to the absence of any available account of the base rate of "other subtypes of depression", however it is clear that any current design must take into account as far as possible the level of negative life events experienced by subjects, and any findings must be interpreted in light of this variable.

This leads therefore to the third hypothesis: that in the presence of negative life events the causal attributions of female subjects will be more internal, stable and global for negative events, and more external, unstable and specific for positive events than will that of males.

A fourth hypothesis, emanating from the established differences in those events which precipitate self-poisoning among women, i.e. their predominantly relational or affiliative nature, and also from the "specific vulnerability" hypothesis of the attributional reformulation of learned helplessness as described by Alloy, is one relating to causal attribution in the affiliative domain: namely, that causal attributions among female subjects in relation to negative affiliative events will be more internal, stable and global than will those of men in the same content domain.

Finally, it has been suggested throughout this work that differences in attributional style are the result not of biological sex, but of sex role socialisation. This assumption has implicit within it the notion that individuals may possess a characteristically female, or male style while not being of that biological sex. If a dysfunctional style is implicated in self-poisoning, then such a style might logically be possessed by male self-poisoners, and, indeed, should be so if the initial proposal is correct. Thus the fifth hypothesis is: that there will be no significant difference between the attributional style of biologically male and biologically female self-poisoners.

Procedure

The study involved three groups—a sample of self-poisoning patients, and two comparison groups. The self-poisoning (SP) sample was composed of patients admitted for deliberate self-poisoning which had occurred within the previous 24 hours. The first comparison group consisted of patients on medical wards for the investigation and treatment of medical conditions who had no history of self-poisoning. These were included in the design in order to control for the possible effects of hospitalisation, and also to provide a comparison group of subjects who had unequivocally experienced at least two negative events—illness and hospitalisation. The reasons for this second requirement will be discussed in more detail later. The third group consisted of non-patient subjects, also with no history of self-poisoning, drawn from various groups of workers and students in the Health and Social Services.

Both patient groups were interviewed in hospital wards, the interview lasting approximately 35 minutes. The non-patient groups were introduced in general terms to the study in a group situation and then given questionnaires to complete when alone—posting them back to the author on completion. Three questionnaires were employed: the Attributional Style Questionnaire (ASQ: Peterson et al., 1982); a Life Events Questionnaire derived from that employed by Paykel (Paykel et al., 1975); and a General Questionnaire which elicited demographic and employment information, and details of drugs taken by self-poisoning patients.

The resultant data was subjected to multivariate, and univariate analysis of variance, correlation and chi-squared analysis using the Statistical Package for the Social Sciences PC (SPSS/PC).

Subjects

Self-poisoning (SP) Group.   60 self-poisoning patients (34 females, 26 males) who had been admitted within the previous 24 hours to a general medical ward were interviewed—their ages ranged between 16 and 60 with a mean age of 30.9 years. This reflects the age distribution of self-poisoners generally, the largest numbers (27.3%) occurring in the age range 25–34, although, as has been described in chapter one, the highest rates occur among those aged 20–24. (Wells, 1981, p.27). 50% reported a previous episode of self-poisoning, which is a rate in keeping with other studies (Bancroft & Marsack, 1977a; Morgan, Pottle, Pocock, & Burns-Cox, 1976). This should not be confused with the repetition rate of individuals which is reported to be in the region of 25% with a clustering in the first month after the initial episode (Morgan et al., 1976).

Patient Comparison Group.   31 patients (15 female and 16 male) with no history of self-poisoning who were in the same medical wards as those to which self-poisoning patients are admitted, were interviewed. They were aged between 16 and 60 with a mean age of 31.2 years. They were short-term patients without life threatening conditions whose circumstances, in these respects, reflected the hospital experience of the SP sample. Additionally no patient was included whose medical condition included a psychiatric component: thus, for example, several young women who were being treated for anorexia and others whose conditions involved hormonal abnormalities were excluded on these grounds. Typically patients who were included were having investigations for such conditions as diabetes or were recovering from viral disorders. No patient who was approached refused to participate.

There were two reasons for including this comparison group. In view of the importance of severe negative events to the emergence of a dysfunctional attributional style the chance occurrence of such events among a non-patient group could not be relied upon and therefore the patient comparison group was included because all such subjects are confronting at least two important events with negative connotations—illness and hospital admission. These events are unequivocal and self-evident and thus knowledge of their occurrence is not dependent on the reports of subjects. Reporting bias is a facet of life events research which is often seen as problematic in view of the possible distortions caused by memory effects and the danger of variables such as mood and number of reported events being confounded—i.e. depressed people may report more negative events and less positive ones because they are depressed, rather than because more have occurred (Teasdale & Fogarty, 1979).

The second reason for the inclusion of this group is that it controls for the effects of hospitalisation. This was considered important in view of our interest in learned helplessness which Raps, Peterson, Jonas, & Seligman (1982) suggested could ensue from being hospitalised, although Baltes and Skinner (1983) subsequently claimed such conclusions were unwarranted on the basis of the results reported.

Non-patient Comparison Group. This group comprised 71 individuals—43 females and 28 males with a mean age of 34.9 drawn from students and workers in health and social services agencies. A homogenous student comparison group, frequently used in such studies, was avoided on the grounds that such a comparison group would probably overrepresent the young, single and middle class.

TABLE 7.1
Comparison of Sample Groups—Age, Sex, Occupation and Marital Status

Group	S	n	%	Mean Age	Man. Occ.	%	Marital status					
							s	%	M	%	Ds	%
SP	M	26	43.3	32.6	20	76.9	12	46.2	8	30.8	6	23.1
	F	34	56.7	29.4	20	58.8	17	50.0	5	14.7	12	35.5
Total		60	100	30.9	40	66.7	29	48.3	13	21.7	18	30.0
Patient	M	16	51.6	36.2	9	56.3	6	37.5	8	50.0	2	12.5
	F	15	48.4	25.7	6	40.0	11	73.3	3	20.0	1	6.7
Total		31	100	31.1	15	48.4	17	54.8	11	35.5	3	9.7
Non-patient	M	28	39.4	34.9	17	60.7	10	35.7	17	60.7	1	3.6
	F	43	60.6	27.7	10	23.3	28	65.1	11	25.6	4	9.3
Total		71	100	30.6	27	38.0	38	53.5	28	39.4	5	7.0

KEY: Man.Occ. = manual occupation   Ds = divorced/separated

NOTE: Figures in % column relate to relevant sample group (e.g. in the first row, SP M 26 43.3% means that 43.3% of the total SP sample of 60 were male). Further along that row man.occ. 20 76.9% means that 76.9% of the male SP sample of 26 were in manual occupation.

Questionnaires

The Attributional Style Questionnaire.   The ASQ is intended to yield scores for individual differences in the tendencies to attribute the causes of good and bad events to internal (versus external), stable (versus unstable), and global (versus specific) factors. Subjects are required to suggest one major cause for each of 12 hypothetical events—6 good and 6 bad outcomes, randomly distributed throughout the questionnaire to avoid order effects. Half the events relate to interpersonal events, described as affiliative, and consisting of such statements as "Your spouse has been treating you more lovingly"; the other half are related to achievement situations such as "you have been looking for a job unsuccessfully for some time". The subject is then asked to "Write down the one major cause" and rate this cause along a 7-point scale corresponding to the internality, stability and globality dimensions.

Peterson et al. (1982) reported reliabilities, intercorrelations and test-retest stabilities which demonstrated that the internal consistency of the composite attributional style scales for good and bad events (each based on 18 items, 6 good events × 3 attributional dimensions) demonstrated alpha coefficients of 0.75 and 0.72 respectively (Cronbach, 1951). Those 6 subscales based on 6 items each, which reflect separate attributional dimensions (e.g. internality for good events × 6; internality for bad events × 6) showed coefficients ranging between 0.44 and 0.69, a mean reliability of 0.54. Thus the reliability of composites at the most general level—collapsing internal, stable and global dimensions for good and bad events respectively—is considerably better than that for the individual dimensions.

For good events the individual attributional dimensions were intercorrelated at a level nearer that of their reliabilities, suggesting that the questionnaire did not succeed in distinguishing them. However for bad events the three dimensions (internal, stable, global) were more adequately distinguished. Test-retest correlations were 0.70 for the composite for good events and 0.64 for the composite bad events ($p < 0.001$).

The Life Events Scale.   Based on the Life Event Questionnaire devised by Paykel and his colleagues (Paykel, Prusoff, & Uhlenhuth, 1971) and since widely used in studies of self-poisoners, this is a 36-item self-report scale of subjectively weighted life events. It consists of discrete, novel events as opposed to chronic difficulties, and covers a diversity of areas of functioning from relationships to financial affairs. Both positive and negative events are represented and are randomly placed so as to avoid order effects. Respondents are asked to rate events occurring within the previous 7 days according to the severity of the effect it had upon them on a scale from 0 to 3, 0 being no effect, 1 short-term and mild, 2 longer lasting and greater effect, and 3 very powerful effect whether short-term or longer lasting.

Scores are obtained by simply adding up the events ticked—the same event marked in more than one time period is, however, counted only once. Three different estimations of event occurrence can be arrived at therefore according to time scale, event severity and a combination of both. For reasons to be described below, the present study will be concerned mainly with events marked as 2 or more on the severity scale and occurring within the previous 7 days.

Previous work has demonstrated that events considered by subjects to be of moderate to severe effect more clearly differentiate parasuicides from depressive or normal control groups (Paykel et al., 1975; Slater & Depue, 1981) and also it is these events which most clearly demonstrate the peaking effect with closer proximity to the act (Katschnig, 1980). Combining events of all distress levels in analyses has been found to obscure significant differences between groups (Slater & Depue, 1981, p.280).

Although some aspects are novel this questionnaire is based on Paykel's list of 32 events, on the basis of which he reported that "attempted suicides" reported a mean of 3.3 events per person in the 6 months prior to their act, whereas depressed controls reported 2.1 and general population subjects 0.8. All the differences between pairs were significant at $p < 0.01$ or better (Paykel et al., 1975).

Certain life event scales are based upon the notion that all events involve readjustment or change and that this may be conceived of as stressful—whether the events involved are positive or negative. The Social Readjustment Rating Scale of Holmes and Rahe (1967) is one such example. Our present interest is in negative event occurrence as this type of event has been most consistently related to self-poisoning, and, increasingly, attributional theory in relation to learned helplessness has concentrated on negative events as provocative of the dysfunctional attributional style. In addition the ASQ is most reliable in relation to hypothetical negative events. Furthermore, it has been shown that levels of positive event occurrence do not differentiate between parasuicides and control groups (Paykel et al., 1975). None the less it was felt advisable to retain the positive events in the schedule in order to obscure from respondents the nature of the present interest. To list only negative ones might have encouraged a "negative mental set" in respondents who might therefore mark negative events in order to meet what they considered to be the expectations of the research.

Although there are undoubtedly more complex methods of weighting events such as the "Life Change Units" employed in the Recent Life

Change Questionnaire (Rahe, 1975) and the "Contextual Threat Rating" employed in the Life Event Schedule (Brown & Harris, 1978), several studies have shown that such complex measures produce essentially the same results as less complicated ones (Katschnig, 1980; Dohrenwend & Dohrenwend, 1981; Brown, 1974, p.115).

In terms of the reliability of the present self-report measure, it is true that such measures have been criticised due to the danger of bias resulting from factors such as the affective state of the respondent—for example, depressed subjects might overreport negative events. Many life event questionnaires are complex constructions designed to minimise such bias: however, Slater and Depue (1981) in their study of clinically depressed self-poisoners interviewed not only the self-poisoners but also their closest associates employing a straightforward self-report measure. They found 93% agreement between the two groups of respondents. They refer to Brown's comparable finding of a 92% agreement when employing the LES as further support for the use of their less involved self-report measure.

Another source of alleged bias is that derived from the interdependence of events and affective states—i.e. does the depression of depressed subjects cause the excess of negative events they report by leading, for example, to marital disharmony and arguments. These events would be regarded as "dependent" and could not exercise a causative role, whereas "independent" ones such as the death of a relative could not be caused by the respondent's depression but could therefore have a role in causing it. Despite this danger, Slater and Depue found that similar results occurred in terms of the excess of events experienced by parasuicides versus depressed controls who had not harmed themselves, whether or not they included only those events regarded as independent.

Results

The General Questionnaire. The demographic and employment data closely reflect those reported elsewhere and described in earlier chapters. This may be summarised as showing the expected preponderance of the single and divorced, and, in this sample, particularly divorced women; those in manual occupations, and unemployed men. The mean age of the total sample reflects the national data on the percentage distribution according to age of self-poisoners, with the group 25–34 providing the greatest contribution of any group—27.3%, and males being somewhat older than females (Wells, 1981, p.27).

In terms of the nature of the drugs taken in overdose the consumption of prescribed medication in the current sample at 53.2%

mirrors the 58.9% described for Oxford subjects in 1984 by Platt et al.,
1988. The percentage of male and female subjects taking such
medication was 53.8% and 52.8% respectively. This lack of difference
between the percentages of male and female subjects taking prescribed
medication in self-poisoning apparently contradicts much of the earlier
discussion on the relationship between prescribing and sex differences
in rates of self-poisoning. However, closer analysis of the type of drugs
taken gives a different impression entirely, with 23.1% of males and
47.1% of females taking psychotropic medication in the episode. This is
in keeping with the known 2:1 predominance of women among the
recipients of such medication—a fact rarely discussed in the
self-poisoning literature, but a situation which might contribute to their
similar predominance among self-poisoners, as we have argued earlier
in the present work.

These results support the contention of earlier chapters that
self-poisoners are representative of those who are young, female,
frequently unemployed or in occupations with little autonomy, and
therefore are among those in society least able to control their own
outcomes. The history of loss through family breakdown and death of
parents, and the common experience of psychiatric disorder and
previous self-poisoning known to characterise such groups, coupled with
current relational and family problems, further adds to the argument
that this group is especially vulnerable to helplessness in the face of
multiple adversity.

The Life Events Questionnaire.   This scale serves two main functions.
First it provides data to compare with data reported elsewhere,
especially in terms of the sex differences found in the incidence of life
event occurrence and the overall rate of occurrence in the week before
self-poisoning. Secondly, it enabled the association between the
occurrence of adverse events and causal attributions to be explored. It
will be recalled that only those events which were adverse and scored
as 2 or 3 on the subjective effect scale were included in the analysis for
two reasons: (a) the findings of Paykel et al., (1975) and Slater and
Depue (1981, p.280) that only adverse events of moderate to severe
intensity differentiated between "attempted suicides" and either
depressed or "normal" controls; and (b) the most recent learned
hopelessness attributional literature which asserts that only the
occurrence of negative events rated as important by subjects will
provoke the emergence of a dysfunctional attributional style (Alloy et
al., 1988).

The relative frequency of adverse events shown here reflects those
found by others (Paykel et al., 1975; O'Brien & Farmer, 1980; Katschnig,

TABLE 7.2

Adverse Event Occurrence (Rated 2 or More)

Time-scale/group	SP		Patient Comparison		Non-patient Comparison	
	M	F	M	F	M	F
Previous 7 days	1.4	1.4	0.7	1.0	0.4	0.3

1980) with the SP group showing more adverse events than both comparison groups. The somewhat elevated score of patient controls reflects their illness and hospitalisation as negative events.

A finding of considerable importance to our interest in the association between adverse events and attributions is the very low level of adverse events in the non-patient group in the seven days prior to completion of the questionnaire. This is a point to which we shall return when describing the results derived from the ASQ in the light of the most recent discussion by Alloy of the role of adverse events as provoking agents of dysfunctional attributions.

In terms of the nature of the events described by the self-poisoning group the results reflect the findings of other research in that interpersonal problems in the shape of arguments with key others and major financial problems are the most commonly reported categories for both sexes. Despite this, closer analysis reveals marked sex differences within these categories such that "arguments with boyfriend" is the single largest problem reported by females representing 29.8% of all their problems, whereas the equivalent item for males represents only 11.4%. As 46.2% of the males and 50.0% of the females were single, approximately equal percentages of both groups were "at risk".

A marked sex difference occurs again with the item "court appearance for offence" which represents 8.6% of male problems but is not reported at all by females. Finally, important differences occurred under the item "other" with males reporting 8.6% of their problems here: all were work related such as "argument with boss", whereas no single type of problem emerged within the 2.2% of the problems which females subsumed under this category.

Those studies which have found sex differences in the nature of events associated with self-poisoning have reported that women predominantly experience problems in the relational or private domain and men in the financial, work and legal or public domain (Beck et al., 1973; Weissman, 1974; Bancroft et al., 1977b; Morgan, 1980). We have noted a parallel dichotomy in the attributional literature between those concerns described as "affiliative" and "achievement" oriented. If the events described in Table 7.3 are subsumed under these categories as in

TABLE 7.3
Comparative Percentage of Affiliative and Achievement Events Among Self-Poisoners—Previous 7 Days

	Private/affiliative	Public/achievement
Male	60.1	40.1
Female	76.8	21.3

TABLE 7.4
Attributional Style Questionnaire, Means and Standard Deviations—Females

Item/group		SP n=34		Patient n=15		Non-patient n=43	
		Mean	s.d.	Mean	s.d.	Mean	s.d.
Total ASQ	+	4.8	0.57	4.8	0.62	4.7	0.51
Total ASQ	−	4.5	0.71	4.2	0.42	4.1	0.67
Locus	+	4.7	0.79	4.9	1.20	4.6	0.81
Locus	−	4.4	1.00	4.5	0.86	4.4	0.84
Stability	+	4.8	0.66	4.8	0.84	4.8	0.57
Stability	−	4.5	0.75	4.2	0.59	4.1	0.77
Globality	+	5.0	0.89	4.8	0.95	4.6	0.86
Globality	−	4.6	1.00	4.1	0.98	3.7	1.20
Affiliative	+	5.0	0.60	5.0	0.80	5.0	0.54
Affiliative	−	4.3	0.84	3.9	0.62	3.8	0.75
Achievement	+	4.7	0.77	4.7	0.89	4.3	0.83
Achievement	−	4.8	0.73	4.6	0.59	4.3	0.86

TABLE 7.5
Attributional Style Questionnaire, Means and Standard Deviations—Males

Item/group		SP n=25		Patient n=16		Non-patient n=27	
		Mean	s.d.	Mean	s.d.	Mean	s.d.
Total ASQ	+	4.9	0.62	5.3	0.53	4.9	0.70
Total ASQ	−	4.4	0.68	4.2	0.49	4.1	0.74
Locus	+	4.9	0.88	5.3	0.87	4.8	0.93
Locus	−	4.5	0.94	4.4	0.99	4.2	0.91
Stability	+	4.7	0.82	5.3	0.63	5.0	0.78
Stability	−	4.3	0.69	4.2	0.76	4.1	0.78
Globality	+	5.0	0.83	5.2	0.96	4.9	0.91
Globality	−	4.6	1.30	3.9	0.84	4.0	1.30
Affiliative	+	4.9	0.74	5.2	0.41	5.2	0.56
Affiliative	−	4.1	0.86	4.1	0.68	4.0	0.85
Achievement	+	4.9	0.73	5.4	0.79	4.6	0.89
Achievement	−	4.7	0.79	4.2	0.52	4.2	0.83

Table 7.4 further support emerges for the notion of sex differences in the relative importance of event types in the precipitation of self-poisoning. Table 7.3 demonstrates the clear sex differences in problem domain reported in the literature, with females showing much greater concern with affiliative events and their self-poisoning preceded by negative affiliative events more frequently than males. On the other hand achievement concerns preoccupy males considerably more than females and it is here that the greatest differences are evident.

The implications of these results for an attributional approach to self-poisoning will be discussed when considering the findings which emerged from the ASQ and their relationship to the life events data.

The Attributional Style Questionnaire.   Means and standard deviations of the various groups are shown in the tables and the results will be described in detail in relation to the five specific hypotheses which were derived from the attributional model of self-poisoning.

Dysfunctional Attributions and Self-poisoning

The first specific hypothesis was as follows: "The attributional style of self-poisoners will be more internal, stable and global for negative events, and more external, unstable and specific for positive events than that of a non-patient comparison group".

Analysis of variance showed that for negative events self-poisoners differed from non-patients as predicted by the model, their attributions being more internal, more stable, and global than non-patients. Only on the locus dimension did the difference fail to reach statistical significance. There were, however, no significant differences on positive events.

Further analysis showed that much of the significance was contributed by marked differences between female self-poisoners and female non-patients, differences between the respective groups of males being less marked.

Female self-poisoners differ significantly on all negative items except, again, for the locus dimension which fails to discriminate between the groups. Female self-poisoners are significantly more stable and global in their attributions for negative events in both affiliative and achievement domains than are female non-patients. In relation to positive events, again, there is little evident discrimination.

Male self-poisoners differed in the predicted direction on all negative items but, in contrast to the female results, statistical significance was reached only on the composite score for negative achievement events (F (1,50) = 4.843; $p < 0.032$). This difference was due to their markedly

TABLE 7.6
Attributional Style Questionnaire, Means, Standard Deviations and
F-Tests—Self-poisoners vs. Non-patients

Group		SP (n=59)		Non-patient (n=69)			
Item		Mean	s.d.	Mean	s.d.	F	Sig.
Total ASQ	+	4.9	0.59	4.7	0.59	1.4	0.2468
Total ASQ	−	4.5	0.69	4.1	0.69	9.8	0.0022
Locus	+	4.8	0.83	4.7	0.85	1.3	0.2512
Locus	−	4.4	0.99	4.3	0.86	0.2	0.6985
Stability	+	4.7	0.72	4.9	0.67	1.7	0.1948
Stability	−	4.4	0.85	4.1	0.77	5.7	0.0185
Globality	+	5.0	0.86	4.7	0.89	3.6	0.0605
Globality	−	4.6	1.13	3.8	1.20	13.2	0.0004
Affiliative	+	5.0	0.67	5.1	0.55	1.6	0.2097
Affiliative	−	4.2	0.84	3.9	0.79	4.5	0.0350
Achievement	+	4.8	0.76	4.4	0.86	5.5	0.0206
Achievement	−	4.7	0.75	4.2	0.84	12.0	0.0007

greater globality score. Again, there were no significant differences on the positive items.

The lack of discrimination between groups on the locus dimension is a common finding when employing the ASQ and Clive Robins (Robins, 1988) describes the inconsistent results obtained in many studies of the relationship between attributional style and depression. He points, for example, to the review of Coyne and Gottlib (1983) which concluded that internality appeared to receive most support, while Hammen (1985) later asserted that global attributions showed the most consistent support.

TABLE 7.7
Attributional Style Questionnaire,
Female Self-poisoners vs. Female Non-patients

Item		d.f.	F	Sig.
Total ASQ	+	1,74	2.042	0.1571
Total ASQ	−	1,75	7.055	0.0096
Locus	+	1,75	0.476	0.4920
Locus	−	1,75	0.046	0.8296
Stability	+	1,74	0.046	0.8305
Stability	−	1,75	7.341	0.0083
Globality	+	1,74	4.801	0.0316
Globality	−	1,75	11.816	0.0010
Affiliative	+	1,75	0.000	0.9816
Affiliative	−	1,75	5.307	0.0240
Achievement	+	1,74	3.821	0.0544
Achievement	−	1,75	6.992	0.0100

Robins conducted a meta-analysis of the results of 57 attributional studies which had employed the ASQ following which he concluded that inconsistent results owed a lot to statistical shortcomings. Because different statistical tests differ in their power to detect effects of the same size in a sample of a given size many studies that report no significant relations had a very low *a priori* probability of detecting one even had it existed. Thus, in relation to studies employing the Pearson *r*, Robins states that in order to have a 0.80 probability of detecting a small effect of $r = 0.10$, using a two-tailed test a sample of 800 is required. Even a medium effect of $r = 0.30$ requires a sample of 84. Of the 57 analyses Robins examined, only 8 had such a 0.80 probability or better of detecting a small–medium true population effect (e.g. $r = 0.20$). Thus the comparatively small numbers involved in our own sample, especially when split by sex, could contribute to the failure of the results on the locus   dimension   to   demonstrate   greater   internality   among self-poisoners.

None the less following his meta-analysis Robins (1988) still concluded that:

> If one examines studies with relatively high power ... While the proposed role of internal attributions still enjoys little support, stable and global attributions and the composite all enjoy unanimous support.

Further reason to expect that the locus dimension might produce inconclusive results arises because internality is not a unitary factor but confounds the elements of responsibility and cause. An individual may inadvertantly cause something to happen and thus not feel responsible for its effects which were unintentional. Thus Brewin and Shapiro (1984), separating these factors in their Responsibility for Negative Events Questionnaire, found that women accepted more responsibility for negative events than men (i.e. were more internal).

Thus, although the absence of confirmation for the importance of internality for negative events is disappointing, it is unsurprising and in keeping with other findings. The predicted results in relation to stability and globality for negative events similarly reflect earlier findings and are lent added credibility by Robins' extensive analysis and his conclusions.

The possibility   that   differences   between   self-poisoners   and non-patients could be due to the effects of hospitalisation on the self-poisoners is discounted by analysis of variance comparing the scores of female patient comparison subjects and female non-patients, with no significant differences being found. Similarly with males, although as will be shown later, differences were found between male non-patients and patient comparisons these were of a different nature from those found between non-patients and self-poisoners, again suggesting that hospitalisation can be discounted as a cause for the difference between self-poisoners and non-patients.

There is no support in these results for the hypothesis in relation to good events. The failure of positive items on the ASQ to discriminate between groups is a commonly reported aspect of the attributional literature which has increasingly taken the view that differences in attributional styles may only emerge in the presence of highly salient, negative events. This, in conjunction with the lower reliability for the positive stability and globality dimensions found by Peterson et al. (1982), has led to the abandonment of positive items in the recently published revised ASQ (Peterson & Villanova, 1988) in favour of a questionnaire with more, and only negative items.

Sex Differences in Attributions

In view of the equal level of adverse events reported by male and female self-poisoners, these results support the proposed sex differences in attributional response to real adversity. Female self-poisoners who had experienced high levels of adverse events in the previous seven days, differed from female non-patients, with low levels on all negative items except locus. However male self-poisoners, also with high levels of adverse events, differed from male non-patients with low levels only on the negative achievement item. This suggests, in keeping with the literature on sex differences in attributions and coping skills reviewed in Chapter Six, that negative events provoke more dysfunctional attributions in women, resulting in greater disruption of coping skills and commensurately greater vulnerability to helplessness.

Further though not unequivocal support for this comes from the findings in relation to the second specific hypothesis derived from the attributional model of self-poisoning which was that: "The attributional style of female non-patients will be more internal, stable, and global for negative events, and more external, unstable and specific for positive events than that of male non-patients".

Differences are evident in relation to positive events in the predicted direction—males showing a more internal, stable and global style than females on all positive items. Despite the fact that none reach statistical significance these results reflect that literature which demonstrated a self-serving or ego-enhancing attributional style among males in relation to success.

For negative events, however, no such consistent pattern emerges. This could be the result of the extremely low level of negative life events reported by the non-patient comparison group for it has recently been asserted by Alloy and her colleagues (Alloy et al., 1988) that differences such as those predicted by this hypothesis will not manifest themselves in the absence of negative life events. Thus, negative events are necessary "provoking agents" of the dysfunctional style.

Negative Events as Provoking Agents

The possibility that the absence of provoking events among non-patients has masked real sex differences in attributional style for negative events is enhanced by results relating to the third specific hypothesis: "In the presence of negative life events the causal attributions of female comparison subjects will be more internal, stable and global for hypothetical negative events and more external, unstable and specific for good events than will those of males".

In view of the fact that both male and female patient comparison subjects have experienced the similar adverse events of illness and hospitalisation, comparison of their ASQ results would be considered a more valid test of differences in attributional style. However no significant differences emerged between the groups for negative events. This result is disappointing but may be due to the fact that illness and hospitalisation do not provide sufficiently salient negative events to provoke dysfunctional attributions in relation to negative events. For example, the type of non-life threatening, usually minor illness and short-term hospitalisation encountered by these subjects would not necessarily threaten self-esteem.

There is a suggestion that this account may be valid in that for positive events sex differences did emerge. As predicted, male attributions were more internal, stable and global on all items with differences reaching significance on the composite item for positive events (F $(1,29)$ = 4.515; p<0.0422) and positive achievement events (F $(1,29)$ = 5.351; p<0.028)—results suggestive of a self-serving male bias, with male patient comparisons demonstrating a more ego-enhancing attributional style in the face of real adversity than females.

This impression is reinforced further when male comparison patients are compared with male non-patients, who, it will be remembered reported a low level of adverse events. For positive events the attributions of male comparison patients were more internal, stable and global and these differences reached statistical significance on the composite positive events item (F $(1,41)$ = 4.402; p<0.0421) and composite positive achievement events (F $(1,41)$ = 7.450; p<0.009). No such differences emerged between the respective female groups, with female comparison patients showing no such ego-enhancing response to their similar adversity.

Thus there is mounting support for our model to the effect that males possess a more functional attributional style in the face of adversity than do females. When confronted with illness and hospitalisation males show an adaptive, ego-building pattern of internal, stable, global attribution for good events, which promotes coping by enhancing self-esteem, raising expectancy for future success and thereby promoting persistence and task centredness in current problem-solving attempts. Females, on the other hand, as predicted, show no such ego-building patterns of attribution.

That such attributional differences were disclosed in the patient control group—i.e. in the presence of real adverse events—and not in the non-patient comparison group—in their comparative absence —supports Alloy's contentions in relation to the role of negative events as provoking agents for the emergence of the dysfunctional style (Alloy et al., 1988).

Life Events, Attributions and Specific Vulnerability

The fourth hypothesis relates to sex differences in events precipitating self-poisoning, with female episodes being more commonly preceded by events in the private realm and those of males by events in the public domain. It was proposed therefore that: "The causal attributions of females in relation to negative hypothetical events in the affiliative realm will be more internal, stable and global than will those of males in the same content domain".

No significant differences were found between males and females within any group on this item, but sex differences are apparent between groups in the manner of their attributional response. Again, where adverse event occurrence is low, no differences emerge. However when comparing the response of male and female self-poisoners, who reported high levels of negative events, with male and female non-patients, who reported low levels of such events, differences begin to emerge.

It will be recalled that self-poisoners of both sexes reported high levels of adverse event occurrence in the affiliative realm: males reported 60.1% of their problems were in this area, and females 76.8%. However male self-poisoners demonstrated no significant differences in their ASQ scores in this domain when compared with male non-patients, whereas female self-poisoners compared with female non-patients did show significant differences—being more internal, and significantly more stable and global on the negative affiliative events item.

In view of the previously reported finding of no significant difference on any item between male and female non-patients and their comparable low level of adverse events (male 0.4/female 0.3) these results again point to sex differences in attributional response to adversity and, furthermore to the specific vulnerability proposed by Alloy. In this instance the ASQ scores for negative affiliative items of male self-poisoners show no differences in the face of real adversity in the affiliative realm, whereas those of women show significant differences in the predicted direction of greater internality, stability and globality on this composite item—a more "helpless" style, and, in terms of coping with these events, a more dysfunctional one.

The notion of a specific vulnerability is further supported in the finding that the only significant difference between male self-poisoners and male non-patients occurred on the composite item for negative achievement events. These results accord with the literature reviewed earlier, and with our own findings in relation to sex differences in the nature of precipitant events associated with self-poisoning.

Females report more adverse affiliative events, and males more in the achievement domain in the week before their self-poisoning. The finding that males show a dysfunctional style in relation to negative achievement events, but not to negative affiliative ones suggests an explanation for this widely reported sex difference in precipitant events. Due to male sex role socialisation, failure in the stereotypically masculine achievement domain is extremely salient to the maintenance of male self-esteem and self-image. Dysfunctional attributions, where they exist due to the particular normative or non-normative learning history of an individual, are more likely to be provoked by such threatening, personally salient events. Thus males generally might be expected to be vulnerable to failure in the achievement domain, and certain groups of males—those with a history of economic disadvantage and family breakdown—might be specifically vulnerable due to their possession of the dysfunctional attributional style that such experiences foster.

The sex role socialisation of women promotes the endorsement of helplessness as a stereotypic attribute of femininity. This helplessness, in the sense of it being an attribute of femininity, is not domain specific—women are expected to "be" helpless, not merely to act helpless in particular situations, although this is part of the stereotype and is especially true in their relationships with men, as the achievement of femininity depends in part on maintaining heterosexual relationships. The normative socialisation of women, as we have seen, promotes the development of a helpless attributional style which is adaptive in maintaining such relationships but is dysfunctional when it comes to coping with their loss.

Thus the vulnerability of women is not domain specific as that of men appears to be, and hence self-poisoning females show dysfunctional attributions in both affiliative and achievement domains. However affiliative relationships are central to the maintenance of stereotypic femininity, and (particularly among women with few alternative roles) central also to the maintenance of self-image and self-esteem. Due, therefore, to the personal salience of breakdown in these relationships, such women would be particularly vulnerable to the emergence of dysfunctional attributions in response.

The pattern of sex differences in results on the ASQ and Life Events Scale is in keeping with the literature describing sex differences in precipitant events and suggests an account not only of these but of the predominance of women among self-poisoners. Quite simply, women are vulnerable to a wider range of adverse events capable of provoking dysfunctional attributions and the coping deficits associated with them.

Sex, Gender and Attribution

The final specific hypothesis derived from the attributional model of self-poisoning related to the significance of sex role socialisation in the origins of a dysfunctional style. It proposed: "That there will be no significant difference in the attributional style of biologically male and biologically female self-poisoners".

As predicted, no significant differences in ASQ scores were found between male and female self-poisoners. This result is in keeping with the literature on psychological androgeny and sex and gender differences in attribution reviewed in Chapter Six. Attributional style is not biologically determined but, rather, is a social construction in part related to gender and sex role socialisation, but more fundamentally the product of social learning, both normative and non-normative.

Thus, although women would more commonly show a dysfunctional style, males with particular learning histories, characterised by extreme non-contingency, could develop the style which females acquire through normative socialisation into the "helpless" female role. The history of early parent loss and family breakdown, and the current lower class, underqualified and unemployed status of self-poisoning males suggests prolonged experience of an inability to determine one's own outcomes—of non-contingency. This non-contingency is seminal to the development of helplessness and, the attributional model suggests, would account for their presence among self-poisoning patients.

Summary

The results of this empirical study clearly suggest that self-poisoning patients possess a more dysfunctional attributional style in relation to negative events than people who have no history of self-poisoning. There is a considerable literature which we have earlier reviewed demonstrating the cognitive and behavioural deficits associated with this pattern of causal attribution, and that such deficits are present in self-poisoners.

Although the present results in relation to sex differences in attributional style are not as unequivocal, they are in accord with the large body of theoretical and empirical work which shows that females, and males high in feminine attributes, more commonly possess a dysfunctional attributional style and the coping deficits associated with it. This, along with the greater prescription of psychotropic medication to women, would account for the female predominance among self-poisoners. In view of the multiple adversity known to confront these patients it is, therefore, unsurprising that they react with that helplessness of which unconsciousness and surrender to medical care is an extreme expression.

In Chapter Two, while developing a social/psychological account of self-poisoning through a critique of existing theories, it became apparent that a truly interactive model would need to meet three main requirements, as Nicholas Braucht (1979, p.665) had proposed in his own review:

1. That such real life behaviours cannot adequately be understood by recourse to either individual difference variables alone or environmental variables alone.
2. That neither individuals nor environments can be understood to be pathological in themselves.
3. That behaviour is not viewed as sick or well, but is defined as transactional—an outcome of reciprocal interactions between specific social situations and the individual.

There is certainly sufficient support from this initial empirical study to suggest that the attributional model of self-poisoning meets these requirements and in so doing provides a viable alternative to the pathology paradigm on which much earlier theory has been based. In that it is not dependent on the assumed psychopathology of the individual it can provide a much more comprehensive account of this phenomenon capable of embracing both the social and psychological domains. In that it invokes a social/psychological process which is socially constructed rather than biologically determined, it offers an account also of historical patterns in the epidemiology of self-poisoning which is unavailable within the pathology paradigm.

Theory has an importance beyond the merely descriptive, however, and in relation to human behaviour and distress it has particular importance as a guide to intervention. In the field of self-poisoning professional intervention has apparently met with little success in terms of either primary prevention through the medium of suicide prevention centres, or secondary intervention through various forms of counselling. During the period of the growth in prevention centres, self-poisoning continued to increase at an unprecedented rate, and no form of counselling has succeeded in reducing the repetition rate among such patients. While it would be unrealistic to assume that the pathology pardigm with its emphasis on psychopathology has been entirely responsible for this therapeutic failure, it has probably inhibited the growth of interventive practice based upon other models.

It therefore remains in our final chapter to briefly review the literature describing the outcomes of some current interventions and to consider the implications of our own findings for primary and secondary intervention in this still considerable social problem.

CHAPTER 8

Intervention

The present work has not sought to provide a practice guide to intervention in self-poisoning. Rather, it has been concerned to examine the theoretical basis upon which much interventive practice is based and to disclose its inadequacy. An alternative theoretical model based upon attribution theory has been proposed, and supported by evidence drawn from the literature and the results of an initial study of causal attribution among self-poisoners.

However, if dysfunctional attributions are implicated in the coping deficits observed among self-poisoners and if, as an extensive literature seems to suggest, there are sex differences in attributions which render women particularly vulnerable to such deficits, the implications of an attributional approach for primary and secondary intervention merit consideration here. This is especially so in a field where existing interventions have seemed markedly unsuccessful.

PREVENTION

In relation to the prevention of suicide and self-poisoning, organisations such as the Samaritans in Britain and Crisis Intervention Centres in America have increased their presence enormously since the early 1970s—this despite the fact that evidence of their efficacy in reducing the rates of either completed suicide or self-poisoning is scant, and comparing rates of suicidal behaviour in populations with and without such services has produced equivocal results. An early British study of 15 towns with and without Samaritans' services concluded that there was a significant reduction in suicide rates in those with Samaritans compared with matched towns without (Bagley, 1968).

However a later study by Jennings, Barraclough, and Moss (1978) questioned the basis upon which the towns in the first study had been matched and pointed out that the first study had used two methods of selecting control towns. One of these methods had in fact resulted in the control towns selected showing no significant difference in the suicide rate. Jennings—using different selection criteria—achieved closer matching, had a larger sample of towns and a longer time scale for its suicide statistics. He concluded that no significant difference existed between Samaritan and control towns and noted that over the period 1970–1974 the number of Samaritans' clients had increased by over 150% (70,000–190,000) but the suicide rate had barely declined, going from 8.1 per 100,000 to 7.9. Neither study reported on rates of non-fatal self-poisoning but of course its incidence increased dramatically throughout the period of both, and Holding (1974) found that although television coverage of Samaritans' services increased calls there was no accompanying decline in attempted or actual suicide rates.

An American study by Miller, Coombs, Leeper, and Barton (1984) found that a significant reduction in suicide rates had occurred among young, white women during the period of the greatest growth in crisis intervention centres (1968–1973) and that this group constituted the largest user of such centres. A meta-analysis by Dew, Bromet, and Brent (1987) of the results of 18 studies produced no evidence of centre effects on community suicide rates.

A possible reason for the apparent ineffectiveness of prevention centres is that they may not attract those individuals most at risk of suicide or self-poisoning. Whereas the Dew study found that American crisis intervention centres do attract individuals at high risk of suicide, Kreitman and Chowdhury (1973), in comparing parasuicides (mainly self-poisoners) with Samaritans' clients, found distinct differences between the two groups. Samaritans' clients were predominantly male (2:1)—the reverse being the case among the parasuicides, and clients were less distressed and less likely to be receiving treatment for psychological symptoms than were parasuicides.

Impressed by the sex difference in composition of the two groups, Kreitman and Chowdhury suggested that sex differences in styles of coping and help-seeking might account for this. Women, they supposed, might favour more "expressive" activity when confronted with multiple problems, involving emotional appeal or attempts to "intermit an intolerable state of mind", whereas men would prefer "instrumental" activity geared to solving an objectifiable problem—by seeking advice and guidance in this case rather than self-poisoning. As self-poisoning is a predominantly female behaviour and the supposedly more rational activity of consulting the Samaritans appears not to appeal to women, this might account for their ineffectiveness in reducing self-poisoning.

The suggestion that, at least in the case of the Samaritans, individuals at risk of self-poisoning are not using the service is reinforced by Bancroft et al. (1977b) finding that 75% of one sample of self-poisoners had heard of the Samaritans but that only 4% had contacted them in the week prior to the self-poisoning.

In relation to other possible sources of primary intervention, Hawton and Blackstock (1976) found that over half of their sample had contacted one agency or another and that General Practitioners were the most commonly contacted within the week prior to self-poisoning. Most of these patients had social and interpersonal difficulties and many received minor tranquillisers which they then took in overdose a short time afterwards. Hawton and Catalan (1982a) reviewing the study some years later pointed out that (p.27):

> ... of those who did not contact their GP beforehand 25% said that he had been unhelpful in the past or would be unsympathetic or disapproving of their problems, and 17% thought that he would be too busy to deal with such problems.

This impression of conflicting expectations of helpers and help-seekers is confirmed in a study of the contacts of adolescent self-poisoners in Oxford (Hawton et al., 1982c). It was found that half the subjects had consulted their GP within a month and one-quarter within a week prior to the episode. However only two of those who had seen a GP within the month prior to their self-poisoning reported having discussed the problems which precipitated it, despite the fact that five had been prescribed psychotropics. Of the 12 who had seen a social worker a similar picture emerges, with only 3 discussing the problems which subsequently precipitated the self-poisoning. Perhaps even more suggestive of mutual misperception is the finding that of the 13 subjects who visited the family doctor within a month following the episode only 6 reported any discussion of it, although all the GPs concerned had been informed of their patient's self-poisoning.

Similar results emerged from Turner's (1980) study of patterns of help-seeking prior to deliberate self-harm in which 69% of self-poisoners had heard of Samaritans and the Social Services Department, but only 20% had consulted either. 36% of the patients had contacted their General Practitioner and, of these, 83% had been prescribed psychotropic drugs; 88% of the patients prescribed these drugs subsequently used them in their self-poisoning and 83% of those who had sought help from their GP felt they needed further help. Turner suggests that (p.183):

> ... it would seem that having found that this kind of help has failed to meet their needs they do not know where to turn next. The subsequent deliberate self-harm may be explicable, in some degree, as a challenge to the patient's general practitioner to provide a different solution to his problem.

and he later concludes:

> If we are to make any progress with regard to primary prevention of deliberate self-harm then the various ways in which patients perceive the help that they need and its optimal form of presentation must obviously be taken into account.

SECONDARY INTERVENTION

The literature is no more reassuring in relation to the success of secondary intervention—that following self-poisoning—as the high rate of repetition bears witness; it is estimated variously at between 15% (Morgan et al., 1976) and 25% (Bancroft et al., 1977a) in the 12 months following an initial episode. The high rate of drop out from treatment—60% of those who began outpatient appointments in Turner's (1980) study—similarly casts doubt on the efficacy of intervention, and the fact that 1 in 60 self-poisoners will die by suicide within 12 months (Kessel, 1966) adds urgency to to the search for more effective methods.

Attitudes Towards Self-poisoners

Following self-poisoning the approach adopted by medical, nursing and social work staff who become involved and, indeed, who among these groups does become involved, is likely to influence outcomes. At this stage too there is ample evidence of misperception between patient and professional, helper and helped.

Patel (1975) studied the attitudes of the junior doctors and nurses who have most contact with self-poisoners in the hospital setting, and found that they had "unfavourable attitudes towards these patients". Patel began his paper by quoting several statements reported in earlier studies as typical of the attitudes found, these included:

Their admissions may be regarded with disfavour, treatment may be narrowly confined to their physical condition, provision for aftercare or psychiatric investigation haphazard or ignored (Woodside, 1959).

Viewed as attempts at self-destruction, many of these episodes appear to be half-hearted or histrionic, and the medical staff who have to deal with them sometimes feel a sense of irritation which they find hard to conceal (BMJ, 1971, leading article).

Attempted suicide is of course the most unpopular of all complaints with the medical profession, and even the normally angelic nurses can turn quite waspy at the sight of a living attempt (Bernard, 1974).

The fashion is to treat them with contempt and discharge them as soon as possible (Murray, 1974).

Patel, in addition to eliciting attitudes, enquired as to the match between the beliefs of staff about the disposal of self-poisoners and the actual disposal. Thus most medical staff were under the impression that almost all such cases were admitted to wards and declared the opinion that most should be—whereas only 75% were. Similarly most medical and nursing staff believed that most such patients received psychiatric assessment before discharge—only 64% did in fact receive it.

This disjunction between belief and actuality is perhaps illuminated by the finding that both doctors and nurses considered these patients not personally satisfying to treat or nurse and doubted whether they benefited from their stay in hospital, and that half the junior medical staff and two-fifths of the nurses expressed hostile attitudes to them. In general staff believed that self-poisoning results from social rather than psychiatric problems and Patel concluded that such patients receive such a hostile reception because they are not regarded as "true medical problems".

Attribution of Motivation

Shula Ramon and her colleagues (Ramon, Bancroft, & Skrimshire, 1975) in a vignette study sought to enquire further into the origins of these unfavourable attitudes and discovered that sympathy levels among doctors and nurses varied according to the motives which they attributed to the self-poisoners. Those patients who were considered to have "depressive" motivation (i.e. communicating despair and aimed at withdrawal, escape or death) were more acceptable, and evoked more sympathy and readiness to help than those whose motives were considered to be "manipulative" (i.e. aimed at eliciting a response from others). Nurses were in general more accepting and sympathetic than doctors—a difference also found by Ghodse (1978) and Hawton,

Marsack, & Fagg (1981). Doctors made a clearer distinction between those patients they considered genuinely suicidal—to whom they were relatively accepting—and the manipulative to whom they were less so. Doctors attributed attention seeking and manipulative motives to patients significantly more frequently than did nurses, who more commonly attributed self-poisoning to personal problems such as family, work and "boyfriend" (sic).

The authors suggest that these marked differences between doctors and nurses may be due to sex differences, and it will be recalled from the discussion in Chapter Two of Linehan's (1973) social acceptability theory of sex differences in suicidal behaviour that females are in general more sympathetic to both male and female suicidal target figures than are males who appear least sympathetic to troubled female target figures whether suicidal or not (Stillion et al., 1986; White & Stillion, 1988).

Ramon and her colleagues, however, did not explore this possibility either theoretically or by reporting sex as a variable in their own data. It is clear, however, from the use of personal pronouns that the doctors in the study were predominantly male and nurses female (Ramon et al., 1975, p.262). This lack of interest in sex as a study variable, as we have seen, is not untypical of the self-poisoning literature, but it is unusual to find such clearly expressed evidence of the sex role stereotyping which underpins much of this literature and for this reason the concluding remarks of this paper are reproduced here in some detail:

> We are not in a position to explain these differences between doctors and nurses from the available data, but informal comments from the staff interviewed, as well as common sense interpretation, suggest that this difference may be consistent with their respective roles. The doctor carries greater responsibility for decision making, in particular the decision whether the patient requires medical care. He (sic) is perhaps more likely to feel ambivalent about patients whose immediate problems are self-induced and are usually not the manifestation of illness, and who frequently present relatively insoluble problems to the would-be helper. The nurse on the other hand, can continue to keep to her (sic) traditional role of the warm, sympathetic supporter without being troubled by the question whether the patient qualifies for help or not.

Apart from the evident sex role stereotypy contained in these assertions, it is not made clear whether the barely concealed moral judgements about the deservingness of the patient who "qualifies for help or not" are the authors' or those of the doctors and nurses. Important issues are therefore raised by this paper and we shall return to consider whether judgements involved in the attribution of motives to self-poisoners are in fact moral rather than medical and whether sex and gender may influence them.

For the moment, however, there is further evidence to consider of the clash in perspective between helper and helped which has been an emerging feature of this literature and one which Ramon describes as a lack of "shared meaning".The author suggests that if self-poisoning is an act aimed at communication it must involve assumptions by the self-poisoner about the likely reactions to it—assumptions about its shared meaning which there is reason to believe are ill-founded.

Bancroft et al., 1979 gave a list of motives to 41 self-poisoning patients and the same list to 3 psychiatrists who were given transcripts of interviews and clinical details of these patients. They discovered marked differences between the reasons the patients gave for their self-poisoning and those attributed to them by psychiatrists: while the psychiatrists agreed with the one-third of the patients who claimed no suicidal intent, they disagreed with half of those who claimed such intention. In general the psychiatrists differed most markedly in their willingness to attribute hostile and manipulative reasons to self-poisoners who themselves least commonly used such explanation. Thus one of the motives most commonly chosen by psychiatrists (71%) was "frighten or get your own back on somebody/make people sorry for the way they have treated you", whereas this was among the least commonly chosen by patients (10%) who most frequently attributed their actions to the need for relief from a "terrible state of mind" (44%) or to the fact that "the situation was so unbearable" that they "did not know what else to do" (56%). Only 15% of patients and psychiatrists employed the motive of seeking help as an explanation.

If the process of helping begins with such profound mutual misperception it is unsurprising that it has been shown to continue with such limited effectiveness.

A review of interventions by Hirsch, Walsh, and Draper (1982) described evaluative studies of methods ranging from inpatient behaviour modification and insight oriented therapy (Liberman & Eckman, 1981) to intensive social work follow-up with outpatients (Gibbons, Butler, Urwin, & Gibbons, 1978). They found little evidence that any method had convincingly demonstrated its effectiveness in reducing the repetition rate. Perhaps because of this the conclusion arrived at seems to suggest a disillusionment with the psychopathology paradigm and a turning towards social-psychological forms of explanation (Hirsch et al., 1982, p.310):

If Liberman (Liberman & Eckman, 1981) is correct in asserting that suicidal behaviour is learned and maintained by social consequences ... a radically different approach will be necessary and ... ethno-cultural influences may prove to be the most important in the long run, as indicated by the rapid changes in the incidence of parasuicide which we have witnessed over the past 25 years, despite attempts of primary and secondary prevention.

It is becoming clear from this review of what is known about patterns of help-seeking, and primary and secondary intervention that the apparent ineffectiveness of both may be in part due to a disjunction between the implicit models individuals hold of help-seeking and help-giving. Kreitman suggests that the model of helping and coping espoused by the Samaritans may not be that held by the largest group of self-poisoners—women. Hawton found that self-poisoners who did not contact their GP beforehand assumed that their problems would not be seen by him or her as appropriately brought for discussion. A significant percentage had previous experience of this response, and the patients' beliefs seem justified by the additional finding that the problems which had precipitated self-poisoning were rarely discussed when patients saw their GPs after hospital treatment. Turner concluded that much self-poisoning might actually represent a rejection of the type of help previously received from the GP and that a closer match between patients' perception of the help they need and the help they are offered is required, while Ramon found evidence of a lack of "shared meaning" about the behaviour.

In summary, doctors and to a lesser extent nurses are unsympathetic to such patients unless genuine suicidal motives are attributed to the behaviour. The unfavourable attitudes may, therefore, be a reflection of the fact that only a minority of patients actually claim and even less are perceived by medical staff as possessing such motivation. In addition troubled women—who constitute two-thirds of the patients—are viewed unsympathetically by men who, at least until recently, predominated among the doctors. It seems likely that sex role stereotypy will have some influence in this process of motive attribution and the fact that such women have been referred to as "harridans" (McCulloch & Philip, 1972, p.62), and as "hysterical" when there is no professional justification for the first and no clinical evidence for the second (Goldney, 1981a) reinforces this suspicion. That there is no "shared meaning" between helper and helped at least at the point of entry to the helping process is abundantly clear from the clash in attributions for motives between them, and may well contribute to the apparent ineffectiveness of much secondary intervention.

The possibility that the inefficacy of various forms of helping may be due, at least in part, to clashes in attributional patterns between helpers and help-seekers is one which Phillip Brickman and his colleagues considered in their Attributional Model of Helping and Coping. This suggests that people hold implicit models of helping and coping which differ according their characteristic attributions of the cause of problems and of the responsibility for their solution. This model therefore may be enlightening in relation to self-poisoning—especially so as it has been subsequently shown that gender differences exist in the respective models of helping and coping possessed by men and women.

An Attributional Model of Helping and Coping

The authors introduce the model by asserting (Brickman et al., 1982, p.368) that the focus of interest is: "How people decide whether material aid, exhortation, discipline, emotional support or some other form of help is most appropriate and what the consequences of these choices are".

A key variable in this is the attribution of responsibility both for the cause of problems and their solution, but responsibility involves two separate issues—blame and control. In attributional terms blame is determined by whether the cause of a problem is seen as internal or external to the individual, and control according to whether the cause is stable or unstable—unstable causes, such as lack of effort are thought of as controllable. However, as we have seen earlier in this work, some internal causes, such as disease, do not result in blame and some unstable causes such as bad luck are uncontrollable. The confusion of blame and control, Brickman and his colleagues point out, may have unfortunate consequences such as the assumption that looking for a solution to a problem involves finding someone to blame, or that if the variables causing a problem cannot be changed then no solution can be found.

The proposal is therefore that we conceptually separate the two issues of blame for the cause of problems and responsibility for their solution: thus, individuals may be perceived as having high or low responsibility for the cause of their problem and high or low responsibility for its solution. This results in (p.370):

... four fundamentally different orientations to the world, each internally coherent, each in some measure incompatible with the other three. These different models of helping and coping exist in the minds of helpers, aggressors and recipients of help or aggression. They are also embodied in social institutions that mete out help or punishment ... each set of assumptions makes it easier to solve certain problems and harder to solve others. For example, the assumptions in most doctor/patient relationships facilitate the acceptance of information and instructions by the patient but make it hard for patients to assert their own opinions.

Later it is asserted that the importance of this approach is not whether or not helping occurs but whether the helpers and helped share an implicit model of the process and the consequences of both for effective helping. Different types of psychotherapy, the authors suggest, embody one of each of the four models—which are as follows.

The Moral Model. High responsibility is attributed to individuals for both the cause and solution of their problems. Help-seekers are expected to accept that the blame for their predicament lies within themselves, their character or lack of effort. Help is limited to reminding them of this and of their responsibility to change it if they wish to solve their problem. The benefit to the client in this model is that it emphasises self-reliance and avoids dependency; the disadvantage is that it can lead potential helpers into blaming the victim, and help-seekers to underutilise external sources of help. It is proposed that rational-emotive therapy and existential therapy embrace this model.

The Compensatory Model. Low responsibility is attributed to the individual for the cause of their problem, but high responsibility for its solution. Thus clients may be viewed as being disadvantaged through no fault of their own, but are regarded as being responsible for acquiring the skills and attributes they need to solve their problem. Help involves encouragement and tuition in the skills of problem solving. Advantages to clients include empowerment of the client, encouragement to direct their energy outwards adopting a problem-solving orientation rather than an inward looking self-blaming attitude. In addition clients are enabled to retain the respect of others in that they are seen as not responsible for their problem but using their own initiative to solve it. Individuals with this orientation may tire of trying to solve problems for which they do not feel responsible and "burn-out" may result. Cognitive-behaviour therapy which emphasises skill acquisition by the client is typical of this model.

The Medical Model. Individuals are attributed low responsibility for both their problem and its resolution. Help-seekers are viewed as victims of factors beyond their control and therefore blameless, and help is perceived as submission to the will of the expert helper who is the sole agent of change. Individuals who hold this model perceive themselves and are perceived as ill or incapacitated, as the authors state (Brickman et al., 1982, p.373):

> They are expected to accept this state, which in turn involves exempting them from their ordinary social obligations ... the other actors ... are experts who have been trained to recognise what the problem is and to provide what treatment or service is available.

The advantage of this model to the client is that they can accept help without being blamed for the problem or expected to solve it: "The same symptoms that would be punished under another model are entitled to treatment under the medical model" (p.373). The disadvantage is that help is deskilling and creates dependency. The traditional relationship between doctor and diseased patient is an example of this model, and traditional insight oriented psychotherapy based on psychodynamic principles is said to embody its assumptions.

The Enlightenment Model.   Individuals are responsible for the cause of their problems but not their solution. Clients are encouraged to accept their responsibility for causing their problems through their own shortcomings and help is perceived as enlightening the client as to these internal origins of the problem and helping them to overcome their inadequacy by the helper imposing control from without. Alcoholics Anonymous may be viewed as exemplary of this model.

ATTRIBUTION AND PRIMARY
INTERVENTION—PREVENTION

Brickman and his colleagues propose that difficulties in helping relationships may be due either to dysfunctional, dependency inducing collusion betwen the models of helper and helped, or to clashes between their implicit models. There is little doubt from our review of the literature dealing with both primary and secondary intervention that such clashes exist between the clients and helpers in this context.

The finding of our own study that self-poisoners—particularly females—tend to attribute negative events more internally, stably and globally than non-patients, suggests that they regard uncontrollable, characterological aspects of themselves to have caused their problems and that they are therefore not responsible for them. In view of the perceived stability and globality of the causes of their problems which would limit their control over them and adversely affect any attempts they might make to change them it seems equally unlikely that self-poisoners would feel either competent to resolve their problems or responsible for so doing.

Thus the implicit model of coping and helping implied by this pattern of attribution is the Medical Model, whereby people are neither responsible for their problems nor their solution. In this context it is interesting that attitudinal studies among the general population (Ginsburg, 1971) and of the reasons self-poisoners give for their act (Bancroft et al., 1979) suggest that behaviour regarded as suicidal is conceived as something that happens to an individual rather than being brought about by them, as Brickman and his fellow authors assert (Brickman et al., 1982, p.372):

> The Medical Model ... refers not only to cases in which people are thought to be victims of disease but to all cases in which people are considered subject to forces beyond their control.

If self-poisoners do possess this implicit model then it is unsurprising that the GP is the source of help most commonly sought beforehand. Unfortunately, however, GPs are often untrained in psycho-social counselling, have very little time per consultation and sometimes feel that counselling in any case is not their appropriate task. Thus many such patients, as we have seen, are offered little opportunity to discuss their problems and receive psychotropic drugs instead.

While for the GP this may well be in keeping with the conventional Medical Model of diagnosis and symptomatic treatment, the experience for the troubled, but not necessarily sick, patient may be more akin to that of the Moral Model in which they are held to be responsible for both problem and solution. The prescription of psychotropic drugs, rather than relieving the patient of their sense of inadequacy, reinforces it by its implication that the origin of the problem is the internal, psychological state of the patient rather than external, social or relational ones. The message of the apparent reluctance to discuss their problems and the seemingly hurried prescription of drugs is that they are seen as both responsible for their problem and its solution.

Studies have shown that self-poisoners who consulted their GP beforehand frequently felt dissatisfied with the help received and in need of further help. The possibility that such a clash in attributional perspectives underlies this dissatisfaction is supported by accounts of prior contacts with helpers obtained from female self-poisoners in O'Brien's study. Referring to their consultations with GPs and others, the following descriptions (O'Brien, 1986, p.47) clearly indicate significant disparity between expectation and actuality:

I did say I was having matrimonial problems and things, I didn't think I could cope and my nerves were very on edge, and I needed something to calm me down. He didn't talk to me. He just said take these tablets when required and that was Valium.

He thinks I'm a neurotic woman, so out comes the Valium.

I mean they are supposed to be there to help you, they are supposed to care, but they don't give a fuck, so they get rid of you with tablets.

There are similar descriptions of encounters with other potential helpers. For example two women described their expectations of psychiatrists prior to their consultation in this way:

Well I went in there with the attitude of "OK, you sort out this mess for me".

There he was with all his degrees and things and I felt I was stupid and nothing, but that he must have all the answers.

In relation to the Samaritans there is again evidence of a clash in expectations of help and that actually received:

They were very nice and all, gave me a cup of tea, and I talked for about three hours. But all she did was listen and ask the odd question. I wanted her to say something back to me, but they are not supposed to do that. I got the feeling that she didn't really know what I was on about.

Turner (1980) suggested that, finding the response of their GP unhelpful, self-poisoning may represent a challenge to the doctor to produce a more acceptable solution and a further comment from one of O'Brien's subjects (at p.48) lends credibility to this possible consequence of the clash in perspective:

You keep going back to him ... you've got to keep trying. You think because they are doctors they can come up with something. It's the only hope. But so often you come away feeling what's the point, they can't do anything. That's the worst time, when your last resort has gone and you feel really alone.

One disadvantage of the Medical Model is that it fosters dependency when shared by both helper and helped. Brickman and his colleagues point to the work of Langer and Benevento (1978) demonstrating that once people are made to feel dependent on others they may lose the ability to do even those things they once did well. The dependency implicit in this woman's statements and the dangers of further deskilling which it implies are apparent in her assumption that if the doctor cannot resolve the problem no one can and the last resort is gone. Ironically, if, as O'Brien's findings suggest, the next stage is self-poisoning then the unfavourable and sometimes hostile response from hospital medical and nursing staff will further reinforce the disparity between the implicit Medical Model of helping and coping held by the patient and that shown by the helpers—which may more closely resemble the Moral Model.

The attributional model of helping and coping contributes, therefore, to our understanding of the apparent anomaly whereby most patients have recently consulted sources of possible help, usually a doctor, but none the less still poison themselves. The interaction between doctor and patient may be seen as a clash between the patient's Medical Model and the Moral Model which seems to underpin the doctor's perceived disinterest, leading to feelings of shame and further hopelessness in the patient. Alternatively it may be seen as an unfortunate collusion whereby both doctor and patient hold an implicit Medical Model which leads to the prescription of psychotropics by the doctor and—when the drugs fail to solve the problem—leads the patient to disappointment, further hopelessness, and possibly self-poisoning.

That Brickman's model has particular relevance to female self-poisoning is suggested by the results of two further pieces of empirical research. The first we have explored already in discussing sex differences in attribution. This is Brewin and Shapiro's (1984) finding that women took responsibility for negative events more readily than did males, thereby being more vulnerable to the adverse effects of shame and guilt when encountering a helper possessing an implicit Moral Model. The second is a study which specifically sought to establish whether there are gender differences in the extent to which individuals accept responsibility for solutions.

Mitchell (1987) proposed that sex role socialisation has important implications for the conceptualisation of problems and the choice of solutions. She suggests that masculinity is stereotypically associated with competence, decisiveness, self-reliance and stoicism, whereas femininity is associated with greater dependency and the more ready expression of distress. On this basis she hypothesised that subjects high in femininity (whether male or female) would endorse the Enlightenment or Medical Models as they stress low internal attribution of responsibility for problem solving.

Using the Personal Attributes Questionnaire (Spence & Helmreich, 1978) and a scale devised to tap the four models (Rabinowitz, 1978), Mitchell found that as predicted, femininity showed a consistent positive association with measures of the Enlightenment and Medical

Models. This finding might contribute to the explanation of the greater utilisation of health services by women, as it suggests that femininity may legitimise help-seeking. In the present context, however, the endorsement of a Medical Model of coping and helping by troubled women might also render them more vulnerable to hopelessness when their expected model is disconfirmed by their experience of medical help. Furthermore, by promoting medical help-seeking for social and relational problems the endorsement of the Medical Model exposes them to the risks associated with the prescription of psychotropic medication.

These attributional insights clearly lead to some recommendations in relation to primary intervention. If GPs are the most favoured source of help sought by potential self-poisoners it seems essential that either they have the training and time to devote to the proper psycho-social assessment and counselling of such patients, or that there is someone else within the primary care team who does. While few people appear to seek the counsel of social workers before self-poisoning, O'Brien found that those who had done so expressed greater satisfaction with the help they received (O'Brien, 1985, p.55). Although GPs are increasingly receiving initial training in counselling their time per consultation in the surgery is inadequate to allow its practice. It would seem logical therefore that the attachment of a social worker to GP surgeries might improve the match between the sort of help people expect and that which they receive. In addition, if GPs are able to obtain immediate counselling and practical assistance for their patients from surgery based social workers they may be less inclined to prescribe the pharmaceutical first aid of psychotropic medication.

There is reason to believe that reducing the rate of psychotropic prescription by any means would constitute a most effective form of primary intervention. Since 1976 self-poisoning has been declining in Great Britain with a 15% reduction in England alone between 1978 and 1985 (Wells, 1988). During the period from 1976 the rate of prescription of psychotropic drugs has shown a similarly impressive decline and both have been most marked among women (Platt et al., 1988; DHSS, 1987). This apparent correlation lends credence to the explanation for both the increase and the decline in self-poisoning offered by Brewer and Farmer (1985) to the effect that psychotropic prescription is causally implicated in self-poisoning—and others have reached a similar conclusion (Forster & Frost, 1985). One explanation for this decline in prescription may be the evidence emerging from the early-1970s that benzodiazepines, previously regarded as entirely safe drugs, cause dependency and, while having both medium- and long-term side effects have only short-term benefits.

The use of paracetemol—a highly dangerous drug in overdose but none the less readily available without prescription—is common among younger self-poisoners of both sexes and although its use declines with age among females there is no such decline among males (Hawton & Goldacre, 1982d, p.168). If, indeed, there is a causal relationship between the availability of drugs and self-poisoning then restricting the availability of analgesics and antipyretics could represent the first stage of effective intervention.

ATTRIBUTION AND SECONDARY INTERVENTION—THE "DILEMMA OF HELPING"

When people fail to distinguish between attribution of responsibility for a problem and for a solution, they must choose between two unsatisfactory alternatives: holding actors responsible for both problem and solution and not giving help; or holding actors responsible for neither ... and giving help on terms that undermine actors sense of competence and control and their ability to make effective use of the help itself (Brickman et al., 1982, p. 376).

Quite clearly the busy doctor's dilemma is at least in part resolved by psychotropic prescription. This is in keeping with the Medical Model but so too is the unfortunate dependency and deskilling encouraged by its acceptance and, at least in some cases, the hopelessness resulting from its failure to solve the problem. Drug prescription is not the only form of intervention embodying the Medical Model and possessing its attendant dangers, however, and the attributional model of helping and coping offers some explanation also of the apparent ineffectiveness of certain forms of counselling when employed in secondary intervention with self-poisoners.

Brickman and his colleagues proposed that forms of insight-oriented counselling based on psychodynamic principles also entail the disadvantages of a Medical Model. Thus the failing client must seek and accept the insights of the "expert" counsellor/therapist in order to improve their functioning—an inherently dependent, passive role, which is potentially deskilling.

Within the attributional model of helping and coping, the dilemma of helping without undermining coping is resolved in counselling by employing the Compensatory Model. This is the only one which both justifies helping (since actors have not caused their own problem), and enables the helped to remain involved in its resolution, for which they are ultimately responsible. In this way the dangers of dependency and deskilling may be minimised.

The Compensatory Model is contrasted with interventions based upon psychoanalytic theory which seem to embody the assumptions of the Medical Model in that the causes of neurosis are thought to be hidden in the depths of time and the unconscious and are therefore inaccessible to clients without the expert help of the therapist. Thus, although they are not responsible for causing their problems, neither are they able to take an active role in their resolution. As another of O'Brien's (1985) subjects reported (p.51) in relation to treatment from a psychiatrist:

> I always felt that you were the patient and they were the ones who were all right and that whatever you said or did was always seen with the idea that you were basically sick and they weren't sick. They weren't interested in breaking down what their role was.

It has been the contention of this book that the pathology paradigm underlying much of the theory and practice applied to self-poisoning is flawed, particularly in relation to the psychodynamic account of female self-poisoning. Its biologically based theory of women as inherently masochistic and self-defeating is unsupported by research and its assumption of psychopathology is out of keeping with the comparative absence of such pathology among self-poisoners. The alternative attributional theory has been proposed because it does not rely on the asocial assumption of individual pathology, and it can embrace both the social and the psychological. Thus, the dysfunctional attributional style possessed by self-poisoners is not the product of internal pathology, but of normative sex role socialisation, socio-economic status and non-normative life experiences.

It suggests that the dysfunctional attributional style found commonly among women and self-poisoning patients—consisting of internal, stable and global attributions for negative events—impedes problem solving by promoting self-preoccupation and diverting attention from strategic activity. In relation to intervention, therefore, the insight-oriented practice of counselling based on psychodynamic theory is entirely inappropriate. By encouraging introspection and self-preoccupation it adds to the attentional deficits resulting from dysfunctional attributions by directing attention away from external sources of difficulty and strategic problem-solving activity. The apparent ineffectiveness of much current counselling with self-poisoning patients might therefore be expected.

There is further justification in the attributional literature for the employment of forms of counselling with self-poisoners which are based upon a Compensatory Model. Numerous studies have demonstrated that people who attribute improvement in a variety of conditions to internal causes—such as their own efforts—maintain that improvement longer than those who attribute it to external ones such as medication (Davison & Valins, 1969; Valins & Nisbett, 1971; Liberman, 1978; Chamblis & Murray, 1979). Clients who hold an implicit Medical Model will attribute any improvement in their situation, not to their own efforts, but to those of the expert counsellor. Improvement may, therefore, be shortlived as such a pattern of external attribution for positive events will not enhance persistence in the face of future problems; neither will it promote the development of those problem-solving skills which self-poisoners have been shown to lack.

These insights from attributional research suggest three techniques which might usefully be included in the assessment phase of secondary intervention with self-poisoning patients:

1. Assessment of models of helping and coping held by client and counsellor.
2. Assessment of the client's attributional style.
3. Assessment of the particular problem-solving deficits which the client may possess.

Models of Helping and Coping.   Counsellors seeking to begin by exploring models of helping and coping are cautioned to remember some of the characteristics of self-poisoners identified in the literature and discussed in earlier chapters of this book. In advocating a Compensatory Model the counsellor should be prepared in the negotiating process for some resistance—this might be expected from female clients, still the majority of self-poisoners—on the basis of Mitchell's (1987) finding that femininity correlated highly with possession of implicit Medical or Enlightenment Models.

In addition it should be remembered from previous chapters that high status individuals respond attributionally as do those with high self-esteem and high expectancy of success—assuming responsibility for solving problems and taking an active role in devising strategies to solve them, rather than being preoccupied with blaming themselves for causing them. The working class status of most self-poisoners might mean therefore that they will not initially share the Compensatory Model of their predominantly middle class helpers. The possibility of resistance and the potential for either a collusive and dysfunctional sharing of an inappropriate Medical Model, or for a clash between Medical and Compensatory Models makes exploration and negotiation not only a more delicate exercise but a more important one.

Attributional Style. In relation to the assessment of attributional style the revised Attributional Style Questionnaire described by Peterson and Villanova (1988) is an accessible and easily employed instrument which enjoys greater reliability than its predecessor. The neglect of clients' attributional style may, as we have suggested, reduce the efficacy of any intervention as those who attribute any success to external rather than internal factors are less likely to maintain improvement.

This may explain the puzzling finding of Gibbons, Butler, Urwin, & Gibbons (1978) that, although self-poisoning patients receiving problem-oriented task-centred case work showed some improvement in social functioning, their repetition rate was no lower than that of a control group who received a routine follow-up service—referral back to GP, to a psychiatrist, or "other referral". If such clients attributed the improvement in their social functioning to the therapist's intervention then—although the problems initially presented may have been ameliorated—the client would none the less not have developed the enhanced persistence and problem-solving skills which a more adaptive attributional style would promote following such success. New problems arising later would, therefore, evoke the same dysfunctional attributions and consequent hopelessness which may then result in repetition.

If, as seems likely from the results of our own research, the client is found to possess a dysfunctional attributional style then there are several accounts of successful attributional retraining in the literature which will be described in more detail later.

Problem-solving Deficits. The third aspect of assessment suggested by an attributional approach is that clients should be involved not only in the assessment of their particular problems—as Hawton and Catalan (1982a) and Gibbons et al. (1978) propose—but also in the assessment of deficits in their problem-solving techniques. This could employ measures such as the Means–Ends Problem Solving Procedure (Platt, Spivack, & Bloom, 1975) and the Alternative Uses Test (Wilson et al., 1975) already extensively used in research with such patients.

Again, the limited success of even those forms of intervention which embody the Compensatory Model (such as problem-oriented task-centred counselling which do involve clients in responsibility for finding solutions) may be more understandable when it is realised that focussing on particular problems and their solutions may not result in the enhancement of problem-solving skills as such. Thus when new and different problems arise the client is no better equipped to deal with them than before intervention began and—especially in the presence of dysfunctional attributions—hopelessness may again lead to self-poisoning.

COUNSELLING SELF-POISONING CLIENTS

Turning now to techniques of counselling more in keeping with these attributional insights into self-poisoning, it is reassuring to note that Brickman and his fellow authors believe that in relation to counselling the Compensatory Model is fully realised in cognitive-behavioural approaches which teach clients how to alter maladaptive cognitive processes and environmental contingencies. In relation to self-poisoners there are two general accounts of cognitive-behavioural approaches which are designed as guides to practice (Beck, Rush, Shaw, & Emery, 1979; Williams & Wells, 1989). As does the attributional theory of self-poisoning, the cognitive-behavioural approach to intervention assumes the client has deficits in certain skills for which she is not to blame and which she can subsequently control, rather than assuming pathology in personality which, even if not to blame for it, she has little hope of controlling. Two main approaches to counselling the self-poisoner are suggested by this—attributional retraining and problem-solving training.

Attributional Retraining

The effects of attributional manipulation on persistence and quality of performance in both academic and interpersonal contexts are well documented. For example LaNoue and Curtis (1985) improved women's initial expectations and performance by encouraging effort attributions and in the context of problem solving, Mikulincer and Nizan (1988) convincingly demonstrated the beneficial effects in academic tasks of manipulating failure attributions from global to specific which enhanced attention by reducing off-task cognitions. In the interpersonal sphere Anderson (1983) showed that encouraging unstable, specific attributions to effort as opposed to stable, global attributions to personality enhanced persistence and performance by focussing attention away from characterological introspection towards behavioural strategy.

In view of the fact that the present volume is the first extensive exploration of an attributional approach to self-poisoning it is not surprising that no example of attributional retraining specifically with these clients appears to be available. However, a detailed report of the technique is provided by Layden (1982), and a review of 15 attributional retraining studies by Forsterling (1985) concluded that such intervention is effective in producing changes on both cognitive and behavioural levels, increasing the subjects' attributions for failure to lack of effort, and improving performance as well as persistence.

Problem-solving Training

The dysfunctional attributional style possessed by self-poisoners may result in problem-solving deficits in the face of adversity. This occurs not only through decrements in persistence but also through attentional deficits which limit their ability to identify more effective strategies. There are several accounts of coping skills training programmes with various client groups in the literature and a useful review is that of Elizabeth Marx (1988). A recent example of effective, relatively short-term coping skills training is described in Ronald Smith's (1989) study of exam phobic students. Five fortnightly sessions of only 60 minutes each succeeded in achieving significant reductions in anxiety and improvements in academic performance.

There are also several examples of such training with parasuicides. Clum, Patsiokas, and Luscomb (1979), whose work in relation to problem-solving deficits in self-poisoners was described in Chapter Two, suggest that an "empirically-based comprehensive treatment programme for parasuicide" would concentrate on cognitive restructuring as the primary goal of treatment. As problem-solving deficits are central to the aetiology of self-poisoning, they propose the adoption of D'Zurrilla and Goldfried's (1971) five-step approach to resolving such deficits. The steps are:

1. Accepting that problem situations are a normal part of life and learning that first impulses to solve them should be resisted;
2. Defining the problem in operational terms;
3. Generating alternative solutions to the problem;
4. Making a decision regarding which course to follow;
5. Verifying one's choice of an alternative in the problem situation.

Clum et al. (1979. p.944) asserts that: "Such an approach would directly train the unsuccessful suicide, who has had previous trouble in problem solving, in techniques for solving problems".

Three further research-based studies exist which demonstrate the beneficial effects of problem-solving therapies—those of Fraser (1987), Linehan (1988) and Salkovskis, Atha, and Storer, (1990).

Fraser set out to assess interpersonal problem-solving ability in self-poisoners and the relative efficacy of a variety of subsequent interventions. Comparing self-poisoners with mixed psychiatric outpatients and normal controls on a measure of means–ends problem solving, he found, as others had before, that self-poisoners produced significantly fewer relevant means, story directed responses and sufficient narratives compared to both control groups. On time and obstacle recognition self-poisoners were significantly more deficient than either control group and greater social dysfunction, stress and affective disturbance was associated with poorer interpersonal problem solving among them. Three types of intervention of eight weeks duration were employed—Cognitive Therapy, Problem-Solving Training and Psychiatric Aftercare. The problem-solving abilities of self-poisoners improved most in the problem-solving group and the maintenance of affective change at follow-up was related to the extent of improvement in such abilities. Problem-solving training had the most effect on improving social functioning, was as effective in reducing suicidal rumination as the other forms of intervention, and no repetition occurred.

Linehan (1988) described Dialectical Behaviour Therapy (DBT) specifically as reducing the risk of self-harm. The therapy has a double focus: (a) A behavioural/problem-solving focus, enhancing capabilities, a collaborative approach to generating alternative coping strategies, contingency clarification and contingency management, and an emphasis on the "observable" present; and (b) A focus on the dialectical aspects of both the patient's experience - which might include feeling everything very intensely whilst simultaneously invalidating these feelings by expecting not to have them or blaming oneself for having them—and a focus on the dialectical aspect of therapy with its encouragement to accept things as they are while also trying to change.

Patients take part in individual psychotherapy and group psychotherapy, the focus of each being slightly different. The group concentrates on problem-solving skills (interpersonal effectiveness, emotional regulation and distress tolerance respectively). In individual therapy, therapist and patient investigate in great detail the circumstances surrounding any suicidal thought, feeling or behaviour. The client keeps a record of alcohol and drug abuse (prescribed and non-prescribed), rates degrees of suicidal urges and depression and any episodes of self-harm. In therapy the diary is discussed, the aim being to dissociate emotional upsets from suicidal behaviour, and no such behaviour, no matter how apparently insignificant, is ignored. Every movement of thought and behaviour is exhaustively assessed and the chain of thought, feeling and behaviour leading to self-harm is made explicit. Only then are alternative strategies discussed.

Salkovskis, Atha, and Storer (1990) carried out a controlled trial in which patients at high risk of repeated suicide attempts (as measured by the Buglass and Horton (1974) Scale) were randomly allocated to either cognitive-behavioural problem-solving treatment or a "treatment as usual" control condition. Effectiveness was assessed not only by rate of repetition but also with repeated measures using the Beck Suicidal Intent Scale (Beck, Schuyler, & Herman, 1974), the Personal

Questionnaire Rapid Scaling Technique (Mulhall, 1977) designed to assess the extent of problems and their relative severity, the Profile of Mood States (McNair, Lorr, & Droppelman, 1971) and the Beck Hopelessness Scale (Beck et al., 1974c).

The experimental problem-solving approach followed a format first described by Bancroft (1986) and involved five sessions of treatment of at least one hour given first at the time of the attempt, three days later, after one and two weeks, and finally after one month. In addition "homework" assignments were used. Patients were taught how to identify and specify problems and prioritise problem-solving efforts; to employ the brainstorming technique to generate alternative solutions and then decide on concrete and attainable goals which would represent significant improvement in their own terms. Following this, strategies for attaining their goals were devised and means of obtaining feedback on success, with an emphasis being placed on the need to be flexible on judgements of success and failure and being open to revising goals and strategies as required. Thus the emphasis throughout was on learning techniques of problem solving applicable to any problem rather than on the resolution of any particular problem. Assessments and treatment were carried out in the patients' own homes which the authors felt resulted in none dropping out of treatment—an unusual finding among self-poisoners.

The experimental group showed significantly more improvement on all problems identified by the PQRST, there was significant, substantial and enduring reduction in depression and hopelessness, and also a lower rate of repetition up to 6 months but not at 18 months. The mean time to repeat, however, was 9.3 months in the experimental group compared with 3 months in the control (treatment as usual) group. Although these findings must be treated with caution as the sample contained only 20 patients of whom 12 were in the experimental group, it none the less provides further encouragement for the study of problem-solving interventions, especially as all the patients were deemed at high risk of repetition.

In her detailed review of problem-solving therapies, Elizabeth Marx (1988, p.49) suggests that "since we cannot prevent the occurrence of problems, the promotion of patients to become their own therapist certainly seems a most valuable target". This is a view wholly consistent with our prediction that Brickman's Compensatory Model (which stresses the responsibility of the patient for problem resolution) is likely to prove most successful in therapy for parasuicide patients. Thus, cognitively-based, problem-solving training is evidently an approach worthy of further research and application. However, Brickman's analysis and our own finding of a dysfunctional attributional style among self-poisoners suggest that this should constitute but one stage of a programme of intervention. In order to maximise effectiveness such programmes should perhaps begin with negotiation of mutual expectations of the helping process, proceed through attributional assessment, and, if necessary retraining, and only finally culminate in problem solving training.

SEX ROLE SOCIALISATION, SOCIAL CHANGE, AND FEMALE SELF-POISONING

Hirsch, Walsh, and Draper, whose paper on the apparent inefficacy of primary and secondary intervention we have already discussed (Hirsch et al., 1982), concluded a second, similarly pessimistic review (Hirsch et al., 1983) thus:

> ... one wonders whether socio-cultural influences prove more important than any treatment approach and whether a real reduction in the parasuicide rate will only come when the nature of society itself changes.

There is ample evidence both that the rate of self-poisoning has declined in Britain over the past 13 years, and that there have been changes in certain aspects of British society. The nature of evidence at this level of analysis is inevitably less convincing than that with which we have been dealing thus far, at best seeking to establish correlation rather than causality. However, the importance of placing self-poisoning within its historical and cultural context has been emphasised earlier in this work and some review of this context will be helpful before addressing the question of the relationship between recent social changes and self-poisoning.

In Chapter Four, the relatedness of historical changes and trends in the incidence of self-poisoning were discussed in terms of women's roles in society and sex role socialisation. Direct parallels were drawn between the 19th century epidemic of female hysteria and the mid-20th century one of female self-poisoning. Showalter's (1985) analysis of female hysteria interpreted it as emanating from the disparity between mid-19th century women's increasing aspirations for education and rewarding employment and their limited access to such opportunity.

Rigidly ascribed sex roles and inflexible stereotypes of appropriate masculine and feminine attributes and behaviours meant that to reject normatively ascribed roles risked losing the feminine identity which was the only vehicle through which women attained any status in male dominated society. Stereotypical attributes of mid-19th century femininity, as Showalter demonstrates through the popular literature of the day, included frailty, passivity and dependence, and the invalidism and dependence of the hysterical woman are interpreted by Showalter as the only means available to many women to withdraw from socially sanctioned roles without losing their feminine identity. Thus normative sex role socialisation formed female deviance as well as conformity.

Female hysteria is seen in this analysis therefore as a "silent protest" and an "inarticulate body language" and the mid-20th century epidemic of female self-poisoning has been interpreted in this work in much the same way as a response to the disparity between women's aspirations and expectations following the Second World War and the social roles available to them. The particular nature of this female malady, as with hysteria before it, is here seen as the result of normative sex role socialisation. This identifies femininity as helplessness and asserts that women are both directly socialised to be helpless in order to fulfil the stereotype of femininity, and indirectly socialised through their experience of powerlessness to both expect and possess limited control over their own outcomes—to be helpless. Through the increasingly powerful social institution of medicine (with which women have considerably more involvement than men) prescribed psychotropic medication became the remedy, sanctioned by the sex role system, for the social and emotional consequences of this female helplessness.

As a result, when confronted with multiple adversity, helpless women responded in the normatively prescribed fashion—by self-medication taken to its extreme of self-poisoning. While permitting withdrawal from and protest against her situation, self-poisoning allows the woman to retain her feminine identity by assuming the passive, dependent and helpless role of the unconscious patient. The epidemic of self-poisoning did not begin in the early-1960s as much commentary suggests, for the first sudden increase occurred in 1947 (the year the National Health Service commenced and drugs became readily available to working class people). From then until 1976 the rate of self-poisoning increased inexorably.

The demographic and social changes accompanying this trend are discussed in Chapter Four and the evidence for their relatedness to self-poisoning assessed. In the interests of brevity this will not be repeated here other than to suggest that many of the factors associated with self-poisoning during the period of its increase have now been found to have diminished during its decline.

In Great Britain in 1977 the incidence of self-poisoning fell, the first time this had happened in 30 years, and it has declined yearly since then. During this comparatively short period changes have emerged in some socio-economic and other variables which had been associated particularly with the increase in female self-poisoning. The prescription of psychotropic drugs decreased for the first time in at least a decade in 1977, and it has declined at an increasing rate since. There have been decreases in male participation in the labour force and increases in that of females, and a 50% decrease in teenage marriages. Not only has there been a general decline in incidence but rates among women have decreased more rapidly than those of men, such that in one study the sex ratio had almost reached parity (Robinson et al., 1986).

Kessler and McRae (1983) found similar trends in America between 1940 and 1980 and suggest that this is due to women having increased access to non-traditional roles outside the home, in part facilitated by deferred childbearing, smaller families and more employment being available. They describe other research showing that women with these characteristics (especially those in employment) demonstrate lower rates of psychological distress than do women in more traditional roles, and propose that women in conventional roles have less effective coping styles than non-traditional women. When confronted with problems in family and relational spheres women in traditional roles rely on other people for emotional support and do not know how to garner help when this is not available. Referring to Martin Seligman's work, they suggest that this style is one of "learned helplessness". Having more diverse roles allows women access to greater coping resources when adversity occurs, and they are therefore less reliant on male support both economic and emotional.

Males may experience these developments as challenging their traditional domination in certain public and private roles, and suffer a loss of self-esteem and effective coping as a result. This might be especially true where high levels of male unemployment prevail, as they have done in the past decade. Thus, Kessler and McRae assert there is a "convergence of coping styles" with males more frequently demonstrating that style traditionally characteristic of female coping, and that, as styles have converged so too has the rate of male and female self-poisoning.

This notion receives further support from a theoretical paper by Marecek (1979) who suggests that what she describes as "biosocial trends" in the 1970s have led to greater androgeny among women. Thus, rising rates of divorce may require women to develop competence in both masculine and feminine spheres, and fewer children and fewer child rearing years encourage and permit women to seek alternative sources of self-esteem outside the family. Individuals with a broader range of skills and more flexible attitudes might be expected to attain greater achievement. In this way more role models of female success become available and a cycle of reinforcement for female achievement is established. Certainly Wong, Kettlewell, and Sproule (1985) found that women with a masculine sex role orientation demonstrated greater career achievement, and possessed the attributional style of internal, stable and global attribution in relation to that success which we have shown to be associated with the possession of coping skills.

More evidence of attitudinal change in the 1970s among American women which could have significance for coping behaviour comes from Sutherland and Veroff (1985). They measured the "need for achievement" of two cohorts of young Americans and found that adolescent females demonstrated higher achievement scores in 1979 than did adolescent girls in 1972, although the reverse was true for males (see Table 4.1 and Figs 4.2 and 4.3). As we reported in Chapter Four their conclusion was:

> ... something very critical happened during the 1970s that changed the achievement orientations in adolescent boys and girls ... the later cohort groups of each sex deviated from the patterns created by the earlier, more traditional, cohort groups. The later birth cohorts showed result patterns similar to those of the opposite sex in the earlier cohort group. Whether this means that the younger generation is becoming androgynous with respect to achievement motivation is not clear ... we may very well be at a transition period. Once we pass this transition point, when the expectations for both men and women in their roles will be truly parallel, perhaps the results for both men and women will be similar.

The authors propose that this change might have been promoted by the increasing discussion of sex roles in schools and in the mass media, and that more specific attention was being paid to androgeny as a value. It is at this point that convergence occurs between Kessler and McCrae's proposals on the change of female coping style, Sutherland and Veroff's report of changes in female achievement motivation, and that body of attributional research by Dweck and others demonstrating the effects of teacher feedback on the attributional style of pupils.

Dweck and Licht (1980) summarised this work, reporting its finding that teachers attributed boys' failures to a lack of motivation eight times as often as they did girls' failures, and that girls demonstrated a helpless attributional style significantly more often than boys. Thus girls mirrored the teachers' attributions and made internal, stable, global attributions for their failures which, as we have seen, adversely affects performance and persistence following failure in a variety of ways. Dweck successfully reversed this pattern of attribution and enhanced helpless students' performance by manipulating attributional feedback. Children—regardless of sex—who experienced the contingencies that boys experience in the classroom did not attribute their failures to lack of ability; those who received the pattern of feedback experienced by girls did do so. Dweck concluded that these results confirm that teachers' feedback does indeed influence the attributional style of pupils.

It seems eminently possible therefore that an increasing awareness in the 1970s and 1980s among educators of the impact of sex role stereotypy has, indeed, led to modification of teachers' expectations and their attributions. This would have resulted in a convergence of male and female attributional style with women acquiring a more masculine style which is associated with higher initial expectancy of success, greater persistence and improved performance—in short, enhanced coping skills.

There is another way in which social change involving the membership of another powerful institution might influence the decline in self-poisoning among women and this relates to the medical profession and the trend we have earlier explored of a reduction in the prescription of psychotropic medication. It has been suggested that the discovery of previously unexpected side effects of the benzodiazepines has led to this reduction. However, it is possible that a diminution of sex role stereotypy among the medical profession has led to more reluctance to internally attribute the cause of female distress, and hence to the reduction of psychotropic prescription to women who have predominantly social and relational problems.

Constance Thomas (1985) points out that of 15 studies on the effects of sex role stereotypes on clinical judgements reported prior to 1975 nearly all showed that both male and female mental health therapists held traditional stereotypes which afforded normal women a lower status of mental health than men. Since 1975, however, Thomas found no study to have shown that female therapists hold traditional biases and as a result she speculates that the women's movement began to have an impact on female therapists in the mid 1970s. She therefore determined to establish whether this apparent change had continued and whether it had extended to male therapists.

The Sexual Stereotype Questionnaire (Rosenkrantz, Vogel, Bee, & Broverman, 1968) which was used in the the the seminal Broverman research in 1970 (Broverman et al., 1970) and, Thomas claims, in most studies since, was sent to 116 male and female psychiatrists and psychologists. She found that in 1982, when her study was carried out, there remained no evidence of sex role stereotyping in either female or male mental health professionals, although she cautions that this apparent change in attitude may not indicate commensurate behaviour change.

Lykes and Stewart (1986) explored possible indices of the impact of the women's movement in America which could conceivably facilitate such changes and found that the percentage of PhDs in psychology who are women had risen from 21% in the early 1960s to 45% in 1982. In addition the representation of women on the governing bodies of associations of mental health professions similarly increased between 1975 and 1983. The number of women editors and contributors to professional journals also increased—in 1963, 21% of contributors to the Journal of Personality and Social Psychology were women, by 1983 49% were. Thus the greater presence of women in the profession and the more frequent publication of women psychologists would make pejorative stereotypes harder to maintain and provide successful role models to challenge them.

Although it would be unsound to make too many claims on the basis of this type of evidence, there has been a dramatic decline in female self-poisoning in a short period of time and this has been a time of rapid social change in those spheres which our analysis of self-poisoning has suggested are particularly implicated in its aetiology. Furthermore, the nature of the change in traditional female domestic roles, in education and in medicine has been in directions which our attributional analysis would predict as leading to such a decline in this phenomenon.

This book has sought to disclose the inadequacies of a particular theoretical approach to female self-poisoning. What we have described as the pathology paradigm in relation to this behaviour has not only been out of keeping with the known facts of the phenomenon but has exercised a limiting influence on the emergence of models with potentially greater explanatory value and thus has deprived vulnerable people of the help they need. Its effects have been particularly pernicious for women as it has frequently led to the commonplace attribution of mental or personality disorder to them, although it has been demonstrated that there is little clinical justification for such diagnosis. Any theoretical approach to a predominantly female phenomenon which ignores issues of gender, of sex role stereotypy and sex role socialisation is fatally flawed. Whilst this text is not offered as a practice guide, the attributional theory of self-poisoning does have important implications for its management, for, as one eminent feminist commentator (Lipshitz, 1978, p.108) asserts:

So long as psychological theory, on which psychological treatment is based, does not include the analysis of symptoms in the context of their social and historical conditions, and the myths and stereotypes of our gender ideals, we shall not begin to see how to make changes.

Appendix

Influential texts reviewed with little or no mention of gender issues include the following:

The cry for help. Shneidman, E.S. & Farberow, N.L. (1961). New York: McGraw-Hill.
Suicide and attempted suicide. Stengel, E. (1964). Harmondsworth: Penguin Books.
Suicidal behaviour. McCulloch, J.W. & Philip, A.E. (1972). Oxford: Pergamon Press.
Parasuicide. Kreitman, N. (1977). London: Wiley.
Discovering suicide. Maxwell-Atkinson, J. (1978). London: Macmillan.
Death wishes. Morgan, H.G. (1979). Chichester: Wiley.
The suicide syndrome. Farmer, R. & Hirsch, S.R. (1980). London: Croom-Helm.
Attempted suicide. A practical guide to its nature and management. Hawton, K. & Catalan, J. (1982). Oxford University Press.
The negative scream. O'Brien, S. (1985). London: Routledge and Kegan Paul.
Suicide and attempted suicide among children and adolescents. Hawton, K. (1986). London: Sage Publications.

References

Abramson, L.Y., Seligman, M.E.P., & Teasdale, J.D. (1978). Learned helplessness in humans: Critique and reformulation. *Journal of Abnormal Psychology, 81 (1),* 49–74.

Alagna, S.W. (1982). Sex role identity, peer evaluation of competition and the responses of women and men in a competitive situation. *Journal of Personality and Social Psychology, 43,* 546–554.

Alderson, M.R. (1985). National trends in self-poisoning in women. *The Lancet,* April 27th.

Alloy, B., Abramson, L.Y., Metalsky, G.I., & Hartlage, S. (1988). The hopelessness theory of depression: Attributional aspects. *British Journal of Clinical Psychology, 27,* 5–21.

Alloy, B., Peterson, C., Abramson, L.Y., & Seligman, M.E.P. (1984). Attributional style and the generality of learned helplessness. *Journal of Personality and Social Psychology, 46,* 681–687.

Altemeyer, R.A. & Jones, K. (1974). Sexual identity, physical attractiveness and seating positions as determinants of influence in group discussions. *Canadian Journal of Behavioural Science, 6,* 357–375.

Anderson, C.A. (1983). Motivational and performance deficits in interpersonal situations. *Journal of Personality and Social Psychology, 45,* 1136–1141.

Andrews, G.R. & Debus, R.L. (1978). Persistence and the causal perception of failure: Modifying cognitive attributions. *Journal of Educational Psychology, 70(2),* 154–166.

Antill, J.K. & Cunningham, J.D. (1979). Self-esteem as a function of masculinity in both sexes. *Journal of Consulting and Clinical Psychology, 47,* 783–785.

Antonovsky, A. (1985). *Health, stress and coping.* San Francisco: Jossey Bass.

Armitage, K.J., Schneiderman, L.J., & Bass, R.A. (1979). Response of physicians to medical complaints in men and women. *Journal of the American Medical Association, 241 (2)*, 2186–2187.

Asarnow, J.R., Carlson, G.A., & Gutherie, D. (1987). Coping strategies, self-perceptions, hopelessness and perceived family environments in depressed and suicidal children. *Journal of Consulting and Clinical Psychology, 55(3)*, 361–366.

Atkins, L. & Jarrett, D. (1979). The significance of significance tests. In J. Irvine, I. Miles, & J. Evans, *Demystifying social statistics*. 87–109. Pluto Press.

Bagley, C. (1968). The evaluation of a suicide prevention scheme by an ecological method. *Social Science and Medicine, 2*, 1–14.

Bagley, C.R. (1975). Suicidal behaviour and suicidal ideation in adolescents: A problem for counsellors in education. *British Journal of Guidance and Counselling, 3*, 190–208.

Balter, M.B., Levine, J., & Manheimer, D.I. (1974). *New England Journal of Medicine, 290*, 769–774.

Baltes, M.M. & Skinner, E.A. (1983). Cognitive performance deficits and hospitalisation: Learned helplessness, instrumental passivity of what? Comment on Raps, Peterson, Jonas and Seligman. *Journal of Personality and Social Psychology, 45 (5)*, 1013–1016.

Bancroft, J. (1986). Crisis intervention. In S. Bloch, (Ed.), *An introduction to the psychotherapies* (2nd ed). Oxford University Press.

Bancroft, J., Skirmshire, A., & Simkin, S. (1976). The reasons people give for taking overdoses. *British Journal of Psychiatry, 128*, 538–48.

Bancroft, J. et al. (1979). The reasons people give for taking overdoses: A further enquiry. *British Journal of Medical Psychology, 52*, 353–365.

Bancroft, J. et al. (1975). Self poisoning and self injury in the Oxford area: Epidemiological aspects. *British Journal of Preventive and Social Medicine, 29*, 170–177.

Bancroft, J. & Marsack, P. (1977). The repetitiveness of self-poisoning and self-injury. *British Journal of Psychiatry, 131*, 394–399.

Bancroft, J., Skrimshire, A., Casson, J., Harvard-Watts, O., & Reynolds, F. (1977). People who deliberately poison or injure themselves: Their problems and their contacts with helping agencies. *Psychological Medicine, 7*, 289–303.

Barclay, A. & Casumano, D.R. (1967). Father absence, cross-sex identity and field dependent behaviour in male adolescents. *Child Development, 38*, 243–250.

Barraclough, B., Bunch, J., & Sainsbury, P. (1974). A hundred cases of suicide: Clinical aspects. *British Journal of Psychiatry, 125*, 355–73.

Bar-Tal, D. & Frieze, I.H. (1977). Achievement motivation for males and females as a determinant of attribution for success and failure. *Sex Roles, 3*, 3.

Batchelor, I.R.C. & Napier, M.B. (1953). Broken homes and attempted suicide. *Delinquency, 4*, 99–108.

Battle, E.S. & Rotter, J.B. (1963). Children's feelings of personal control as related to class and ethnic group. *Journal of Personality, 31*, 482–490.

Baucom, D.H. (1976). Independent masculinity and femininity scales in the California Psychological Inventory. *Journal of Consulting and Clinical Psychology, 44*, 876.

Baucom, D.H. & Danker-Brown, P. (1979). Influence of sex roles on the development of learned helplessness. *Journal of Consulting and Clinical*

Psychology, 47 (5), 928–936.

Beck, A.T. (1963). Thinking and depression: 1. Idiosyncratic content and cognitive distortions. *Archives of General Psychiatry, 9,* 324–335.

Beck, A.T. (1967). *Depression: Clinical experimental and theoretical aspects.* New York: Hoebner Medical Division, Harper and Row.

Beck, A.T. (1983). Cognitive therapy of depression: New perspectives. In P. Clayton, & J. Barrett, (Eds.), *Treatment of depression: Old controversies and new approaches.* New York: Raven Press.

Beck, A.T., Beck, R., & Kovacs, M. (1975). Classification of suicidal behaviours: I. Quantifying intent and medical lethality. *American Journal of Psychiatry, 132, 3,* 285–287.

Beck, A.T. & Greenberg, R.L. (1974). Cognitive therapy with depressed women. In V. Franks, & V. Burtle, (Eds.), *Women in therapy: New psychotherapies for a changing society.* New York: Brunner/Mazel.

Beck, A.T., Kovacs, M., & Weissman, A. (1975). Hopelessness and suicidal behaviour. *Journal of the American Medical Association, 234, 11,* 1146–1149.

Beck, A.T., Lester, D., & Kovacs, M. (1973). Attempted suicide by males and females. *Psychological Reports, 33,* 965–966.

Beck, A.T., Rush, A.J., Shaw, B.F., & Emery, G. (1979). *Cognitive therapy of depression.* New York: Guilford Press.

Beck, A.T., Schuyler, D., & Herman, I. (1974). Development of suicidal intent scales. In A.T. Beck, H.L.P. Resnick, & D. Lettieri, (Eds.), *The prediction of suicide.* Bowie, MD: Charles Press.

Beck, A.T. et al. (1974b). The measurement of pessimism: The hopelessness scale. *Journal of Consulting and Clinical Psychology, 42,* 861–865.

Bell, G.C. & Schaffer, K.F. (1984). The effects of psychological androgyny on attributions of causality for success and failure. *Sex Roles, 11 (11/12),* 1045–1055.

Bellantuono, C., Reggi, V., Tognoni, G., & Garattini, S. (1980). Benzodiazepines: Clinical pharmacology and therapeutic use. *Drugs, 19,* 195.

Bem, S.L. (1974). The measurement of psychological androgeny. *Journal of Consulting and Clinical Psychology, 42,* 155–162.

Bem, S.L. (1975). Sex role adaptability: One consequence of psychological androgyny. *Journal of Personality and Social Psychology, 31 (4),* 634–43.

Bernard, J. (1974). *Observer Magazine,* 28th April.

Bille-Brahe, U. & Wang, A.G. (1985). Attempted suicide in Denmark: 2. Social integration. *Social Psychiatry, 20,* 163–70.

Billings, A.C. & Moos, R.H. (1981). The role of coping responses and social resources in attenuating the stress of life events. *Journal of Behavioural Medicine, 4,* 139–157.

Birtchnell, J. (1970). The relationship between attempted suicide, depression and parent death. *British Journal of Psychiatry, 116,* 307–313.

Birtchnell, J. & Floyd, S. (1974). Attempted suicide and the menstrual cycle—A negative conclusion. *Journal of Psychosomatic Research, 18,* 361–369.

Blake, W. (1973). The influence of race on diagnosis. *Smith College Studies in Social Work, 43,* 184–192.

Blatt, S.J., Quinlan, D.M., Chevron, E.S., McDonald, C., & Zuroff, D. (1982). Dependency and self-criticism: Psychological dimensions of depression. *Journal of Consulting and Clinical Psychology, 50,* 113–124.

British Medical Journal. (1971). *Leading article, 1,* 419.

Bond, L.A. (1981). Perceptions of sex-role deviations: An attributional analysis. *Sex Roles, 7,* 107–115.

Bond, L.A. & Deming, S. (1982). Childrens' causal attributions for performance on sex stereotypic tasks. *Sex Roles, 8,* 12.

Bradley, G.W. (1978). Self-serving biases in the attribution process: A re-examination of the fact or fiction question. *Journal of Personality and Social Psychology, 36,* 56–71.

Braucht, G.N. (1979). Interactional analysis of suicidal behaviour. *Journal of Consulting and Clinical Psychology, 47 (4),* 653–669.

Brewer, C. & Farmer, R. (1985). Self-poisoning in 1984: A prediction that did not come true. [Letter] *British Medical Journal, 290,* 391.

Brewin, C.R. (1985). Depression and causal attributions: What is their relationship? *Psychological Bulletin, 98 (2),* 297–309.

Brewin, C.R. & Shapiro, D.A. (1984). Beyond locus of control: Attribution of responsibility for positive and negative outcomes. *British Journal of Psychology, 75,* 43–49.

Brickman, P., Rabinowitz, V.C., Karuza, J., Coates, D., Cohn, E., & Kidder, L. (1982). Models of helping and coping. *American Psychologist, 37 (4),* 368–384.

Broverman, D.M., Broverman, I.K., Clarkson, F.E., Rosenkrantz, P.S., & Vogel, S.R. (1970). Sex role stereotypes and clinical judgements of mental health. *Journal of Consulting and Clinical Psychology, 34 (1),* 1–7.

Broverman, I.K., Vogel, S.R., Broverman, D.M., Clarkson, F.E., & Rosenkrantz, P.S. (1972). Sex-role stereotypes: A current appraisal. *Journal of Social Issues, 28 (2),* 59–78.

Brown, G. & Harris, T. (1978). *Social origins of depression. A study of psychiatric disorder in women.* London: Tavistock.

Brown, G.W. (1974). Meaning, measurement, and stress of life events. In B.S. Dohrenwend, & B.P. Dohrenwend, (Eds.), *Stressful life events: Their nature and effects.* New York: Wiley.

Browne, T. Sir. (1716). *Christian Morals.*

Bryant, B.K. & Trockel, J.F. (1976). Personal history of psychological distress related to locus of control orientation among college women. *Journal of Consulting and Clinical Psychology, 44 (2),* 266–271.

Buglass, D. & Horton, J. (1974). A scale for predicting subsequent suicidal behaviour. *British Journal of Psychiatry, 124,* 573–578.

Buglass, D. & McCulloch, J.W. (1970). Further suicidal behaviour: The development and validation of predictive scales. *British Journal of Psychiatry, 116,* 483–491.

Bulman, R.J. & Wartman, C.B. (1977). Attributions of blame and coping in the "real world": Severe accident victims react to their lot. *Journal of Personality and Social Psychology, 35,* 351–363.

Cafferata, G., Kasper, J., & Bernstein, A. (1983). Family roles, structure and stressors in relation to sex differences in obtaining psychotropic drugs. *Journal of Health and Social Behaviour, 24,* 132–143.

Callichia, J.P. & Pardine, P. (1984). Attributional style: Degree of depression, respondents' sex, and nature of the attributional event. *The Journal of Psychology, 117,* 167–175.

Cantor, P.C. (1976). Personality characteristics found among young female suicide attempters. *Journal of Abnormal Psychology, 85 (3),* 324–329.

Caplan, P.J. (1986). *The myth of women's masochism.* London: Methuen.

Cartwright, A. (1974). Prescribing and the relationship between patients and doctors. In R. Cooperstock, (1974) op.cit.

Carver, C.S. & Ganellen, D.J. (1983). Depression and components of self-punitiveness: High standards, self-criticism and overgeneralisation. *Journal of Abnormal Psychology, 92 (3),* 330–337.

Cavell, M. (1974). Since 1924: Toward a new psychology of women. In J. Strouse, (Ed.), *Women and analysis.* New York: Dell.

Chaiton, A. et al. (1976). Patterns of medical drug use: A community focus. *Canadian Medical Association Journal, 114,* 33.

Chambliss, C. & Murray, E.J. (1979). Cognitive procedures for smoking reduction: Symptom attribution vs. efficacy attribution. *Cognitive Therapy and Research, 3,* 91–95.

Chapin, M. & Dyck, D.G. (1976). Persistence in children's reading behaviour as a function of *N* length and attribution retraining. *Journal of Abnormal Psychology, 85,* 511–515.

Chesler, P. (1972). *Women and Madness.* Garden City, N.Y.: Doubleday.

Chetwynd, J. & Hartnett, O. (Eds.). *The sex role system.* London: Routledge and Kegan Paul.

Chevron, E.S., Quinlan, D.M., & Blatt, S.J. (1978). Sex roles and gender differences in the expression of depression. *Journal of Abnormal Psychology, 87,* 680–683.

Clancy, K. & Gove, W. (1974). Sex differences in mental health: An analysis of response bias in self-reports. *American Journal of Sociology, 80,* 205–216.

Clifton, A.K. & Lee, D.E. (1976). Self-destructive consequences of sex-role socialisation. *Suicidal and Life Threatening Behaviour, 6,* 1.

Clingman, J.M. & Musgrove, W.J. (1977). The attitudes towards women held by practitioners in medicine and law. *Sex Roles, 3,* 185–188.

Cloward, R.A. & Piven, F.F. (1979). Hidden protest: The channeling of female innovation and protest. *Signs: Journal of Women in Culture and Society, 4 (4),* 651–669.

Clum, G.A., Patsiokas, A.T., & Luscomb, R.L. (1979) Empirically based comprehensive treatment programme for parasuicide. *Journal of Consulting and Clinical Psychology, 47(5),* 937–945.

Cohen, J. (1977). *Statistical power analysis for the behavioural sciences (rev.ed.).* New York: Academic Press.

Coie, J.D., Pennington, B.F., & Buckley, H.H. (1974). Effects of situational stress and sex roles on the attribution of psychological disorder. *Journal of Consulting and Clinical Psychology, 42 (4),* 559–568.

Cole, D.A. (1989). Psychopathology and adolescent suicide: Hopelessness, coping beliefs and depression. *Journal of Abnormal Psychology, 98 (3),* 248–255.

Cooperstock, R. (1971). Sex differences in the use of mood modifying drugs: An exploratory model. *Journal of Health and Social Behaviour, 12,* 238–244.

Cooperstock, R. (1974). *Social aspects of the medical use of psychotropic drugs.* Toronto, Canada: Addiction Research Foundation of Ontario.

Cooperstock, R. (1978). Sex differences in psychotropic drug use. *Social Science and Medicine, 12 (3b),* 179–186.

Cooperstock, R. (1982). Research on psychotropic drug use: A review of findings and methods. *Social Science and Medicine, 16,* 1179–1196.

Costrich, N., Feinstein, J., Kidder, L., Maracek, J., & Pascale, L. (1975). When stereotypes hurt: Three studies of the penalties for sex role reversals. *Journal of Experimental and Social Psychology, 11,* 520–530.

Coyne, J.C. & Gotlib, I.H. (1983). The role of cognition in depression: A critical appraisal. *Psychological Bulletin, 94 (3)* 472–505.

Crandall, V.C. (1969). Sex difference in expectancy of intellectual and academic reinforcement. In C.P. Smith, (Ed.), *Achievement Related Motives in Children.* New York: Russell Sage.

Crombie, G. (1983). Women's attribution patterns and their relation to achievement: An examination of within-sex differences. *Sex Roles, 9 (12),* 1171–1182.

Cronbach, L.J. (1951). Coefficient alpha and the internal construction of tests. *Psychometrica, 16,* 297–334.

Crook, T. & Raskin, A. (1975). Association of childhood parental loss with attempted suicide and depression. *Journal of Consulting and Clinical Psychology, 43,* 277.

Cutrona, C.E. (1983). Causal attributions and perinatal depression. *Journal of Abnormal Psychology, 92,* 161–172.

Dalton, K. (1959). Menstruation and acute psychiatric illness. *British Medical Journal, 1,* 148–149.

Dalton, K. (1980). Cyclical criminal acts in premenstrual syndrome. *The Lancet, November 15,* 1070–1.

Darley, J.M. & Gross, P.H. (1983). A hypothesis-confirming bias in labelling effects. *Journal of Personality and Social Psychology, 44,* 20–33.

Davis, F.B. (1968). Sex differences in suicide and attempted suicide. *Diseases of the Nervous System, 29,* 193–194.

Davison, G.C. & Valins, S. (1969). Maintenance of self-attributed and drug attributed behaviour change. *Journal of Personality and Social Psychology, 11,* 25–33.

Deaux, E. & Emswiller, T. (1974). Explanations of successful performance on sex-linked tasks. What is skill for the male is luck for the female. *Journal of Personality and Social Psychology, 29,* 80–85.

Deaux, K. & Farris, E. (1976). Sex: A perspective on the attribution process. In J.H. Harvey, et al. (Eds.), *New Directions in Attribution Research, Vol. 1.* Hillsdale, N.J.: Lawrence Erlbaum Associates Inc.

Deaux, K. & Farris, E. (1978). Attributing causes for one's own performance: The effects of sex, norms and outcomes. Reported in I. Ickes, & M.A. Laydon, *Attributional Styles.* In J.H. Harvey, et al. (Eds.), *New directions in attribution research, Vol. 2,* Hillsdale, N.J.: Lawrence Erlbaum Associates Inc., 119–152.

Deaux, K., White, L., & Farris, E. (1975). Skill vs. luck: Field and laboratory studies of male and female preferences. *Journal of Personality and Social Psychology, 32,* 629–636.

Delamont, S. (1980). *The Sociology of Women. An Introduction.* London: George Allen & Unwin, 14–29.

Dent, J. & Teasdale, J.D. (1988). Negative cognition and the persistence of depression. *Journal of Abnormal Psychology, 97 (1),* 29–34.

Deutsch, H. (1945). *The psychology of women* New York: Grune & Stratton.

Dew, M.A., Bromet, E.J., & Brent, D. (1987). A quantitative literature review of the effectiveness of suicide prevention centres. *Journal of Consulting and Clinical Psychology, 55 (2),* 239–244.

DHSS. (1984). Health notice. *The Management of Deliberate Self-Harm.* HN(84)5, December.

DHSS. (1987). *Prescription Analysis.* [Personal communication.]

Diekstra, R.F.W. (1982). Epidemiology of attempted suicide in the EEC. *Biblthca Psychiat., 162,* 1–16, Karger: Basel.

Diekstra, R.F.W. et al. (1978). Attitudes towards suicide and incidence of suicidal behaviour in a general population. In *Modern Civilization.* Jerusalem: Academic Press.

Diener, C.I. & Dweck,C.S. (1978). An analysis of learned helplessness: Continuous changes in performance, strategy and achievement cognitions following failure. *Journal of Personality and Social Psychology,* reported in C.S. Dweck, & T.E. Goestz, op.cit., 1978.

Dohrenwend, B.P. & Dohrenwend, B.S. (1976). Sex differences in psychiatric disorders. *American Journal of Sociology, 81 (6)* 1447–1453.

Dohrenwend, B.S. & Dohrenwend, B.P. (1981). *Stressful life events and their contexts.* New York: Rutgers University Press.

Dohrenwend, B.P., Shrout, P.E., Egri, G., & Mendelsohn, S.F. (1980). Measures of non-specific psychology distress and other dimensions of psychopathology in the general population. *Archives of General Psychiatry, 37,* 1229–26.

Dunnel, K. & Cartwright, A. (1972). *Medicine takers, prescribers and hoarders.* London: Routledge and Kegan Paul.

Dweck, C.S. (1975). The role of expectations and attributions in the alleviation of learned helplessness. *Journal of Personality and Social Psychology, 31,* 674–685.

Dweck, C.S. & Bush, E.S. (1976). Sex differences in learned helplessness: 1. Differential debilitation with peer and adult evaluators. *Developmental Psychology, 12,* 147–156.

Dweck, C.S. & Gilliard, D. (1975). Expectancy statements as determinants of reactions to failure: Sex differences in persistence and expectancy change. *Journal of Personality and Social Psychology, 33 (6),* 1077–84.

Dweck, C.S. & Licht, B.G. (1980). Learned helplessness and intellectual achievement. In J. Garber & M.E.P. Seligman, (Eds.), *Human Helplessness; Theory and Applications, Chapter 8,* 197–221. New York: Academic Press.

Dweck, C.S. & Repucci, N.D. (1973). Learned helplessness and reinforcement responsibility in children. *Journal of Personality and Social Psychology, 25,* 109–116.

Dweck, S.W. & Goetz, T.E. (1978). Attributions and learned helplessness. In J.H. Harvey, W.J. Ickes, & R.F. Kidd, (Eds.), *New Directions in Attribution Research, Vol. 2,* 157–179, Hillsdale, N.J.: Lawrence Erlbaum Associates Inc.

Dyer, J., Duffy, J., & Kreitman, N. (1978). *Parasuicide in Edinburgh.* Unpublished report. Edinburgh M.R.C. Unit for Epidemiological Studies in Psychiatry.

D'Zurrilla, T. & Goldfried, M. (1971). Problem solving and behaviour modification. *Journal of Abnormal Psychology, 78,* 107–126.

Elkind, D. (1967). Egocentrism in adolescence. *Child Development, 38,* 1025–1034.

Elkind, D. (1985). Egocentrism redux. *Developmental Review, 5,* 218–226.

Equal Opportunities Commission of Northern Ireland. *Gender differences in infant classes.* Belfast: EOC.

Erikson, E. (1964). *Identity, youth and crisis.* New York: Norton.

Erkut, S. (1983). Exploring sex differences in expectancy, attributions and academic achievement. *Sex Roles, 9 (2),* 217–231.

Esquirol, L. (1838). *Des malades mentales.* Paris: Baillière.

Evans, . (1967). Deliberate self-poisoning in the Oxford area. *British Journal of Preventive and Social Medicine, 21 (3),* 97–107.

Eysenck, H. (1986). *Decline and fall of the Freudian empire.* London: Pelican.

Farberow, N.L., & McEvoy, T. (1966). Suicide among patients with diagnoses of anxiety reaction or depressive reaction in general medical and surgical hospitals. *Journal of Abnormal Psychology, 71,* 287–299.

Farmer, R. & Hirsch, S.R. (1980). *The suicide syndrome.* London: Croom Helm.

Feather, N.T. (1966). Effects of prior success and failure on expectations of success and subsequent performance. *Journal of Personality and Social Psychology, 3,* 287–298.

Feather, N.Y. (1969). Attribution of responsibility and valence of success and failure in relation to initial confidence and perceived locus of control. *Journal of Personality and Social Psychology, 13,* 129–144.

Feather, N.T. & Simon, J.G. (1971). Attribution of responsibility and valence of outcome in relation to initial confidence and success and failure of self and others. *Journal of Personality and Social Psychology, 18,* 173–188.

Feather, N.T. & Simon, J.G. (1975). Reactions to male and female success and failure in sex-linked cultures. *Journal of Personality and Social Psychology, 31,* 20–31.

Ferguson, D.M. & Horwood, L.J. (1987). Vulnerability to life events exposure. *Psychological Medicine, 17,* 739–749.

Fidell, S. (1980). Sex role stereotypes and the American physician. *Psychology of Women Quarterly, 4 (3),* 313–329.

Firth, R. (1971). Suicide and risk taking in Tikopia society. In A. Giddens, (Ed.), *The sociology of suicide.* London: Cass & Co.

Fisher, S. & Greenberg, R.P. (1985). *The scientific credibility of Freud's theories and therapy.* New York: Columbia University Press.

Fitch, G. (1970). Effects of self esteem, perceived performance, and choice on causal attributions. *Journal of Personality and Social Psychology, 16 (2),* 311–315.

Fleishman, J.A. (1984). Personality characteristics and coping patterns. *Journal of Health and Social Behaviour, 25,* 229–244.

Ford, M.R. & Widiger, T.A. (1989). Sex bias in the diagnosis of hystrionic and anti-social personality disorders. *Journal of Consulting and Clinical Psychology, 57 (2),* 301–305.

Forster, D.P. & Frost, C.E.B. (1985). Medicinal self-poisoning and prescription frequency. *Acta Psychiatrica Scandinavia, 71,* 567–574.

Forsterling, F. (1985). Attributional retraining: A review. *Psychological Bulletin, 98 (3),* 495–512.

Forsyth, D.R. (1980). The functions of attributions. *Social Psychology Quarterly, 43 (2),* 184–189.

Foulds, G.A. & Hope, K. (1968). *Manual of the Symptom Sign Inventory (S.S.I.).* London: University of London Press.

Fourestie, V., Lignieres, B., Roudot-Thoraval, F., Fulli-Lemaire, I., Cremniter, D., Nahoul, K., Fournier, S., & Lejonc, J-L. (1986). Suicide attempts in hypo-oestrogenic phases of the menstrual cycle. *The Lancet,* December 13, 1357–1360.

Fox, J.W. (1980). Gove's specific sex role theory of mental illness: A research note. *Journal of Health and Social Behaviour, 21,* 260–267.

Fraser, D.M. & Lawson, A.A.H. (1975). Acute poisoning in young women 1965–73. *Health Bulletin, 33 (3),* 97–101.

Fraser, S.G. (1987). Cognitive and behavioural strategies in the management of suicidal behaviour. *ASLIB index to theses: Volume 36, part 4,,* 1425. PhD., Leicester University.

Freud, S. (1959). Some psychological consequences of the anatomical distinction between the sexes. In J. Strachey, (Ed.), *Collected papers of Sigmund Freud, Volume 5,* 186–197. New York: Basic Books.

Freud, S. (1965). Femininity. In J. Strachey, (Ed.), *New Introductory Lectures on Psychoanalysis,* 112–135. New York: Norton. Referred to in J.B. Rohrbaugh, *Women Psychology's Puzzle,* 84. Abacus, 1981.

Freud, S. (1982). Some psychical consequences of the anatomical distinction between the sexes. *Standard edition of the complete works of Sigmund Freud. Volume 19.* London: Hogarth Press. Referred to in J. Sayers, op.cit. 126.

Fromm, E. (1947). *Man for himself.*

Gannon, L., Heiser, P., & Knight, S. (1985). Learned helplessness versus reactance: The effects of sex role stereotypy. *Sex Roles, 12 (7/8),* 791–806.

Gatchel, R.J., Paulus, P.B., & Maples, C.W. (1975). Learned helplessness and self-reported affect. *Journal of Abnormal Psychology, 84,* 732–734. Reported in I.W. Miller, & W.H. Norman, (1979). Learned helplessness in humans: A review and attribution theory model. *Psychological Bulletin, 86 (1),* 93–189.

Ghodse, A.H. (1978). Recommendations by accident and emergency staff about drug overdose patients. *Social Science and Medicine, 13A,* 169–173.

Gibbons, J.S., Butler, J., Urwin, P., & Gibbons, J.L. (1978). Evaluation of social work service for self-poisoning patients. *British Journal of Psychiatry, 133,* 111–118.

Ginsberg, G.P. (1971). Public conceptions and attitudes about suicide. *Journal of Health and Social Behaviour, 12,* 200–207.

Goffman, E. (1971). *Relations in Public.* New York: Harper & Row.

Goldacre, M. (1982). Hospital admissions for adverse effects of medicinal agents (mainly self-poisoning) among adolescents in the Oxford region. *British Journal of Psychiatry, 141,* 106–170.

Goldie, N. (1979). Review article in *Sociology of Health and Illness, 1,* 352–357.

Goldney, R. (1981a). Are young women who attempt suicide hysterical? *British Journal of Psychiatry, 138,* 141–146.

Goldney, R. (1981b). Attempted suicide in young women: Correlates of lethality. *British Journal of Psychiatry, 139,* 382–390.

Goldney, R. & Pilowsky, . (1980). Depression in young women who have attempted suicide. *Australian and New Zealand Journal of Psychiatry, 14,* 202–211.

Goldney, R.D. (1981c). Parental loss and reported childhood stress in young women who attempt suicide. *Acta Psychiatrica Scand., 64,* 34–59.

Goldney, R.D. (1982). Locus of control in young women who have attempted suicide. *The Journal of Nervous and Mental Disease, 126,* 198–201.

Golin, S., Sweeney, P.D., & Shaeffer, D.E. (1981). The causality of causal attributions in depression. A cross-lagged panel correlational analysis. *Journal of Abnormal Psychology, 90,* 14–22.

Gove, W.R. (1972). Sex, marital status and suicide. *Journal of Health and Social Behaviour, 13,* 204–213.

Gove, W.R. (1978). Sex differences in mental illness among adult men and women. *Social Science and Medicine, 12B,* 187–198.

Greer, S. (1966). Parental loss and attempted suicide: A further report. *British Journal of Psychiatry, 112,* 465–470.

Hamid-Ghodse, A. (1979). Recommendations by accident and emergency staff about drug overdose patients. *Social Science and Medicine, 13A,* 169–73.

Hamilton, S., Rothbart, M., & Dawes, R. (1986). Sex bias, diagnosis and DSM III. *Sex Roles, 15 (5/6),* 269–274.

Hammen, C.L. (1985). Predicting depression: A cognitive-behavioural perspective. In P.C. Kendall (Ed.), *Advances in cognitive behavioural research and therapy, Volume 4,* New York: Academic Press.

Hamsher, J.H., Geller, J.D., & Rotter, J.B. (1968). Interpersonal trust, internal-external control, and the Warren commission. Report, *Journal of Personality and Social Psychology, 9,* 210–215.

Hansen, R.D. & O'Leary, V.E. (1985). Sex determined attributions. In V.E. O'Leary, et al. *Women, gender and social psychology,* Hillsdale, N.J.: Lawrence Erlbaum Associates Inc.

Harvey, J.H., Ickes, W.J., & Kidd, R.F. (1978). *New Directions in Attribution Research, Vol. II,.* Hillsdale, N.J.: Lawrence Erlbaum Associates Inc.

Hastie, R. (1984). Causes and effects of causal attribution. *Journal of Personality and Social Psychology, 46,* 44–56.

Hawton, K. (1979). Domiciliary and outpatient treatment following deliberate self-poisoning. In R. Farmer, op.cit. 246–258.

Hawton, K. (1986). *Suicide and Attempted Suicide among Children and Adolescents,* 61. Sage Publications.

Hawton, K. & Blackstock, E. (1976). General practice aspects of self-poisoning and self-injury. *Psychological Medicine, 6,* 571–575.

Hawton, K. & Blackstock, E. (1977). Deliberate self-poisoning: Implications for psychotropic drug prescription in general practice. *Journal of the Royal College of General Practitioners, 27,* 560–563.

Hawton, K. & Catalan, J. (1982). *Attempted suicide. A practical guide to its nature and management,* 7. Oxford University Press.

Hawton, K. & Goldacre, M. (1982). Hospital admissions for adverse effects of medicinal agents (mainly self-poisoning) among adolescents in the Oxford region. *British Journal of Psychiatry, 141,* 166–170.

Hawton, K., Marsack, P., & Fagg, J. (1981). The attitudes of psychiatrists to deliberate self-poisoning: Comparison with physicians and nurses. *British Journal of Medical Psychology, 54,* 341–348.

Hawton, K., O'Grady, J., Osborn, M., & Cole, D. (1982a). Adolescents who take overdoses: Their characteristics, problems and contacts with helping agencies. *British Journal of Psychiatry, 140,* 118–123.

Hawton, K., Cole, D., O'Grady, J., & Osborn, M. (1982b). Motivational aspects of deliberate self-poisoning in adolescents. *British Journal of Psychiatry, 141,*

286–291.

Heilman, M.E. & Sarawatari, L.R. (1979). When beauty is beastly: The effect of appearance and sex on evaluations of job applicants for managerial and non-managerial jobs. *Organisational Behaviour and Human Performance, 23,* 360–372.

Heshusius, L. (1980). Female self-injury and suicide attempts: Culturally reinforced techniques in human relations. *Sex Roles, 6(6),* 843–855.

Hiroto, D.S. (1974). Locus of control and learned helplessness. *Journal of Experimental Psychology, 102,* 187–193.

Hirsch, S.R., Walsh, C., & Draper, R. (1982). Parasuicide: A review of treatment interventions. *Journal of Affective Disorders, 4,* 299–311.

Hirsch, S.R., Walsh, C., & Draper, R. (1983). The concept and efficacy of the treatment of parasuicide. *British Journal of Clinical Pharmacology, 15,* 189S–194S.

Hite, S. (1976). *The Hite report: A nationwide study of female sexuality.* New York: Dell.

HMSO. (1968). *Hospital Treatment of Acute Poisoning.* London.

HMSO. (1987). *Social Trends, 17.* London.

HMSO. (1988). *Social Trends, 18.* London.

Hoffman, L.W. (1975). Early childhood experiences and women's achievement motives. In M.T.S. Mednick, S.S. Tangri, & L.W. Hoffman, (Eds.), *Women and Achievement,* 129–149. New York: Wiley.

Holden, R.R., Mendonca, J.D., & Serin, R.C. (1989). Suicide, hopelessness and social desirability: A test of an interactive model. *Journal of Consulting and Clinical Psychology, 57(4),* 500–504.

Holding, T.A. (1974). The BBC 'Befrienders' series and its effects. *British Journal of Psychiatry, 124,* 470–472.

Holmes, T.H. & Rahe, R.H. (1967). The social readjustment rating scale. *Journal of Psychosomatic Research, 11,* 213–218.

Holstein, R.M. (1970). *Patient and therapist initial expectancies for psychotherapeutic change as they relate to treatment outcomes.* Unpublished doctoral dissertation. Boston University.

Hopkins, F. (1937). Attempted suicide: An investigation. *Journal of Mental Science, 83,* 71–94.

Horner, M. (1972). Toward an understanding of achievement related conflicts in women. *Journal of Social Issues, 28,* 157–175.

Horwitz, A. (1977). The pathways into psychiatric treatment: Some differences between men and women. *Journal of Health and Social Behaviour.* 18 June, 169–178.

Husaini, B.A. & Neff, J.A. (1981). Social class and depressive symptomatology: The role of life change events and locus of control. *The Journal of Nervous and Mental Disease, 169(10),* 638–647.

Ickes, W. & Layden, M.A. (1984). Attributional styles. In J.H. Harvey, et al. op.cit. (1978).

Jackson, D.N. (1984). *Personality research form manual (3rd ed.).* Port Huron, M.I.: Research Psychologists Press.

Janoff-Bulman, R. (1979). Characterological versus behavioural self-blame: Inquiries into depression and rape. *Journal of Personality and Social Psychology, 37,* 1798–1809.

Jarvis, K.J., Ferrence, R.G., Johnson, F.G., & Whitehead, P.C. (1976). Sex and age patterns in self-injury. *Journal of Health and Social Behaviour, 17,* 146–155.

Jennings, C., Barraclough, B.M., & Moss, J.R. (1978). Have the samaritans lowered the suicide rate? A controlled study. *Psychological Medicine, 8,* 413–422.

Jones, D.I.R. (1977). Self-poisoning with drugs: The past twenty years in Sheffield. *British Medical Journal, i,* 28–29.

Jones, E.E. & Nisbett, R.E. (1972). The actor and the observer: Divergent perceptions of the causes of behaviour. In E.E. Jones et al. (Eds.), *Attribution: Perceiving the Causes of Behaviour.* Morristown N.J.: General Learning Press.

Katschnig, H. (1980). *Measuring life stress: A comparison of two methods.* In R. Farmer, & S. Hirsch, (Eds.), op.cit.

Kelley, H. (1967). Attribution theory in social psychology. In D. Levine, (Ed.), *Nebraska Symposium on Motivation.* Lincoln: University of Nebraska Press.

Kennedy, P. (1972). Efficacy of a regional poison treatment centre in Edinburgh. *British Medical Journal, 4,* 255–257.

Kennedy, P.F. & Kreitman, N. (1973). An epidemiological study of parasuicide (attempted suicide) in general practice in Edinburgh. *British Journal of Psychiatry, 123,* 23–24.

Kessel, N. (1965). Self-poisoning—Part one. *British Medical Journal,* 27 November.

Kessel, N. (1966). The respectability of self-poisoning and the fashion of survival. *Journal of Psychosomatic Research, 10,* 29–36.

Kessel, N. & McCulloch, W. (1966). Repeated acts of self-poisoning and self-injury. *Proceedings of the Royal Society of Medicine, 59,* 89–92.

Kessler, R.C., Brown, R.L., & Broman, C.L. (1981). Sex differences in psychiatric help-seeking: Evidence from four large-scale surveys. *Journal of Health and Social Behaviour, 22,* 49–64.

Kessler, R.C. & McRae, J.A. (1983). Trends in the relationship between sex and attempted suicide. *Journal of Health and Social Behaviour, 24,* 98–110.

Keyes, S. (1984). Gender stereotypes and personal adjustment: Employing the PAQ, TSBI and GHQ with samples of British adolescents. *British Journal of Social Psychology, 23,* 173–180.

King, E. (1980). Sex bias in psychoactive drug advertisements. *Psychiatry, 43,* 129–137.

Klein, D.C. & Seligman, M.E.P. (1976). Reversal of performance deficits and perceptual deficits in learned helplessness and depression. *Journal of Abnormal Psychology, 85,* 11–26.

Koumjian, K. (1981). The use of valium as a form of social control. *Social Science and Medicine, 15e,* 245–249.

Krausen, N. & Stryker, S. (1984). Stress and well-being: The buffering role of locus of control beliefs. *Social Science and Medicine, 18(9),* 783–790.

Kreitman, N. (Ed.) (1977). *Parasuicide.* Chichester: John Wiley.

Kreitman, N. & Chowdhury, N. (1973). Distress behaviour: A study of selected samaritans clients and parasuicides (attempted suicide patients). *British Journal of Psychiatry, 123,* 1–8.

Kreitman, N. & Schreiber, M. (1979). Parasuicide in young Edinburgh women, 1968–75. *Psychological Medicine, 9,* 469–479.

Kreitman, N. et al. (1969). Parasuicide. [Letter to the] *British Journal of Psychiatry, 115,* 746–7.

Lack, D. (1980). Pain differences, similarities found. *Science News, 118,* 182–183.

Lambley, P. & Silbowitz, M. (1973). Rotter's internal-external scale and prediction of suicide contemplators among students. *Psychological Reports, 33,* 585–586.

Lamke, L.K. (1982). The impact of sex role orientation on self-esteem in early adolescence. *Child Development, 53,* 1530–1535.

Landfield, A. (1976). A personal construct approach to suicidal behaviour. In P. Slater, *Explorations in Interpersonal Space, Vol. 1.* London: Wiley.

Langer, E.J. (1982). *Minding matters: The mindlessness/mindfulness theory of cognitive activity.* Paper presented at the meeting of the Society for Experimental Social Psychology. Nashville: Indiana. Reported in R.D. Hanson, & V.E. O'Leary et al. (Eds.), op.cit. 1985.

Langer, E.J. & Benevento, A. (1978). Self-induced dependence. *Journal of Personality and Social Psychology, 36,* 886–893.

LaNoue, J.B. & Curtis, R.C. (1985). Improving women's performance in mixed-sex situations by effort attributions. *Psychology of Women Quarterly, 9(3),* 337–356.

Lapsley, D. (1985). Elkind and egocentrism. *Developmental Review, 5,* 227–236.

Laws, S., Hey, V., & Eagan, A. (1985). *Seeing Red. The Politics of pre-menstrual Tension.* London: Hutchinson.

Layden, M.A. (1982). Attributional style therapy. In C. Antaki, & C.R. Brewin, (Eds.), *Attributions and Psychological Change, Chp. 4.* New York: Academic Press.

Lazarus, R. (1981). The costs and benefits of denial. In B.S. Dohrenwend, & B.P. Dohrenwend, *Stressful Life Events and Their Contexts,* 131–156. New York: Rutgers University Press.

Lefcourt, H.M. (1981). Locus of control and stressful life events. In B.S. Dohrenwend, & B.P. Dohrenwend, *Stressful Life Events and Their Contexts.* New York: Rutgers University Press.

Lendrum, R.C. (1933). A thousand cases of attempted suicide. *American Journal of Psychiatry, 90,* 479–500.

Levenson, M. (1972). *Cognitive and Perceptual Factors in Suicidal Individuals.* Unpublished Ph.D., University of Kansas.

Levine, R., Gillman, M-J., & Reis, H. (1982). Individual differences for sex differences in achievement attributions. *Sex Roles, 8(4),* 455–465.

Lewinsohn, P., Steinmetz, J., Larson, D., & Franklin, J. (1981). Depression related cognitions: Antecedent or consequence? *Journal of Abnormal Psychology, 90,* 213–219.

Lewis, C. (1986). Early sex-role socialisation. In D.J. Hargreaves, & A.M. Colley, (Eds.), *The Psychology of Sex Roles,* 95–117. London: Harper & Row.

Liberman, B.L. (1978). The role of mastery in psychotherapy: Maintenance of improvement and prescriptive change. In J.D. Frank, et al. (Eds.), *The Effective Ingredients of Successful Psychotherapy.* New York: Brunner-Mazel.

Liberman, R.P. & Eckman, T. (1981). Behaviour therapy vs. insight oriented therapy for repeated suicide attempters. *Archives of General Psychiatry, 38,* 1126–1130.

Linehan, M.M. (1971). Sex differences in suicide and attempted suicide: A study of differential social acceptability and expectations. Doctoral Dissertation, Loyola University of Chicago. *Dissertation Abstracts International 3036-B*, University Microfilms no. 71–28, 130.

Linehan, M.M. (1973). Suicide and attempted suicide: Study of perceived sex differences. *Perceptual and Motor Skills, 37*, 31–34.

Linehan, M.M. (1988). Dialectical behaviour therapy for personality disorder: Theory and method. *Bulletin of the Meninger Clinic, 51*, 261–276.

Linehan, M., Goodstein, J., Nielsen, S., & Chiles, J. (1983). Reasons for staying alive when you are thinking of killing yourself: The reasons for living inventory. *Journal of Consulting and Clinical Psychology, 51*, 276–286.

Lipshitz, S. (1978). Women and psychiatry. In J. Chetwynd, & O. Hartnett, (Eds.), *The Sex Role System: Psychological and Sociological Perspectives, Chp. 8*. London: Routledge & Kegan Paul.

Lochel, E. (1983). Sex differences in achievement motivation. In J.A. Jaspers, F.D. Fincham, & M. Hewstone (Eds.), *Attribution Theory and Research Conceptual, Developmental and Social Dimensions, 192–222*. New York: Academic Press.

Lopez, S.R. (1989). Patient variable biases in clinical judgement. Conceptual overview and methodological considerations. *Psychological Bulletin, 106(2)*, 184–203.

Lorr, M. et al. (1961). Meprobamate and chlorpromazine in psychotherapy. *Archives of General Psychiatry, 4*, 381–389.

Luscomb, R.L., Clum, G.A., & Patsiokas, A.T. (1980). Mediating factors in the relationship between life stress and suicide attempting. *The Journal of Nervous and Mental Disease, 168(11)*, 644–650.

Lykes, M.B. & Steward, A.J. (1986). Evaluating the feminist challenge to research in personality and social psychology: 1963–1983. *Psychology of Women Quarterly, 10*, 393–412.

Maccoby, E.E. & Jacklin, C. (1974). *The Psychology of Sex Difference*. Stanford, California: Stanford University Press.

Magos, A. & Studd, J. (1987). Suicide attempts and the menstrual cycle. *The Lancet*, January 24, 217.

Mandell, A.J. & Mandell, M.P. (1967). Suicide and the menstrual cycle. *Journal of the American Medical Association, 200*, 792–3.

Mant, A., Broom, D., & Duncan-Jones, P. (1983). The path to prescription: Sex differences in psychotropic drug prescribing for general practice patients. *Social Psychiatry, 18*, 185–192.

Maracek, J. (1979). Social change, positive mental health and psychological androgeny. *Psychology of Women Quarterly, 3(3)*, 241–247.

Maris, R.W. (1971). Deviance as therapy: The paradox of the self-destructive female. *Journal of Health and Social Behaviour, 12*, 113–124.

Martin, V. & Nivens, M.K. (1987). The attributional response of males and females to non-contingent feedback. *Sex Roles, 16(9/10)*, 453–462.

Marx, E. (1988). Problem solving therapy. In F.N. Watts, (Ed.), *New Developments in Clinical Psychology, Vol. 2*. Chichester: Wiley.

Masuda, M. & Holmes, T.H. (1978). Life events: Perceptions and frequencies. *Psychosomatic Medicine, 40(3)*, 236–261.

Matthew, H. (1966). Poisoning in the home by medicaments. *British Medical*

Journal, 2, 788.

Matthew, H. & Lawson, A.A.H. (1967). *Treatment of Common Acute Poisonings.* Edinburgh: Livingstone.

McCulloch, J.W. & Philip, A.E. (1972). *Suicidal Behaviour. Oxford:* Pergamon Press.

McFarland, C., Ross, M., & DeCourville, N. (1989). Women's theories of menstruation and biases in recall of menstrual symptoms. *Journal of Personality and Social Psychology, 57(3),* 522–531.

McGhee, P. & Crandall, V.C. (1968). Beliefs in internal-external control of reinforcements and academic performance. *Child Development, 39,* 91–102.

McHugh, M.C., Frieze, I.H., & Hanusa, B.H. (1982). Attributions and sex differences in achievement: Problems and new perspectives. *Sex Roles, 8(4),* 467–479.

McIntosh, J.L. (1985). *Research on Suicide. A Bibliography,* 1. New York: Greenwood Press.

McKinlay, J.B. (1975). Who is really ignorant—physician or patient? *Journal of Health and Social Behaviour, 16,* 3–11.

McNair, D.M., Lorr, M., & Droppelman, L.F. (1971). *The Profile of Mood States.* San Diego CA: Educational and Industrial Testing Service.

Mechanic, D. (1965). Perception of parental responses to illness. *Journal of Health and Social Behaviour, 6,* 253–257.

Mehrabian, A. (1968). Male and female scales of the tendency to achieve. *Educational and Psychological Measurement, 28,* 493–502.

Mellinger, G.D. (1978). Psychic distress, life crisis, and use of psychotropic medications. *Archives of General Psychiatry, 35,* 1045–1052.

Metalsky, G.I., Abramson, L.Y., Seligman, M.E.P., Semmel, A., & Peterson, C. (1982). Attributional life styles and events in the classroom: Vulnerability and invulnerability to depressive mood reactions. *Journal of Personality and Social Psychology, 43(3),* 612–617.

Meyer, J.P. (1980). Causal attribution for success and failure: A multivariate investigation of dimensionality, formation and consequence. *Journal of Personality and Social Psychology, 38,* 704–718.

Michela, J.L., Peplau, L.A., & Weeks, D.G. (1982). Perceived dimensions of attributions for loneliness. *Journal of Personality and Social Psychology, 43,* 929–936.

Mikulincer, M. (1986). Attributional processes in the learned helplessness paradigm. The behavioural effects of globality attributions. *Journal of Personality and Social Psychology, 51,* 1248–1256.

Mikulincer, M. & Nizan, B. (1988). Causal attribution, cognitive interference and the generalisation of learned helplessness. *Journal of Personality and Social Psychology, 55(3),* 470–478.

Miller, H.L., Coombes, D.W., Leeper, J.D., & Barton, S.N. (1984). An analysis of the effects of suicide prevention facilities on suicide rates in the United States. *American Journal of Public Health, 74(4),* 340–343.

Miller, I.W. & Norman, W.H. (1979). Learned helplessness in humans: A review and attribution theory model. *Psychological Bulletin, 86(1),* 93–118.

Miller, W.R. & Seligman, M. (1975). Depression and learned helplessness in man. *Journal of Abnormal Psychology, 84,* 228–238.

Mills, J. et al. (1974). The epidemiology of self-poisoning in Hobart, 1968–1972.

Australian and New Zealand Journal of Psychiatry, 8, 167–172.

Minkoff, K., Bergman, E., Beck, A.T., & Beck, R. (1973). Hopelessness, depression, and attempted suicide. *American Journal of Psychiatry, 130,* 455–459.

Mitchell, C.L. (1987). Relationship of femininity, masculinity and gender to attribution of responsibility. *Sex Roles, 16(3/4),* 151–163.

Money, J.W. & Erhardt, A.A. (1972). *Man and Woman, Boy and Girl: The differentiation and dimorphism of gender identity from conception to maturity.* Baltimore: Johns Hopkins University Press.

Morgan, H.G. (1979). *Death Wishes. The understanding and management of deliberate self-harm.* Chichester: Wiley.

Morgan, H.G. (1980). Social correlates of deliberate self-harm. In R.D.T. Farmer, & S. Hirsch, (Eds.), *The Suicide Syndrome,* 90–102. London: Croom Helm.

Morgan, H.G., Burns-Cox, C.J., Pocock, H., & Pottle, S. (1975). Deliberate self-harm: Clinical and socio-economic characteristics of 368 patients. *British Journal of Psychiatry, 126,* 564–574.

Morgan, H.G., Pottle, S., Pocock, H., & Burns-Cox, C.J. (1976). A follow up study of 279 patients. *British Journal of Psychiatry, 128,* 361–368.

Mulhall, D. (1977). *Personal Questionnaire Rapid Scaling Technique* (manual). Windsor: National Foundation for Educational Research.

Murray, M. (1974). Unpublished dissertation. University of Glasgow.

Nathanson, C.A. (1977). Sex, illness, and medical care. A review of data, theory, and method. *Social Science and Medicine, 11,* 13–25.

National Institute of Health and Medical Research (France). (1988). Adolescent health. Reported in the *Times Educational Supplement,* January 8.

Neuringer, C. (1976). Current developments in the study of suicidal thinking. In E.S. Shneidman, (Ed.), *Suicidology: Contemporary developments.* New York: Grune & Stratton.

Neuringer, C. & Lettieri, D. (1982). *Suicidal women—their thinking and feeling patterns.* New York: Gardner.

Newmann, J. (1984). Sex differences in symptoms of depression: Clinical disorder or normal distress? *Journal of Health and Social Behaviour, 25, (June),* 136–159.

Newson, J. & Newson, E. (1976). *Seven Years Old in the Home Environment,* 100. London: Allen & Unwin.

Newson-Smith, J.G.B. & Hirsch, S.R. (1979). Psychiatric symptoms in self-poisoning patients. *Psychological Medicine, 9,* 493–500.

Nicholls, J.G. (1975). Causal attributions and other achievement related cognitions: Effects of task outcome, attainment value and sex. *Journal of Personality and Social Psychology, 31,* 379–389.

Nolen-Hoeksema, S. (1987). Sex differences in unipolar depression: Evidence and theory. *Psychological Bulletin, 101, 2,* 259–282.

Norwood-East, W. (1913). On attempted suicide, with an analysis of 1,000 consecutive cases. *Journal of Mental Science, 59,* 428–478.

Nowacki, S. & Duke, M.P. (1974). A locus of control scale for non-college as well as college adults. *Journal of Personality Assessment, 38,* 136–137.

Nowacki, S. & Poe, C.A. (1973). The concept of mental health as related to sex of person perceived. *Journal of Consulting and Clinical Psychology, 40(1),* 160.

Oatley, K. & Bolton, W. (1985). A social-cognitive theory of depression in reaction to life events. *Psychological Review, 92(3),* 372–388.

O'Brien, S. (1986). *The Negative Scream.* London: Routledge & Kegan Paul.

O'Brien, S.E.M. & Farmer, R.D.T. (1980). The role of life events in the aetiology of episodes of self-poisoning. In R.D.T. Farmer, & S. Hirsch, (Eds.), *The Suicide Syndrome,* 124–130. London: Croom Helm.

Olejnik, A.B. (1980). Socialisation of achievement: Effects of sex and age on achievement evaluations by adults. *Personality and Social Psychology Bulletin, 6,* 68–73.

Osgood, C.E., Suci, G.J., & Tannenbaum, P.H. (1957). *The Measurement of Meaning.* Urbana, Illinois: University of Illinois Press.

Pallis, D.J. & Sainsbury, P. (1976). The value of assessing intent in attempted suicide. *Psychological Medicine, 6,* 487–492.

Parish, P. (1971). The prescribing of psychotropic drugs in general practice. *Journal of Royal College of General Practitioners, 21, supplement 4,* 1–77.

Parker, A. (1981). The meaning of attempted suicide to young parasuicides: A repertory grid study. *British Journal of Psychiatry, 139,* 306–312.

Parloff, M.B., Kelman, H.C., & Frank, J.D. (1954). Comfort, effectiveness and self-awareness as criteria for improvement in psychotherapy. *American Journal of Psychiatry, 111,* 343–351.

Parry, G. & Brewin, C. (1988). Cognitive style and depression: Symptom related, event related or provoking factor? *British Journal of Clinical Psychology, 27,* 23–35.

Parry, H.J.I., Cisin, M., Balter, M., Mellinger, G., & Manheimer, D. (1974). Increasing alcohol intake as a coping mechanism for psychic distress. In R. Copperstock, (Ed.), *Social Aspects of the Medical Use of Psychotropic Drugs.* Toronto: Alcoholism and Drug Addiction Research Foundation of Ontario.

Pasahow, R.J. (1980). The relation between an attributional dimension and learned helplessness. *Journal of Abnormal Psychology, 89,* 358–367.

Passer, M.W. (1977). *Perceiving the causes of success and failure revisited: A multidimensional scaling approach.* Unpublished doctoral dissertation. Los Angeles: University of California.

Patel, A.R. (1975). Attitudes towards self-poisoning. *British Medical Journal, 2,* 426–430.

Patsiokas, A.T., Clum, G.A., & Luscomb, R.L. (1979). Cognitive characteristics of suicide attempts. *Journal of Consulting and Clinical Psychology, 47(3),* 478–484.

Paykel, E.S., Myers, J.K., Lindethal, J.J., & Tanner, J. (1974). Suicidal feelings in the general population: A prevalence study. *British Journal of Psychiatry, 124,* 460–69.

Paykel, E.S., Prusoff, B.A., & Myers, J.K. (1975). Suicide attempts and recent life events: A controlled comparison. *Archives of General Psychiatry, 32,* 327–333.

Paykel, E.S., Prusoff, B.A., & Uhlenhuth, E.H. (1971). Scaling of life events. *Archives of General Psychiatry, 25,* 340–347.

Peller, S. (1932). Zur Statistik der Selbstmordhandlung. *Allgemeines Statistiches Archiv., 32,* 434.

Penfold, P.S. & Walker, G.A. (1984). *Women and the Psychiatric Paradox.* Open University Press.

Peterson, C., Luborsky, L., & Seligman, M.E.P. (1983). Attributions and depressive mood shifts: A case study using the symptom-context method. *Journal of Abnormal Psychology, 92,* 96–103.

Peterson, C., Schwartz, S.M., & Seligman, M.E.P. (1981). Self blame and depressive symptoms. *Journal of Personality and Social Psychology, 41,* 253–259.

Peterson, C., Semmel, A., von Baeyer, C., Abramson, L.Y., Metalsky, G.I., & Seligman, M.E.P. (1982). The attributional style questionnaire. *Cognitive Therapy and Research, 6,* 287–300.

Peterson, C. & Villanova, P. (1988). An expanded attributional style questionnaire. *Journal of Abnormal Psychology, 97,* 87–89.

Peterson, C. et al. (1985). Depressive symptoms and unprompted causal attributions: Content analysis. *Behaviour Research Theory, 23(4),* 379–382.

Philip, A.E. (1970). Traits, attitudes and symptoms in a group of attempted suicides. *British Journal of Psychiatry, 116,* 475–82.

Phillips, D.L. & Segal, B.E. (1969). Sexual status and psychiatric symptoms. *American Sociological Review, 34,* 58–72.

Pierce, D.W. (1977). Suicidal intent in self-injury. *British Journal of Psychiatry, 130,* 377–85.

Pierce, D.W. (1981). The predictive validation of a suicide intent scale: A five year follow-up. *British Journal of Psychiatry, 139,* 391–396.

Piliavin, J.A. & Unger, R.K. (1985). The helpful but helpless females: Myth or reality? In V.E. O'Leary, R.K. Unger, & B.S. Walston (Eds.), *Women, gender and social psychology.* Hillsdale, N.J.: Lawrence Erlbaum Associates Inc.

Pillard, R.C. & Fisher, S. (1970). Aspects of anxiety in dental clinic patients. *Journal of the American Dental Association, 80,* 1331–1334.

Plaat, J., Spivack, G., & Bloom, W. (1975). *Manual for the means-end problem solving procedure (MEPS): A measure of interpersonal problem solving skill.* Philadelphia: Hahneman Medical College and Hospital, Department of Mental Health Sciences, Hahnemen Community MH/MR Center.

Platt, S. (1983). Unemployment and parasuicide in Edinburgh 1968–82. *Unemployment Unit Bulletin, 10,* 4–5.

Platt, S. (1985). A subculture of parasuicide? *Human Relations, 38,* 257–297.

Platt, S., Hawton, K., Kreitman, N., Fagg, J., & Foster, J. (1988). Recent clinical and epidemiological trends in parasuicide in Edinburgh and Oxford. *Psychological Medicine,* in press.

Platt, S. & Kreitman, N. (1985). Parasuicide and unemployment among men in Edinburgh 1968–82. *Psychological Medicine, 15,* 113–123.

Prather, J.E. & Fidell, L.S. (1975). Sex differences in the content and style of medical advertisements. *Social Science and Medicine, 9,* 23–26.

Prescott, L.F. (1985). Drugs prescribed for self-poisoners. *British Medical Journal, 290,* 1633.

Rabinowitz, V.C. (1978). Orientations to help in four natural settings. Doctoral dissertation, *Dissertations Abstracts International, University Microfilms no. 79–07,* 928. North Western University.

Rahe, R.H. (1975). Epidemiological studies of life change and illness. *International Journal of Psychiatry in Medicine, 6,* 133–46.

Ramon, S., Bancroft, J., & Skrimshire, A.M. (1975). Attitudes towards self-poisoning among physicians and nurses in a general hospital. *British Journal of Psychiatry, 127,* 257–264.

Raps, C.S., Peterson, C., Jonas, M., & Seligman, M.E.P. (1982). Patient behaviour in hospitals: Helplessness, reactance or both? *Journal of Personality and Social Psychology, 42,* 1036–1041.

Roberts, H. (1985). *The Patient Patients. Women and Their Doctors.* Pandora Press.

Robins, C.J. (1988). Attributions and depression: Why is the literature so inconsistent? *Journal of Personality and Social Psychology, 54,* 880–889.

Robinson, A., Platt, S., Foster, J., & Kreitman, N. (1986). *Parasuicide in Edinburgh 1985—A Report on Admissions to the Regional Poisoning Treatment Centre.* Unpublished Report, October.

Rosenkrantz, P., Vogel, S., Bee, H., Broverman, I., & Broverman, D. (1968). Sex role stereotypes and self-concepts in college students. *Journal of Consulting and Clinical Psychology, 32,* 287–295.

Roth, S. & Kubal, L. (1975). Effects of non-contingent reinforcement on tasks of differing importance: Facilitation and learned helplessness. *Journal of Personality and Social Psychology, 32,* 680–691.

Rothbart, M.K. (1976). Birth order, sex of child, and maternal help-giving. *Sex Roles, 2,* 39–46.

Rotter, J.B. (1966). Generalised expectancies for internal vs. external control of reinforcement. *Psychological Monographs, 80, (whole number 609),* 1–28.

Salkovskis, P.M., Atha, C., & Storer, D. (1990). Cognitive-behavioural problem solving in the treatment of patients who repeatedly attempt suicide: a controlled trial. *British Journal of Psychiatry, 157,* 871–876.

Salmon, T. (1917). The care and treatment of mental diseases and war neuroses ('shell shock') in the British army. In E. Showalter, op.cit. (1985). *New York War Work Committee of the National Committee for Mental Hygiene.*

Sarason, I.G., Sarason, B.R., Keefe, D.E., Hayes, B.E., & Shearin, E.N. (1986). Cognitive interference: Situational determinants and trait like characteristics. *Journal of Personality and Social Psychology, 51,* 215–226.

Sayers, J. (1982). *Biological Politics.* London: Tavistock.

Schneidman, E.S., & Farberow, N.L. (1961) *The cry for help.* New York: McGraw-Hill.

Schotte, D.E. & Clum, G.A. (1982). Suicide ideation in a college population: A test of a model. *Journal of Consulting and Clinical Psychology, 50,* 690–696.

Schotte, D.E. & Clum, G.A. (1987). Problem solving skills in suicidal patients. *Journal of Consulting and Clinical Psychology, 55(1),* 49–54.

Schur, E. (1983). *Labelling Women Deviant—Gender, Stigma and Social Control, Chp. 3.* Temple University Press.

Scull, A. (1982). *Museums of Madness: The Social Organisation of Insanity in 19th Century England.* Harmondsworth: Penguin Books.

Seligman, M.E.P. (1975). *Helplessness: On depression, development and death.* San Francisco: Freeman.

Seligman, M.E.P. (1981). A learned helplessness point of view. In *Behaviour Therapy for Depression.* New York: Academic Press.

Seligman, M.E.P., Abramson, L.Y., Semmel, A., & von Baeyer, C. (1979). Depressive attributional style. *Journal of Abnormal Psychology, 88(3),* 242–247.

Serbin, L.A., O'Leary, K.D., Kent, R.N., & Tonick, I.J. (1973). A comparison of teacher response to problem and pre-academic behaviour of boys and girls.

Child Development, 44, 796–804.

Serbin, L.A. et al. (1978). Environmental control of independent and dependent behaviours in pre-school boys and girls: a model for independence training. *Sex Roles, 4,* 867–875.

Shader, R. (1968). Subjective determinants of drug prescriptions: A study of therapists' attitudes. *Hospital and Community Psychiatry, 19,* 384–387.

Showalter, E. (1987). *The Female Malady,* 101–120. London: Virago.

Skegg, G., Doll, R., & Perry, J. (1977). The use of medicines in general practice. *British Medical Journal, 1,* 1561–1563.

Skegg, K., Skegg, D.C.G., & Richards, S.M. (1983). Incidence of self-poisoning in patients prescribed psychotropic drugs. *British Medical Journal, 286,* 841–843.

Slater, J. & Depue, A.R. (1981). The contribution of environmental events and social support to serious suicide attempts in primary depressive disorder. *Journal of Abnormal Psychology, 90,* 275–285.

Smith, R.E. (1989). Effects of coping skills training on generalised self-efficacy and locus of control. *Journal of Personality and Social Psychology, 56 (2)* 228–233.

Smith-Rosenberg, C. (1972). The hysterical woman: Sex roles and role conflict in 19th century America. *Social Research, 39,* 652–678.

Spence, J.T. & Helmreich, R.L. (1978). *Masculinity and femininity: Their psychological dimensions, correlates and antecedents.* Austin, TX: University of Texas Press.

Spence, J.T., Helmreich, R.L., & Stapp, J. (1975). Ratings of self and peers on sex role attributions and their relation to self esteem and conceptions of masculinity and femininity. *Journal of Personality and Social Psychology, 32,* 29–39.

Squire, C. (1989). *Significant Differences—Feminism in Psychology.* London: Routledge.

Stengel, E. (1952). Enquiries into attempted suicide (abridged). *Proceedings of the Royal Society of Medicine, 45,* 613.

Stengel, E. (1964). *Suicide and Attempted Suicide.* Harmondsworth: Penguin Books.

Stengel, D. & Cook, N.G. (1958). Attempted suicide: Its social significance and effects. *Maudsley Monograph Number Four.* Oxford: Oxford University Press.

Stephan, W.G., Bernstein, W.M., Stephan, C., & Davis, M.H. (1979). Attributions for achievement: Egotism vs. expectancy confirmation. *Social Psychology Quarterly, 42,* 5–17.

Stillion, J.M., McDowell, E.E., & Shamblin, J.B. (1984). The suicide attitude vignette experience: A method for measuring adolescent attitudes toward suicide. *Death Education, 8,* 65–79.

Stillion, J.M., McDowell, E.E., Smith, R.T., & McCoy, P.A. (1986). Relationship between suicide attitudes and indicators of mental health among adolescents. *Death Studies, 10,* 289–296.

Stimson, G.V. (1975). The message of psychotropic drug ads. *Journal of Communication,* Summer, 153–160.

Stipek, D.J. (1984). Sex differences in children's attributions for success and failure on math and spelling tests. *Sex Roles, 11 (11/12),* 969–981.

Stratchey, J. (Ed.), *The Collected Papers of Sigmund Freud. Vol. 5,* 186–197. New York: Basic Books.

Stryker, S. & Gottlieb, A. (1981). Attribution theory and symbolic interactionism: A comparison. In J.H. Harvey, W.J. Ickes, & R.F. Kidd (Eds.), *New Directions in Attribution Research, Vol. 3.* Hillsdale, N.J.: Lawrence Erlbaum Associates Inc.

Sullivan, W.C. (1900). The relationship of alcoholism to suicide in England, with special reference to recent statistics. *Journal of Mental Science,* April, 260–281.

Sutherland, E. & Veroff, J. (1985). Achievement motivation and sex roles. In V.E. O'Leary, et al. (Eds.), *Women, gender and social psychology, Chapter 4.* Hillsdale, N.J.: Lawrence Erlbaum Associates Inc.

Taylor, J.A. (1953). A personality scale of manifest anxiety. *Journal of Abnormal Social Psychology, 40,* 285–290.

Taylor, R.W. & Meredith, S. (Eds.). (1983). Premenstrual syndrome. Proceedings of a workshop held at the Royal College of Obstetricians and Gynaecologists, London, 2nd December 1982. *Medical News Tribune Ltd.* London.

Taylor, S. (1982). *Durkheim and the study of suicide,* 133. London: Macmillan.

Taylor, S. (1983). Adjustment to threatening events. A theory of cognitive adaptation. *American Psychologist,* 1161–1173.

Teasdale, J.D. & Fogarty, S.J. (1979). Differential effects of induced mood on retrieval of pleasant and unpleasant events from memory. *Journal of Abnormal Psychology, 88 (3),* 248–257.

Tennen, H. & Eller, S.J. (1977). Attributional components of learned helplessness and facilitation. *Journal of Personality and Social Psychology, 35,* 265–271.

Tetlock, P.E. & Levi, A. (1982). Attribution bias: On the inconclusiveness of the cognition—motivation debate. *Journal of Experimental Social Psychology, 18,* 68–88.

Thin, R.N. (1968). Premenstrual symptoms in women who attempt suicide. *Journal of the Royal Army Medical Corps, 114,* 1–4.

Thomas, C. (1985). The age of androgeny: The new views of psychotherapists. *Sex Roles, 13 (7/8),* 381–392.

Tuckman, J. & Youngman, W,F. (1968). A scale for assessing suicide risk of attempted suicides. *Journal of Clinical Psychology, 24,* 17–19.

Turner, R.J. (1980). The use of health services prior to non-fatal deliberate self-harm. In R.D. Farmer & S.R. Hirsch, (Eds.), *The suicide syndrome, Chapter 13.* Croom Helm.

Valin, S. & Nisbett, R.E. (1971). *Attribution process in the development and treatment of emotional disorders.* Morristown, N.J.: General Learning Press.

Verbrugge, L.M. (1989). The twain meet: Empirical explanations for sex differences in health and mortality. *Journal of Health and Social Behaviour, 30,* (Sept), 282–304.

Vinoda, N.M. (1969). Personality and the nature of suicidal attempts. *British Journal of Psychiatry, 115,* 791–795.

Vollmer, F. (1986). Why do men have higher expectancy than women? *Sex Roles, 14 (7/8),* 351–362.

Warner, R. (1978). The diagnosis of anti-social and hysterical personality disorders. *The Journal of Nervous and Mental Disease, 166 (12),* 839.

Weideger, P. (1978). *Female Cycles.* London: The Women's Press.

Weiner, B. (1972). *Theories of Motivation.* Chicago: Markham Publishing Co.

Weiner, B. (1985). Spontaneous Causal Thinking. *Psychological Bulletin, 97 (1)*

74–84.
Weiner, B. (1986). An attributionally based theory of motivation and emotion: Focus, range and issues. In R.M. Sorrention & E.T. Higgins, (Eds.), *Handbook of motivation and cognition—Foundations of social behaviour.* Chichester: John Wiley.

Weiner, B. (1988). Attribution theory and attribution therapy: Some theoretical observations and suggestions. *British Journal of Clinical Psychology, 27,* 93–104.

Weinreich, H. (1978). Sex role socialisation. In J. Chetwynd & O. Hartnett, (Eds.), *The sex role system: Psychological and sociological perspectives,* 18–27. London: Routledge & Kegan Paul.

Weiss, J.M.A. (1957). The gamble with death in attempted suicide. *Psychiatry, 20,* 17–25.

Weissman, M.M. (1974). The epidemiology of suicide attempts 1960–71. *Archives of General Psychiatry, 30,* 737–746.

Weissman, M.M. & Klerman, G.L. (1977). Sex differences in the epidemiology of depression. *Archives of General Psychiatry, 34,* 98–111.

Weissman, M.M. & Klerman, G.L. (1981). Sex differences in the epidemiology of depression. In E. Howell & M. Bayes, *Women and mental health,* 160–195. Basic Books.

Weissman, M.M., Paykel, E.S., French, N., Mark, H., Fox, K., & Prusoff, B. (1973). Suicide attempts in an urban community, 1955 and 1970. *Social Psychiatry, 8,* 82–91.

Welch, R., Gerrard, M., & Huston, A. (1986). Gender related personality attributes and reaction to success/failure: An examination of mediating variables. *Psychology of Women Quarterly, 10,* 221–233.

Wells, N. (1981). Suicide and deliberate self-harm. *Office of Health Economics.*

Wells, N. (1988). Associate Director, *Office of Health Economics—Personal Communication.*

Wenz, F.V. (1977). Subjective powerlessness, sex and suicide potential. *Psychological Reports, 40,* 927–928.

Werry, J.S. & Pedder, J. (1976). Self-poisoning in Auckland. *New Zealand Medical Journal, 83,* 183–187.

Westbrook, M.T. & Mitchell, R.G. (1979). Changes in sex-role stereotypes from health to illness. *Social Science and Medicine, 13A,* 297–302.

Westcott, W.W. (1885). *Suicide.* London: Lewis.

Wexler, L., Weissman, M.M., & Kasl, S.V. (1978). Suicide attempts 1970–75: Updating a United States study and comparisons with international trends. *British Journal of Psychiatry, 132,* 180–5.

White, H. & Stillion, J.M. (1988). Sex differences in attitudes towards suicide: Do males stigmatise males? *Psychology of Women Quarterly, 12,* 357–366.

Whitehead, et al. (1973). Measuring the incidence of self-injury: some methodological and design considerations. *American Journal of Orthopsychiatry, 43,* 142–8.

Williams, C.B. & Nickels, J.B. (1969). Internal-external control dimensions as related to accident and suicide proneness. *Journal of Consulting and Clinical Psychology, 33 (4),* 485–494.

Williams, J.B.W. & Spitzer, R.L. (1983). The issue of sex bias in DSM III. *American Psychologist, 38,* 793–798.

Williams, J.E. & Best, D.L. (1982). Measuring sex stereotype: A thirty nation study. Beverly Hills: Sage Publications.

Williams, J.M.G. & Brewin, C.R. (1984). Cognitive mediators of reactions to a minor life crisis: The British driving test. *British Journal of Social Psychology,* *23,* 41–49.

Williams, J.M.G. & Broadbent, K. (1986). Autobiographical memory in suicide attempters. *Journal of Abnormal Psychology, 95,* 144–149.

Williams, J.M.G. & Dritschel, B.H. (1988). Emotional disturbance and the specificity of autobiographical memory. *Cognition and Emotion, 2,* 221–234.

Williams, J.M.G. & Wells, J. (1989). Suicidal patients. In J. Scott, J.M.G. Williams, & A.T. Beck, (Eds.), *Cognitive Therapy in Clinical Practice, Chapter 9.* London: Routledge & Kegan Paul.

Williams, P., Murray, J., & Clare, A. (1982). A longitudinal study of psychotropic drug prescription. *Psychological Medicine, 12,* 201–206.

Wilson, M. (1981). Suicidal behaviour: Towards an explanation of differences in male and female rates. *Suicide and Life Threatening Behaviour, 11 (3),* 131–140.

Wilson, R.C., Christenson, P.R., Merrifield, P.R., & Guildford, J.P. (1975). *Alternative Uses Test.* Beverly Hills, C.A.: Sheridan Psychological Company.

Wimer, S. & Kelley, H.H. (1982). An investigation of the dimensions of causal attribution. *Journal of Personality and Social Psychology, 43,* 1142–1162.

Wold, C. (1971). Sub-groupings in suicidal women. *Omega, 2,* 19–29.

Women On Words and Images. (1972). *Dick and Jane as Victims.* Princeton, N.J.

Wong, P.T.P., Kettlewell, G., & Sproule, C.F. (1985). On the importance of being masculine: Sex role, attribution and women's career achievement. *Sex Roles, 12 (7/8),* 757–769.

Wong, P.T.P. & Weiner, B. (1981). When people ask 'why' questions, and the heuristics of attributional search. *Journal of Personality and Social Psychology, 40 (4),* 650–663.

Woodside, M. (1959). *British Medical Journal, 2,* 411.

World Health Organization. (1982). *Changing Patterns in Suicide Behaviour. (Euro Reports and Studies, No. 74)* Copenhagen.

Zeldow, P.B. (1984). Sex roles, psychological assessment, and patient management. In C.S. Widom, (Ed.), *Sex roles and psychopathology, Chapter 15.* Plenum Press.

Zuckerman, M., Lubin, B., & Robins, S. (1965). Validation of the multiple affect adjective check list in clinical situations. *Journal of Consulting and Clinical Psychology, 29,* 594.

Author Index

Abramson, L.Y., xv, xvi, 123, 125, 126, 127, 128, 129, 140
Alloy, B., xvi, 140, 142, 154, 164, 175, 178, 182, 183, 184, 185, 196, 203, 204, 210, 211
Altemeyer, R.A., 119
Anderson, C.A., 132, 139, 140, 143, 182, 236
Andrews, G.R., 138
Antonovsky, A., 173, 174
Armitage, K.J., 111
Asarnow, J.R., 47, 143
Atha, C., 237, 238

Bagley, C.R., 10, 218
Balter, M., 96
Baltes, M.M., 198
Bancroft, J., xi, 19, 41, 76, 97, 122, 123, 161, 197, 204, 219, 220, 221, 223, 228, 239
Barraclough, B.M., xi, 20, 218
Barton, S.N., 218
Bass, R.A., 112
Batchelor, I.R.C., 165
Battle, E.S., 62, 67
Baucom, D.H., 117,118

Beck, A.T., 48, 49, 50, 52, 53, 56, 57, 58, 59, 61, 66, 67, 98, 115, 123, 130, 138, 142, 161, 166, 170, 204, 236, 238, 239
Beck, R., 48
Bee, H., 244
Bell, G.C., 134
Bellantuono, C., 102
Bem, S.L., 117, 135, 167
Benevento, A., 120, 229
Bernard, J., 221
Bernstein, A., 103
Best, D.L., 167
Bille-Brahe, U., 171, 172
Billings, A.C., 182
Birtchnell, J., 32, 33, 165
Blackstock, E., 94, 96, 98, 219
Blake, W., 110
Blatt, S.J., 102
Bloom, D., 235
Bolton, W., 172, 173, 174, 175, 184
Bond, L.A., 134, 148
Bradley, G.W., 149
Braucht, G.N., 59, 128, 214
Brent, D., 218
Brewer, C., 94, 113, 231

Brewin, C.R., 131, 134, 137, 148, 208, 230
Brickman, P., 225, 227, 228, 229, 230, 232, 236, 239
Bromet, E.J., 218
Broom, D., 111
Broverman, D.M., 29, 102, 109, 167, 169, 244
Broverman, I., 29, 102, 109, 167, 169, 244
Brown, G., 42, 121, 154, 155, 166, 169, 170, 172, 202
Bryant, B.K., 67
Buglass, D., 31, 238
Bunch, J., xi
Burns-Cox, C.J., 197
Bush, E.S., 118
Butler, J., 223, 235

Cafferata, G., 103
Cantor, P.C., 39
Caplan, P.J., 37
Carlson, G.A., 47
Cartwright, A., 110
Catalan, J., xi, 3, 20, 41, 219, 235
Cavell, M., 38
Chambliss, C., 234
Chapin, M., 138
Chesler, P., 52, 54, 71, 120, 153, 169
Chetwynd, J., 38
Chevron, E.S., 102
Chiles, J., 49
Chowdhury, N., 27, 45, 183, 218
Christenson, P.R., 47
Cisin, M., 107
Clare, A., 112
Clarkson, F.E., 109
Clifton, A.K., 69, 70
Clingman, J.M., 110
Cloward, R.A., 22, 23, 24, 26, 53, 60, 63, 70, 71, 81, 113
Clum, G.A., 47, 48, 138, 143, 144, 145, 237
Cohn, E., 225, 227, 228, 229, 230, 232, 236, 239
Cole, D.A., 48, 49, 165
Cook, N.G., 12, 16, 152
Coombes, D.W., 218
Cooperstock, R., ix, 96, 110, 113

Costrich, N., 152
Coyne, J.C., 131, 207
Crandall, V.C., 62, 148
Crombie, G., 137
Crook, T., 165
Curtis, R.C., 138, 151, 236

D'Zurrilla, T., 130, 139, 144, 145, 237
Dalton, K., 31, 32, 33
Danker-Brown, P., 117, 118
Davis, F.B., 99
Davison, G.C., 234
Dawes, R., 111
Deaux, E., 148
Deaux, K., 131, 147, 148
Debus, R.L., 138
DeCourville, N., 32
Delamont, S., 38
Deming, S., 134, 148
Dent, J., 131
Depue, A.R., 164, 201, 202, 203
Deutsch H., 34, 37
Dew, M.A., 218
DHSS., x, 43
Diekstra, R.F.W., 3
Diener, C.I., 180
Dohrenwend, B.P., 27, 42, 202
Dohrenwend, B.S., 27, 42, 202
Doll, R., 96
Draper, R., 223, 240
Droppelman, L.F., 239
Duffy, J., 43
Duke, M.P., 66
Duncan-Jones, P., 111
Dunnel, K., 110
Durkheim, E., 57, 58
Dweck, C.S., 118, 132, 133, 138, 180, 184, 243, 244
Dweck, S.W., 141, 178, 179, 180, 243
Dyck, D.G., 138
Dyer, J., 43

Eagan, A., 33
Eckman, T., 224
Elkind, D., 49
Eller, S.J., 124, 125
Emery, G., 236
Emswiller, T., 148
Erhardt, A.A., 38

Erikson, E., 37
Erkut, S., 134, 135, 136
Esquirol, L., 12
Eysenck, H., 37

Fagg, J., 222
Farmer, R.D.T., 94, 100, 113, 203, 231
Farris, E., 131, 147, 148
Farberow, N.L., 29, 39
Feather, N.T., 131, 147, 152
Feinstein, J., 152
Ferguson, D.M., 156
Fidell, L.S., 103
Fidell, S., 110
Firth, R., 64
Fisher, S., 38
Fitch, G., 136, 149
Fleishman, J.A., 181, 182
Floyd, S., 32, 33
Fogarty, S.J., 198
Ford, M.R., 111
Forster, D.P., 93, 231
Forsterling, F., 236
Forsyth, D.R., 150, 151, 152
Foulds, G.A., 39
Fourestie, V., 32, 33
Fox, J.W., 27
Fox, K., 41
Franklin, J., 131
Fraser, D.M., 161
Fraser, S.G., 237
French, N., 41
Freud, S., 33, 34, 38, 39
Frieze, I.H., 136
Fromm, E., xvii
Frost, C.E.B., 93, 231

Gannon, L., 134, 135
Gatchel, R.J., 117, 124
Gerrard, M., 137
Ghodse, A.H., 221
Gibbons, J.L., 223, 235
Gibbons, J.S., 223, 235
Gilliard, D., 133
Gillman, M-J., 134
Ginsberg, G.P., 228
Goetz, T.E., 141, 178, 179, 180
Goffman, E., 151
Goldacre, M., 101, 232

Goldfried, M., 130, 138, 144, 237.
Goldie, N., 21, 28
Goldney, R., 40, 42, 67, 165, 224
Goodstein, J., 49
Gotlib, I.H., 131, 207
Gottlieb, A., 151
Gove, W.R., 26, 27, 28, 30, 70, 102, 105
Greenberg, R.L., 51
Greenberg, R.P., 38
Greer, S., 165
Guilford, J.P., 47
Gutherie, D., 47

Hamilton, S., 111
Hammen, C.L., 207
Hamsher, J.H., 66
Hanusa, B.H., 136
Harris, T., 42, 121, 155, 166, 170, 172, 202
Hartlage, S., xvi
Hartnett, O., 38
Harvard-Watts, O., 98
Hastie, R., 177
Hawton, K., xi, 3, 19, 20, 41, 94, 96, 98, 101, 165, 219, 222, 224, 232, 235
Hayes, B.E., 140
Heilman, M.E., 119
Heiser, P., 134, 135
Helmreich, R.L., 29, 136, 137, 230
Heshusius, L., 37, 39, 70, 115, 117
Hey, V., 33
Hiroto, D.S., 116
Hirsch, S.R., 41, 100, 223, 240
Hite, S., 37
HMSO, x, 77
Hoffman, L.W., 168, 170
Holden, R.R., 48
Holding, T.A., 218
Holmes, T.H., 155, 166, 201
Hope, K., 39
Hopkins, F., 15, 85
Horner, M., 119, 167
Horton, J., 238
Horwitz, A., 108, 109
Horwood, L.J., 156
Husaini, B.A., 62, 67
Huston, A., 136, 137

Ickes, W.J., 133, 137, 138, 139, 149

Jacklin, C., 118
Jackson, D.N., 48
Jarvis, K.J., 63, 70
Jennings, C., 218
Jonas, M., 198
Jones, K., 119

Karuza, J., 225, 227, 228, 229, 230, 232, 236, 239
Kasl, S.V., ix
Kasper, J., 103
Katschnig, H., 157, 201, 202
Keefe, D.E., 140
Kelley, H., 147, 175, 184
Kennedy, P.F., 99
Kessel, N., 18, 21, 81, 82, 83, 220
Kessler, R.C., 77, 79, 105, 108, 109, 242, 243
Kettlewell, G., 138, 242
Keyes, S., 168
Kidder, L., 152
King, E., 103
Klein, D.C., 126
Klerman, G.L., 41
Knight, S., 134
Koumjian, K., 96
Kovacs, M., 49, 98
Krause, N., 66, 67
Kreitman, N., ix, xi, 3, 18, 24, 25, 26, 27, 28, 30, 38, 40, 43, 45, 55, 70, 77, 99, 152, 153, 183, 218, 224
Kubal, L., 124

Lack, D., 112
Lambley, P., 65
Lamke, L.K., 136
Landfield, A., 174, 178
Langer, E.J., 120, 229
LaNoue, J.B., 138, 151, 236
Lapsley, D., 49
Larson, D., 131
Laws, S., 33
Lawson, A.A.H., 161
Layden, M.A., 133, 137, 138, 139, 149, 236
Lazarus, R., 182, 183
Lee, D.E., 69, 70

Leeper, J.D., 218
Lefcourt, H.M., 62
Lendrum, R.C., 85
Lester, D., 98
Lettieri, D., 45, 46, 50
Levenson, M., 65
Levi, A., 147
Levine, J., 96
Levine, R., 134, 137
Lewinsohn, P., 131
Lewis, C., 169
Liberman, B.L., 234
Liberman, R.P., 224
Licht, B.G., 243
Lignieres, B., 32, 33
Lindethal, J.J., 11
Linehan, M., 28, 30, 31, 49, 222, 237, 238
Lipshitz, S., 245
Lochel, E., 149, 150, 180
Lopez, S.R., 110, 111
Lorr, M., 239
Luscomb, R.L., 47, 65, 237
Lykes, M.B., 244

Maccoby, E.E., 118
Magos, A., 32
Manheimer, D.I., 96
Mant, A., 111
Maples, C.W., 117
Maracek, J., 152, 242
Maris, R.W., 35, 36, 37, 70
Mark, H., 41
Marsack, P., 197, 222
Martin, V., 134
Marx, E., 237, 239
Masuda, M., 155, 166
Matthew, H., x, 3
McCoy, P.A., 29
McCulloch, J.W., 31, 55, 72, 224
McDonald, C., 102
McDowell, E.E., 29
McFarland, C., 32
McGhee, P., 62
McHugh, M.C., 136
McIntosh, J.L., 3, 11
McKinlay, J.B., 110
McNair, D.M., 239
McRae, J.A., 77, 79, 105, 242, 243

Mechanic, D., 110
Mehrabian, A., 137
Mellinger, G.D., 103, 107
Mendonca, J.D., 48
Meredith, S., 32
Merrifield, P.R., 47
Metalsky, G.I., xvi, 130
Mikulincer, M., 139, 140, 141, 143, 182, 236
Miller, H.L., 218
Miller, I.W., 116
Miller, W.R., 117, 124
Minkoff, K., 50
Mitchell, C.L., 230, 234
Mitchell, R.G., 62, 67, 108, 121, 182, 230
Money, J.W., 38
Moos, R.H., 182
Morgan, H.G., xii, xiii, 56, 161, 197, 204, 220
Moss, J.R., 218
Mulhall, D., 239
Murray, E.J., 234
Murray, J., 112
Murray, M., 221
Musgrove, W.J., 110
Myers, J.K., 11, 121

Napier, M.B., 165
Nathanson, C.A., 31
Neff, J.A., 62, 67
Neuringer, C., 43, 44, 45, 46, 51, 56, 57, 58, 59, 60, 67, 130, 138, 141, 142
Newmann, J., 41, 42
Newson, J., 168
Newson-Smith, J.G.B., 41
Nicholls, J.G., 133, 134
Nickels, J.B., 65
Nielsen, S., 49
Nisbett, R.E., 234
Nivens, M.K., 134
Nizan, B., 139, 141, 236
Nolen-Hoeksema, S., 120, 141
Norman, W.H., 116
Norwood-East, W., 14, 15, 74, 83
Nowacki, S., 66, 109

O'Brien, S., 121, 122, 123, 154, 171, 185, 203, 228, 229, 230, 231, 233

O'Grady, J., 165
Oatley, K., 172, 173, 174, 175, 184
Olejnik, A.B., 118
Osborn, M., 165
Osgood, C.E., 44

Parker, A., 174, 178, 184
Parry, G., 131
Parry, H.J.I., 107
Pasahow, R.J., 140
Pascale, L., 152
Patel, A.R., 220, 221
Patsiokas, A.T., 47, 142, 143
Paulus, P.B., 117
Paykel, E.S., 11, 65, 121, 157, 164, 172, 197, 200, 201, 203
Pedder, J., 165
Peller, S., 12
Perry, J., 96
Peterson, C., 140, 197, 198, 200, 209, 235
Philip, A.E., 35, 38, 39, 55, 72, 224
Phillips, D.L., 102
Piliavin, J.A., 12
Pilowsky, G., 42
Piven, F.F., 22, 23, 24, 26, 53, 60, 63, 70, 71, 81, 113
Platt, S., 25, 47, 77, 153, 203, 231, 235
Pocock, H., 197
Poe, C.A., 109
Pottle, S., 197
Prather, J.E., 103
Prescott, L.F., 94, 99
Prusoff, B.A., 121, 200

Quinlan, D.M., 102

Rabinowitz, V.C., 230
Rahe, R.H., 202
Ramon, S., 221, 222, 223, 224
Raps, C.S., 198
Raskin, A., 165
Reis, H., 134
Repucci, N.D., 132
Reynolds, F., 98
Richards, S.M., 98
Roberts, H., 112
Robins, C.J., 207, 208
Robinson, A., 77, 242

Rosenkrantz, P., 244, 109
Ross, M., 32
Roth, S., 124
Rothbart, M., 111
Rothbart, M.K., 119
Rotter, J.B., 61, 64, 67
Rush, A.J., 236

Sainsbury, P., xi
Salkovskis, P.M., 237, 238
Salmon, T., 75
Sarason, B.R., 140
Sarason, I.G., 140
Sarawatari, L.R., 119
Sayers, J., 38
Scaffer, K.F., 134
Schneiderman, L.J., 111
Schotte, D.E., 47, 48, 138, 143, 144, 145
Schreiber, M., 3
Schur, E., 71
Scull, A., 73
Segal, B.E., 102
Seligman, M.E.P., xv, 77, 114, 115, 116, 117, 121, 123, 124, 129, 140, 142, 165, 166, 198, 242
Semmel, A., 129
Serbin, L.A., 118, 119
Serin, R.C., 48
Shader, R., 110
Shamblin, J.B., 29
Shapiro, D.A., 137, 208, 230
Shaw, B.F., 236
Shearin, E.N., 140
Showalter, E., 46, 71, 72, 73, 74, 75, 79, 105, 116, 240, 241
Silbowitz, M., 65
Simon, J.G., 131, 147, 152
Skegg, D.C.G., 96, 98
Skegg, K., 98
Skinner, E.A., 198
Skrimshire, A., 221
Slater, J., 164, 201, 202, 203
Smith, R.E., 237
Smith, R.T., 29
Smith-Rosenberg, C., 74
Spence, J.T., 29, 136, 137, 230
Spitzer, R.L., 102
Sproule, C.F., 138, 242

Squire, C., xvii
Stapp, J., 136
Steinmetz, J., 131
Stengel, E., xi, xii, 12, 14, 16, 17, 18, 19, 39, 70, 85, 152
Stewart, A.J., 244
Stillion, J.M., 29, 222
Stimson, G.V., 103
Stipek, D.J., 133, 134
Storer, D., 237, 238
Stratchey, J., 33
Stryker, S., 66, 67, 151
Studd, J., 32
Suci, G.J., 44
Sullivan, W.C., 12, 14, 74, 83
Sutherland, E., 79, 243

Tannenbaum, P.H., 44
Tanner, J., 11
Taylor, R.W., 32
Taylor, S., 22, 23, 53, 57, 58, 127
Teasdale, J.D., xv, 123, 131, 198
Tennen, H., 124, 125
Tetlock, P.E., 147
Thomas, C., 244
Trockel, J.F., 67
Turner, R.J., 219, 220, 224, 229

Uhlenhuth, E.H., 200
Unger, R.K., 120
Urwin, P., 223, 235

Valins, S., 234
Verbrugge, L.M., 31
Veroff, J., 79, 243
Villanova, P., 209, 235
Vinoda, N.M., 38
Vogel, S., 244, 109
Vollmer, F., 137, 148
von Baeyer, C., 129

Walsh, C., 223, 240
Wang, A.G., 171, 172
Warner, R., 103
Weideger, P., 33
Weiner, B., 176, 177, 178, 184
Weinreich, H., 169
Weiss, J.M.A., 64
Weissman, A., 49

Weissman, A., 49
Weissman, M.M., ix, 41, 161, 204
Welch, R., 136, 137
Wells, J., 236
Wells, N., ix, 1, 77, 90, 197, 231
Wenz, F.V., 65
Werry, J.S., 165
Westbrook, M.T., 62, 67, 108, 121,
   181, 182
Westcott, W.W., 12
Wexler, L., ix, 3, 93
White, H., 29, 30, 222
White, L., 148
Widiger, T.A., 111

Williams, C.B., 65
Williams, J.B.W., 102
Williams, J.E., 167
Williams, J.M.G., 134, 148, 236
Williams, P., 112
Wilson, M., 30, 31, 69
Wilson, R.C., 47, 235
Wold, C., 161
Women On Word and Images 120
Wong, P.T.P., 138, 177, 242
World Health Organization, 1

Zuckerman, M., 117
Zuroff, D., 102

Subject Index

Attribution theory, xv, xvi, 125-128, 188-191
Attributions and
  affiliation, 160, 161-170, 178-181
  depression, 128-130
  coping, xv, xvi, 131-134, 139-145, 178-182
  gender, xvi, 128, 135-138
  intervention in self-poisoning, 225, 227-239
  motivation, 148, 149
  self-concept, 170-175, 192
  self-poisoning, 139-145, 182-185, 188, 193, 206-209
  sex differences, 131-134, 190, 191, 209, 210, 213, 214
Attribution
  causes of, 175-182
  functions of, 147-154, 194,
Attributional style, 127-134, 184, 185
  social origins of, 154, 170-175
Attributional style questionnaire, 198, 200
Attempted suicide
  definitions, xi, 12-19
  epidemiology, ix, x, xii, 1-10

Attempted suicide and
  mental illness, xi
  psychotropic medication, 81-102
  sex differences in, x, xvi, 10, 11, 187

Benzodiazepines, 96, 102
Biology, 31-33

Causal attribution, xv, xvi
Clinical judgement, 109-112
Cognitive theories of self-poisoning, 43-54
Coping skills, xv, xvi, 47-49, 107-109

Depression and
  self-poisoning, 41-43
  sex differences in, 41-43
Deviance, xi, 35, 36, 69-71, 80, 81
Dichotomous thinking, 44-46
Durkheim, 57, 58

Expectancy, 61

Fear of success, 119, 120
Freudian theory, 33-39

Gender, xvi, xvii, 134-138, 166-169, 213

Help seeking, 107-109, 119, 183
Hopelessness, 50, 51, 60, 61, 165, 166, 195, 196
Human development, 168-170
Hysteria, 20, 39, 40, 72-76, 79, 80

Intervention
    effectiveness, 217-220, 223, 224, 240
    primary, 217-220
    secondary, 221-223

Learned helplessness, xv, 115-125
    sex differences in, 117-123
Locus of control, 61-67
Life events, xvi, 145, 146, 154-157
    and helplessness, 165, 166
    and self-poisoning, 157-164, 194
Life events scale, 200-202

Masochism, 33-39
Meaning of self-poisoning, 20-22, 59, 60
Medical model, 226-234
Menstruation, 31-33
Mental disorder, 41-43

Narcissism, 34
National Health Service, xiii, 71
Neurasthenia, 75
Non-contingency, xv, 115-123, 183, 184

Parent loss, xvi, 165, 166
Pathology paradigm, x, xi, xiii, xv, 19, 20, 55-59, 188, 215
Penis envy, 34, 35
Premenstrual syndrome, 32, 33
Problem solving, xv, 130-134, 225-235
Provoking agents, 155, 210
Psychiatry, xi, 19, 20
Psychopathology, xv
    and sex roles, 69-81
Psychotropic drugs and
    self-poisoning, 97-102, 112-114

sex difference in prescription, 95-99, 102-107
Relational problems, xiv
Repertory grid, 174
Risk taking, 64

Samaritans, 183, 217-219, 224
Self-medication, xiv, 241
Self-poisoning
    attitudes to, 220-224
    definition of, xi
    history of, xi, xiii, 12-16, 76-80, 83-93, 240-246
    methods used, 83-93
    normative origins of, xiii, 21-30, 58-61, 63, 67, 69-71, 80, 81
    reasons for, 161, 164
    sex differences in, x, xvi, xvii
Self-poisoning, theories of
    locus of control, 61-67
    dichotomous thinking, 44, 47
    stress, 21-23
    mental disorder, 41-43
    biology, 31-33
    menstruation, 31-33
    personality theory, 33-40
    risk taking, 64
    sex roles, xiv, 26-30, 46, 51-53, 58-60, 69, 76-81
    social change, 69-81
    subcultural, 24-26
Sex roles, xiv, xv
    and clinical judgements, 109-112
    and psychopathology, 69-76, 170
    and psychotropic prescription, 81, 102-107, 112-114
    and social change, xii, xv, 72-81, 240-245
Sex role stereotypes, 166-170
Social psychology, xiv
Specific vulnerability, xvi, 164, 184, 211-213
Stress, 21-23
Sub-culture, 24-26
Suicide, 12-19

Unemployment, 161
Uncontrollability, xv, 165, 166